APOLOGY

FOR THE WOMAN WRITING

and other works

THE
OTHER VOICE
IN
EARLY MODERN
EUROPE

A Series Edited by Margaret L. King and Albert Rabil, Jr.

Marie le Jars de Gournay

APOLOGY
FOR THE WOMAN WRITING
and other works

ॐ

Edited and Translated
by
Richard Hillman
and Colette Quesnel

General and Section Introductions
by
Richard Hillman

THE UNIVERSITY OF CHICAGO PRESS
Chicago and London

Marie le Jars de Gournay, 1565–1645

Richard Hillman is professor of English at the Université François-Rabelais in Tours, France. His previous books include *Self-Speaking in Medieval and Early Modern English Drama.*
Colette Quesnel is affiliated with the Université du Québec à Montréal. She is the author of *Mourir de rire d'après et avec Rabelais.*

Together they translated and edited *Preface to the Essays of Michel de Montaigne by His Adoptive Daughter, Marie le Jars de Gournay.*

The University of Chicago Press, Chicago 60637
The University of Chicago Press, Ltd., London
© 2002 by The University of Chicago
All rights reserved. Published 2002
Printed in the United States of America

11 10 09 08 07 06 05 04 03 02   1 2 3 4 5

ISBN: 0-226-30555-4 (cloth)
ISBN: 0-226-30556-2 (paper)

Library of Congress Cataloging-in-Publication Data
Gournay, Marie Le Jars de, 1565–1645.
 [Selections. English. 2002]
 Apology for the woman writing and other works / Marie de Gournay ; edited and translated by Richard Hillman and Colette Quesnel ; general and section introductions by Richard Hillman.
  p. cm. — (The other voice in early modern Europe)
 Includes bibliographical references and index.
 ISBN 0-226-30555-4 (cloth : alk. paper)—ISBN 0-226-30556-2 (pbk. : alk. paper)
  1. Gournay, Marie Le Jars de, 1565–1645—Translations into English.   2. Women's rights—Early works to 1800. I. Hillman, Richard, 1949– II. Quesnel, Colette. III Title. IV. Series.

PQ1799.G65 A238 2002
848'.309—dc21

2001052272

CONTENTS

THE OTHER VOICE IN
EARLY MODERN EUROPE:
INTRODUCTION TO THE SERIES

Margaret L. King and Albert Rabil, Jr.

THE OLD VOICE AND THE OTHER VOICE

In western Europe and the United States women are nearing equality in the professions, in business, and in politics. Most enjoy access to education, reproductive rights, and autonomy in financial affairs. Issues vital to women are on the public agenda: equal pay, childcare, domestic abuse, breast cancer research, and curricular revision with an eye to the inclusion of women.

These recent achievements have their origins in things women (and some male supporters) said for the first time about six hundred years ago. Theirs is the "other voice," in contradistinction to the "first voice," the voice of the educated men who created Western culture. Coincident with a general reshaping of European culture in the period 1300–1700 (called the Renaissance or early modern period), questions of female equality and opportunity were raised that still resound and are still unresolved.

The other voice emerged against the backdrop of a three-thousand-year history of the derogation of women rooted in the civilizations related to Western culture: Hebrew, Greek, Roman, and Christian. Negative attitudes toward women inherited from these traditions pervaded the intellectual, medical, legal, religious, and social systems that developed during the European Middle Ages.

The following pages describe the traditional, overwhelmingly male view of women's nature inherited by early modern Europeans and the new tradition that the other voice called into being to begin to challenge its assumptions. This review should serve as a framework for the understanding of the texts published in the series The Other Voice in Early Modern Europe. Introductions specific to each text and author follow this essay in all the volumes of the series.

TRADITIONAL VIEWS OF WOMEN, 500 B.C.E.–1500 C.E.

Embedded in the philosophical and medical theories of the ancient Greeks were perceptions of the female as inferior to the male in both mind and body. Similarly, the structure of civil legislation inherited from the ancient Romans was biased against women, and the views on women developed by Christian thinkers out of the Hebrew Bible and the Christian New Testament were negative and disabling. Literary works composed in the vernacular language of ordinary people, and widely recited or read, conveyed these negative assumptions. The social networks within which most women lived—those of the family and the institutions of the Roman Catholic Church—were shaped by this negative tradition and sharply limited the areas in which women might act in and upon the world.

GREEK PHILOSOPHY AND FEMALE NATURE. Greek biology assumed that women were inferior to men and defined them merely as childbearers and housekeepers. This view was authoritatively expressed in the works of the philosopher Aristotle.

Aristotle thought in dualities. He considered action superior to inaction, form (the inner design or structure of any object) superior to matter, completion superior to incompletion, possession superior to deprivation. In each of these dualities, he associated the male principle with the superior quality and the female with the inferior. "The male principle in nature," he argued, "is associated with active, formative and perfected characteristics, while the female is passive, material and deprived, desiring the male in order to become complete."[1] Men are always identified with virile qualities, such as judgment, courage, and stamina, women with their opposites—irrationality, cowardice, and weakness.

Even in the womb, the masculine principle was considered superior. The man's semen, Aristotle believed, created the form of a new human creature, while the female body contributed only matter. (The existence of the ovum, and with it the other facts of human embryology, were not established until the seventeenth century.) Although the later Greek physician Galen believed that there was a female component in generation, contributed by "female semen," the followers of both Aristotle and Galen saw the male role in human generation as more active and more important.

In the Aristotelian view, the male principle sought always to reproduce itself. The creation of a female was always a mistake, therefore, resulting from

1. Aristotle, *Physics* 1.9.192a20–24, in *The Complete Works of Aristotle*, ed. Jonathan Barnes, rev. Oxford trans., 2 vols. (Princeton, N.J., 1984), 1:328.

an imperfect act of generation. Every female born was considered a "defec-
tive" or "mutilated" male (as Aristotle's terminology has variously been translated), a "monstrosity" of nature.[2]

For Greek theorists, the biology of males and females was the key to
their psychology. The female was softer and more docile, more apt to be despondent, querulous, and deceitful. Being incomplete, moreover, she craved
sexual fulfillment in intercourse with a male. The male was intellectual, active, and in control of his passions.

These psychological polarities derived from the theory that the universe
consisted of four elements (air, earth, fire, and water), expressed in human
bodies as four "humors" (black bile, yellow bile, blood, and phlegm) considered respectively dry, hot, damp, and cold and corresponding to mental
states ("melancholic," "choleric," "sanguine," "phlegmatic"). In this schemati-
zation, the male, sharing the principles of earth and fire, was dry and hot; the
female, sharing the principles of air and water, was cold and damp.

Female psychology was further affected by her dominant organ, the
uterus (womb), *hystera* in Greek. The passions generated by the womb made
women lustful, deceitful, talkative, irrational, indeed—when these affects
were in excess—"hysterical."

Aristotle's biology also had social and political consequences. If the male
principle was superior and the female inferior, then in the household, as in
the state, men should rule and women must be subordinate. That hierarchy
does not rule out the companionship of husband and wife, whose coopera-
tion was necessary for the welfare of children and the preservation of property. Such mutuality supported male preeminence.

Aristotle's teacher Plato suggested a different possibility: that men and
women might possess the same virtues. The setting for this proposal is the
imaginary and ideal Republic that Plato sketches in a dialogue of that name.
Here, for a privileged elite capable of leading wisely, all distinctions of class
and wealth dissolve, as do, consequently, those of gender. Without households or property, as Plato constructs his ideal society, there is no need for
the subordination of women. Women may, therefore, be educated to the
same level as men to assume leadership responsibilities. Plato's Republic remained imaginary, however. In real societies, the subordination of women remained the norm and the prescription.

The views of women inherited from the Greek philosophical tradition
became the basis for medieval thought. In the thirteenth century, the supreme scholastic philosopher Thomas Aquinas, among others, still echoed

2. Aristotle, *Generation of Animals* 2.3.737a27–28, in *The Complete Works*, 1:1144.

Aristotle's views of human reproduction, of male and female personalities, and of the preeminent male role in the social hierarchy.

ROMAN LAW AND THE FEMALE CONDITION. Roman law, like Greek philosophy, underlay medieval thought and shaped medieval society. The ancient belief that adult, property-owning men should administer households and make decisions affecting the community at large is the very fulcrum of Roman law.

Around 450 B.C.E., during Rome's republican era, the community's customary law was recorded (legendarily) on twelve tablets erected in the city's central forum. It was later elaborated by professional jurists whose activity increased in the imperial era, when much new legislation, especially on issues affecting family and inheritance, was passed. This growing, changing body of laws was eventually codified in the *Corpus of Civil Law* under the direction of the emperor Justinian, generations after the empire ceased to be ruled from Rome. That *Corpus*, read and commented on by medieval scholars from the eleventh century on, inspired the legal systems of most of the cities and kingdoms of Europe.

Laws regarding dowries, divorce, and inheritance pertain primarily to women. Since those laws aimed to maintain and preserve property, the women concerned were those from the property-owning minority. Their subordination to male family members points to the even greater subordination of lower-class and slave women, about whom the laws speak little.

In the early republic, the *paterfamilias*, or "father of the family," possessed *patria potestas*, "paternal power." The term *pater*, "father," in both these cases does not necessarily mean biological father but, rather, head of household. The father was the person who owned the household's property and, indeed, its human members. The *paterfamilias* had absolute power—including the power, rarely exercised, of life or death—over his wife, his children, and his slaves, as much as his cattle.

Children could be "emancipated," an act that granted legal autonomy and the right to own property. Male children over fourteen could be emancipated by a special grant from the father or, automatically, by their father's death. But females could never be emancipated; instead, they passed from the authority of their father to a husband or, if widowed or orphaned while still unmarried, to a guardian or tutor.

Marriage under its traditional form placed the woman under her husband's authority, or *manus*. He could divorce her on grounds of adultery, drinking wine, or stealing from the household, but she could not divorce him. She could neither possess property in her own right nor bequeath any to her children upon her death. When her husband died, the household property passed not to her but to his male heirs. And when her father died, she had no claim to any family inheritance, which was directed to her brothers or more remote male relatives. The effect of these laws was to exclude women from civil society, itself based on property ownership.

In the later republican and imperial periods, these rules were significantly modified. Women rarely married according to the traditional form but according to the form of "free" marriage. That practice allowed a woman to remain under her father's authority, to possess property given her by her father (most frequently the "dowry," recoverable from the husband's household in the event of his death), and to inherit from her father. She could also bequeath property to her own children and divorce her husband, just as he could divorce her.

Despite this greater freedom, women still suffered enormous disability under Roman law. Heirs could belong only to the father's side, never the mother's. Moreover, although she could bequeath her property to her children, she could not establish a line of succession in doing so. A woman was "the beginning and end of her own family," said the jurist Ulpian. Moreover, women could play no public role. They could not hold public office, represent anyone in a legal case, or even witness a will. Women had only a private existence and no public personality.

The dowry system, the guardian, women's limited ability to transmit wealth, and total political disability are all features of Roman law adopted, although modified according to local customary laws, by the medieval communities of western Europe.

CHRISTIAN DOCTRINE AND WOMEN'S PLACE. The Hebrew Bible and the Christian New Testament authorized later writers to limit women to the realm of the family and to burden them with the guilt of original sin. The passages most fruitful for this purpose were the creation narratives in Genesis and sentences from the Epistles defining women's role within the Christian family and community.

Each of the first two chapters of Genesis contains a creation narrative. In the first "God created man in his own image, in the image of God he created him; male and female he created them" (New Revised Standard Version, Gen. 1:27). In the second, God created Eve from Adam's rib (2:21–23). Christian theologians relied principally on Genesis 2 for their understanding of the relation between man and woman, interpreting the creation of Eve from Adam as proof of her subordination to him.

The creation story in Genesis 2 leads to that of the temptations in Gene-

sis 3: of Eve by the wily serpent and of Adam by Eve. As read by Christian theologians from Tertullian to Thomas Aquinas, the narrative made Eve responsible for the Fall and its consequences. She instigated the act; she deceived
her husband; she suffered the greater punishment. Her disobedience made it
necessary for Jesus to be incarnated and to die on the cross. From the pulpit,
moralists and preachers for centuries conveyed to women the guilt that they
bore for original sin.

The Epistles offered advice to early Christians on building communities
of the faithful. Among the matters to be regulated was the place of women.
Paul offered views favorable to women in Galatians 3:28: "There is neither Jew
nor Greek, there is neither slave nor free, there is neither male nor female; for
you are all one in Christ Jesus." Paul also referred to women as his coworkers
and placed them on a par with himself and his male coworkers (Phil. 4:2–3;
Rom. 16:1–3; I Cor. 16:19). Elsewhere, Paul limited women's possibilities: "But
I want you to understand that the head of every man is Christ, the head of a
woman is her husband, and the head of Christ is God" (I Cor. 11:3).

Biblical passages by later writers (though attributed to Paul) enjoined
women to forgo jewels, expensive clothes, and elaborate coiffures; and they
forbade women to "teach or have authority over men," telling them to "learn
in silence with all submissiveness," as is proper for one responsible for sin,
consoling them, however, with the thought that they will be saved through
childbearing (I Tim. 2:9–15). Other texts among the later Epistles defined
women as the weaker sex and emphasized their subordination to their hus-
bands (I Pet. 3:7; Col. 3:18; Eph. 5:22–23).

These passages from the New Testament became the arsenal employed
by theologians of the early church to transmit negative attitudes toward
women to medieval Christian culture—above all, Tertullian ("On the Ap-
parel of Women"), Jerome (*Against Jovinian*), and Augustine (*The Literal Meaning of Genesis*).

THE IMAGE OF WOMEN IN MEDIEVAL LITERATURE. The philosophi-
cal, legal, and religious traditions born in antiquity formed the basis of the
medieval intellectual synthesis wrought by trained thinkers, mostly clerics,
writing in Latin and based largely in universities. The vernacular literary tradition that developed alongside the learned tradition also spoke about female nature and women's roles. Medieval stories, poems, and epics also portrayed women negatively—as lustful and deceitful—while praising good
housekeepers and loyal wives as replicas of the Virgin Mary or the female
saints and martyrs.

There is an exception in the movement of "courtly love" that evolved in southern France from the twelfth century. Courtly love was the erotic love between a nobleman and noblewoman, the latter usually superior in social rank. It was always adulterous. From the conventions of courtly love derive modern Western notions of romantic love. The phenomenon has had an impact disproportionate to its size, for it affected only a tiny elite, and very few women. The exaltation of the female lover probably does not reflect a higher evaluation of women or a step toward their sexual liberation. More likely it gives expression to the social and sexual tensions besetting the knightly class at a specific historic juncture.

The literary fashion of courtly love was on the wane by the thirteenth century, when the widely read *Romance of the Rose* was composed in French by two authors of significantly different dispositions. Guillaume de Lorris composed the initial four thousand verses around 1235, and Jean de Meun added about seventeen thousand verses—more than four times the original— around 1265.

The fragment composed by Guillaume de Lorris stands squarely in the courtly love tradition. Here the poet, in a dream, is admitted into a walled garden where he finds a magic fountain in which a rosebush is reflected. He longs to pick one rose, but the thorns around it prevent his doing so, even as he is wounded by arrows from the God of Love, whose commands he agrees to obey. The remainder of this part of the poem recounts the poet's unsuccessful efforts to pluck the rose.

The longer part of the *Romance* by Jean de Meun also describes a dream. But here allegorical characters give long didactic speeches, providing a social satire on a variety of themes, including those pertaining to women. Love is an anxious and tormented state, the poem explains, women are greedy and manipulative, marriage is miserable, beautiful women are lustful, ugly ones cease to please, and a chaste woman, as rare as a black swan, can scarcely be found.

Shortly after Jean de Meun completed *The Romance of the Rose,* Mathéolus penned his *Lamentations,* a long Latin diatribe against marriage translated into French about a century later. The *Lamentations* sum up medieval attitudes toward women and provoked the important response by Christine de Pizan in her *Book of the City of Ladies.*

In 1355, Giovanni Boccaccio wrote *Il Corbaccio,* another antifeminist manifesto, though ironically by an author whose other works pioneered new directions in Renaissance thought. The former husband of his lover appears to Boccaccio, condemning his unmoderated lust and detailing the defects of women. Boccaccio concedes at the end "how much men naturally surpass women in nobility" and is cured of his desires.[3]

WOMEN'S ROLES: THE FAMILY. The negative perceptions of women expressed in the intellectual tradition are also implicit in the actual roles that women played in European society. Assigned to subordinate positions in the household and the church, they were barred from significant participation in public life.

Medieval European households, like those in antiquity and in non-Western civilizations, were headed by males. It was the male serf (or peasant), feudal lord, town merchant, or citizen who was polled or taxed or succeeded to an inheritance or had any acknowledged public role, although their wives or widows could stand on a temporary basis as surrogates for them. From about 1100, the position of property-holding males was enhanced further: inheritance was confined to the male, or agnate, line—with depressing consequences for women.

A wife never fully belonged to her husband's family, nor was she a daughter to her father's family. She left her father's house young to marry whomever her parents chose. Her dowry was managed by her husband and normally passed to her children by him at her death.

A married woman's life was occupied nearly constantly with cycles of pregnancy, childbearing, and lactation. Women bore children through all the years of their fertility, and many died in childbirth before the end of that term. They also bore responsibility for raising young children up to six or seven. That responsibility was shared in the propertied classes, since it was common for a wet-nurse to take over the job of breast-feeding, and servants took over other chores.

Women trained their daughters in the household responsibilities appropriate to their status, nearly always in tasks associated with textiles: spinning, weaving, sewing, embroidering. Their sons were sent out of the house as apprentices or students, or their training was assumed by fathers in later childhood and adolescence. On the death of her husband, a woman's children became the responsibility of his family. She generally did not take "his" children with her to a new marriage or back to her father's house, except sometimes in artisan classes.

Women also worked. Rural peasants performed farm chores, merchant wives often practiced their husband's trade, the unmarried daughters of the ur-

---

3. Giovanni Boccaccio, *The Corbaccio, or, The Labyrinth of Love,* trans. and ed. Anthony K. Cassell, rev. ed. (Binghamton, N.Y., 1993), 71

ban poor worked as servants or prostitutes. All wives produced or embellished textiles and did the housekeeping, while wealthy ones managed servants. These labors were unpaid or poorly paid but often contributed substantially to family wealth.

WOMEN'S ROLES: THE CHURCH. Membership in a household, whether a father's or a husband's, meant for women a lifelong subordination to others. In western Europe, the Roman Catholic church offered an alternative to the career of wife and mother. A woman could enter a convent, parallel in function to the monasteries for men that evolved in the early Christian centuries.

In the convent, a woman pledged herself to a celibate life, lived according to strict community rules, and worshipped daily. Often the convent offered training in Latin, allowing some women to become considerable scholars and authors, as well as scribes, artists, and musicians. For women who chose the conventual life, the benefits could be enormous, but for numerous others placed in convents by paternal choice, the life could be restrictive and burdensome.

The conventual life declined as an alternative for women as the modern age approached. Reformed monastic institutions resisted responsibility for related female orders. The church increasingly restricted female institutional life by insisting on closer male supervision.

Women often sought other options. Some joined the communities of laywomen that sprang up spontaneously in the thirteenth century in the urban zones of western Europe, especially in Flanders and Italy. Some joined the heretical movements that flourished in late medieval Christendom, whose anticlerical and often antifamily positions particularly appealed to women. In these communities, some women were acclaimed as "holy women" or "saints," while others often were condemned as frauds or heretics.

In all, though the options offered to women by the church were sometimes less than satisfactory, sometimes they were richly rewarding. After 1520, the convent remained an option only in Roman Catholic territories. Protestantism engendered an ideal of marriage as a heroic endeavor and appeared to place husband and wife on a more equal footing. Sermons and treatises, however, still called for female subordination and obedience.

THE OTHER VOICE, 1300–1700

When the modern era opened, European culture was so firmly structured by a framework of negative attitudes toward women that to dismantle it was a monumental labor. The process began as part of a larger cultural movement that entailed the critical reexamination of ideas inherited from the ancient and medieval past. The humanists launched that critical reexamination.

THE HUMANIST FOUNDATION. Originating in Italy in the fourteenth century, humanism quickly became the dominant intellectual movement in Europe. Spreading in the sixteenth century from Italy to the rest of Europe, it fueled the literary, scientific, and philosophical movements of the era and laid the basis for the eighteenth-century Enlightenment.

Humanists regarded the scholastic philosophy of medieval universities as out of touch with the realities of urban life. They found in the rhetorical discourse of classical Rome a language adapted to civic life and public speech. They learned to read, speak, and write classical Latin and, eventually, classical Greek. They founded schools to teach others to do so, establishing the pattern for elementary and secondary education for the next three hundred years.

In the service of complex government bureaucracies, humanists employed their skills to write eloquent letters, deliver public orations, and formulate public policy. They developed new scripts for copying manuscripts and used the new printing press for the dissemination of texts, for which they created methods of critical editing.

Humanism was a movement led by males who accepted the evaluation of women in ancient texts and generally shared the misogynist perceptions of their culture. (Female humanists, as will be seen, did not.) Yet humanism also opened the door to a reevaluation of the nature and capacity of women. By calling authors, texts, and ideas into question, it made possible the fundamental rereading of the whole intellectual tradition that was required in order to free women from cultural prejudice and social subordination.

A DIFFERENT CITY. The other voice first appeared when, after so many centuries, the accumulation of misogynist concepts evoked a response from a capable woman female defender: Christine de Pizan (1365–1431). Introducing her *Book of the City of Ladies* (1405), she described how she was affected by reading Mathéolus's *Lamentations*: "Just the sight of this book . . . made me wonder how it happened that so many different men . . . are so inclined to express both in speaking and in their treatises and writings so many wicked insults about women and their behavior. . . . These statements impelled her to detest herself "and the entire feminine sex, as though we were monstrosities in nature."[4]

4. Christine de Pizan, *The Book of the City of Ladies*, trans. Earl Jeffrey Richards, foreword by Marina Warner (New York, 1982), 1.1.1 (pp. 3–4), 1.1.1–2 (p. 5).

The remainder of the *Book of the City of Ladies* presents a justification of the female sex and a vision of an ideal community of women. A pioneer, she has not simply received the message of female inferiority but, rather, she rejects it. From the fourteenth to the seventeenth century, a huge body of literature accumulated that responded to the dominant tradition.

The result was a literary explosion consisting of works by both men and women, in Latin and in the vernaculars: works enumerating the achievements of notable women; works rebutting the main accusations made against women; works arguing for the equal education of men and women; works defining and redefining women's proper role in the family, at court, in public, describing women's lives and experiences. Recent monographs and articles have begun to hint at the great range of this phenomenon, involving probably several thousand titles. The protofeminism of these "other voices" constitutes a significant fraction of the literary product of the early modern era.

THE CATALOGS. Around 1365, the same Boccaccio whose *Corbaccio* rehearses the usual charges against female nature wrote another work, *Concerning Famous Women*. A humanist treatise drawing on classical texts, it praised 106 notable women, ninety-eight of them from pagan Greek and Roman antiquity, one (Eve) from the Bible, and seven from the medieval religious and cultural tradition; his book helped make all readers aware of a sex normally condemned or forgotten. Boccaccio's outlook, nevertheless, is unfriendly to women, for it singled out for praise those women who possessed the traditional virtues of chastity, silence, and obedience. Women who were active in the public realm, for example, rulers and warriors, were depicted as usually lascivious and as suffering terrible punishments for entering into the masculine sphere. Women were his subject, but Boccaccio's standard remained male.

Christine de Pizan's *Book of the City of Ladies* contains a second catalog, one responding specifically to Boccaccio's. Where Boccaccio portrays female virtue as exceptional, she depicts it as universal. Many women in history were leaders, or remained chaste despite the lascivious approaches of men, or were visionaries and brave martyrs.

The work of Boccaccio inspired a series of catalogs of illustrious women of the biblical, classical, Christian, and local past, among them Filippo da Bergamo's *Of Illustrious Women*, Pierre de Brantôme's *Lives of Illustrious Women*, Pierre Le Moyne's *Gallerie of Heroic Women*, and Pietro Paolo de Ribera's *Immortal Triumphs and Heroic Enterprises of 845 Women*. Whatever their embedded prejudices, these catalogs of illustrious women drove home to the public the possibility of female excellence.

THE DEBATE. At the same time, many questions remained: Could a woman be virtuous? Could she perform noteworthy deeds? Was she even, strictly speaking, of the same human species as men? These questions were debated over four centuries, in French, German, Italian, Spanish, and English, by authors male and female, among Catholics, Protestants, and Jews, in ponderous volumes and breezy pamphlets. The whole literary phenomenon has been called the *querelle des femmes*, the "woman question."

The opening volley of this battle occurred in the first years of the fifteenth century, in a literary debate sparked by Christine de Pizan. She exchanged letters critical of Jean de Meun's contribution to the *Romance of the Rose* with two French royal secretaries, Jean de Montreuil and Gontier Col. When the matter became public, Jean Gerson, one of Europe's leading theologians, supported de Pizan's arguments against de Meun, for the moment silencing the opposition.

The debate resurfaced repeatedly over the next two hundred years. *The Triumph of Women* (1438) by Juan Rodríguez de la Camara (or Juan Rodríguez del Padron) struck a new note by presenting arguments for the superiority of women to men. *The Champion of Women* (1440–42) by Martin Le Franc addresses once again the negative views of women presented in *The Romance of the Rose* and offers counterevidence of female virtue and achievement.

A cameo of the debate on women is included in the *Courtier,* one of the most read books of the era, published by the Italian Baldassare Castiglione in 1528 and immediately translated into other European vernaculars. The *Courtier* depicts a series of evenings at the court of the duke of Urbino in which many men and some women of the highest social stratum amuse themselves by discussing a range of literary and social issues. The "woman question" is a pervasive theme throughout, and the third of its four books is devoted entirely to that issue.

In a verbal duel, Gasparo Pallavicino and Giuliano de' Medici present the main claims of the two traditions. Gasparo argues the innate inferiority of women and their inclination to vice. Only in bearing children do they profit the world. Giuliano counters that women share the same spiritual and mental capacities as men and may excel in wisdom and action. Men and women are of the same essence: just as no stone can be more perfectly a stone than another, so no human being can be more perfectly human than others, whether male or female. It was an astonishing assertion, boldly made to an audience as large as all Europe.

THE TREATISES. Humanism provided the materials for a positive counterconcept to the misogyny embedded in scholastic philosophy and law and inherited from the Greek, Roman, and Christian pasts. A series of humanist treatises on marriage and family, on education and deportment, and on the nature of women helped construct these new perspectives.

The works by Francesco Barbaro and Leon Battista Alberti—*On Marriage* (1415) and *On the Family* (1434–37), respectively—far from defending female equality, reasserted women's responsibilities for rearing children and managing the housekeeping while being obedient, chaste, and silent. Nevertheless, they served the cause of reexamining the issue of women's nature by placing domestic issues at the center of scholarly concern and reopening the pertinent classical texts. In addition, Barbaro emphasized the companionate nature of marriage and the importance of a wife's spiritual and mental qualities for the well-being of the family.

These themes reappear in later humanist works on marriage and the education of women by Juan Luis Vives and Erasmus. Both were moderately sympathetic to the condition of women, without reaching beyond the usual masculine prescriptions for female behavior.

An outlook more favorable to women characterizes the nearly unknown work *In Praise of Women* (ca. 1487) by the Italian humanist Bartolommeo Goggio. In addition to providing a catalog of illustrious women, Goggio argued that male and female are the same in essence, but that women (reworking from quite a new angle the Adam and Eve narrative) are actually superior. In the same vein, the Italian humanist Maria Equicola asserted the spiritual equality of men and women in *On Women* (1501). In 1525, Galeazzo Flavio Capra (or Capella) published his work *On the Excellence and Dignity of Women.* This humanist tradition of treatises defending the worthiness of women culminates in the work of Henricus Cornelius Agrippa *On the Nobility and Preeminence of the Female Sex.* No work by a male humanist more succinctly or explicitly presents the case for female dignity.

THE WITCH BOOKS. While humanists grappled with the issues pertaining to women and family, other learned men turned their attention to what they perceived as a very great problem: witches. Witch-hunting manuals, explorations of the witch phenomenon, and even defenses of witches are not at first glance pertinent to the tradition of the other voice. But they do relate in this way: most accused witches were women. The hostility aroused by supposed witch activity is comparable to the hostility aroused by women. The evil deeds the victims of the hunt were charged with were exaggerations of the vices to which, many believed, all women were prone.

The connection between the witch accusation and the hatred of women is explicit in the notorious witch-hunting manual *The Hammer of Witches*

(1486), by two Dominican inquisitors, Heinrich Krämer and Jacob Sprenger. Here the inconstancy, deceitfulness, and lustfulness traditionally associated with women are depicted in exaggerated form as the core features of witch behavior. These traits inclined women to make a bargain with the devil—sealed by sexual intercourse—by which they acquired unholy powers. Such bizarre claims, far from being rejected by rational men, were broadcast by intellectuals. The German Ulrich Molitur, the Frenchman Nicolas Rémy, and the Italian Stefano Guazzo all coolly informed the public of sinister orgies and midnight pacts with the devil. The celebrated French jurist, historian, and political philosopher Jean Bodin argued that because women were especially prone to diabolism, regular legal procedures could properly be suspended in order to try those accused of this "exceptional crime."

A few experts raised their voices in protest, such as the physician Johann Weyer, a student of Agrippa's. In 1563, he explained the witch phenomenon thus, without discarding belief in diabolism: the devil deluded foolish old women afflicted by melancholia, causing them to believe that they had magical powers. Weyer's rational skepticism, which had good credibility in the community of the learned, worked to revise the conventional views of women and witchcraft.

WOMEN'S WORKS. To the many categories of works produced on the question of women's worth must be added nearly all works written by women. A woman writing was in herself a statement of women's claim to dignity.

Only a few women wrote anything prior to the dawn of the modern era, for three reasons. First, they rarely received the education that would enable them to write. Second, they were not admitted to the public roles—as administrator, bureaucrat, lawyer or notary, or university professor—in which they might gain knowledge of the kinds of things the literate public thought worth writing about. Third, the culture imposed silence upon women and considered speaking out a form of unchastity. Given these conditions, it is remarkable that any women wrote. Those who did before the fourteenth century were almost always nuns or religious women whose isolation made their pronouncements more acceptable.

From the fourteenth century on, the volume of women's writings crescendoed. Women continued to write devotional literature, although not always as cloistered nuns. They also wrote diaries, often intended as keepsakes for their children; books of advice to their sons and daughters; letters to family members and friends; and family memoirs, in a few cases elaborate enough to be considered histories.

A few women wrote works directly concerning the "woman question," and some of these, such as the humanists Isotta Nogarola, Cassandra Fedele, Laura Cereta, and Olympia Morata, were highly trained. A few were professional writers, living by the income of their pen—the very first among them being Christine de Pizan, noteworthy in this context as in so many others. In addition to *The Book of the City of Ladies* and her critiques of *The Romance of the Rose*, she wrote *The Treasure of the City of Ladies* (a guide to social decorum for women), an advice book for her son, much courtly verse, and a full-scale history of the reign of King Charles V of France.

WOMEN PATRONS. Women who did not themselves write, but encouraged others to do so, boosted the development of an alternative tradition. Highly placed women patrons supported authors, artists, musicians, poets, and learned men. Such patrons, drawn mostly from the Italian elites and the courts of northern Europe, figure disproportionately as the dedicatees of the important works of early feminism.

For a start, it might be noted that the catalogs of Boccaccio and Alvaro de Luna were dedicated to the Florentine noblewoman Andrea Acciaiuoli and Doña María, first wife of King Juan II of Castile, while the French translation of Boccaccio's work was commissioned by Anne of Brittany, wife of King Charles VIII of France. The humanist treatises of Goggio, Equicola, Vives, and Agrippa were dedicated, respectively, to Eleanora of Aragon, wife of Ercole I d'Este, duke of Ferrara; to Margherita Cantelma of Mantua; to Catherine of Aragon, wife of King Henry VIII of England; and to Margaret, duchess of Austria and regent of the Netherlands. As late as 1696, Mary Astell's *Serious Proposal to the Ladies, for the Advancement of Their True and Greatest Interest* was dedicated to Princess Ann of Denmark.

These authors presumed that their efforts would be welcome to female patrons, or they may have written at the bidding of those patrons. Silent themselves, perhaps even unresponsive, these loftily placed women helped shape the tradition of the other voice.

THE ISSUES. The literary forms and patterns in which the tradition of the other voice presented itself have now been sketched. It remains to highlight the major issues around which this tradition crystallizes. In brief, there are four problems to which our authors return again and again, in plays and catalogs, in verse and in letters, in treatises and dialogues, in every language: the problem of chastity, the problem of power, the problem of speech, and the problem of knowledge. Of these the greatest, preconditioning the others, is the problem of chastity.

THE PROBLEM OF CHASTITY. In traditional European culture, as in those of antiquity and others around the globe, chastity was perceived as woman's quintessential virtue—in contrast to courage, or generosity, or leadership, or rationality, seen as virtues characteristic of men. Opponents of women charged them with insatiable lust. Women themselves and their defenders—without disputing the validity of the standard—responded that women were capable of chastity.

The requirement of chastity kept women at home, silenced them, isolated them, left them in ignorance. It was the source of all other impediments. Why was it so important to the society of men, of whom chastity was not required, and who, more often than not, considered it their right to violate the chastity of any woman they encountered?

Female chastity ensured the continuity of the male-headed household. If a man's wife was not chaste, he could not be sure of the legitimacy of his offspring. If they were not his, and they acquired his property, it was not his household, but some other man's, that had endured. If his daughter was not chaste, she could not be transferred to another man's household as his wife, and he was dishonored.

The whole system of the integrity of the household and the transmission of property was bound up in female chastity. Such a requirement only had an impact on property-owning classes, of course. Poor women could not expect to maintain their chastity, least of all if they were in contact with high-status men to whom all women but those of their own household were prey.

In Catholic Europe, the requirement of chastity was further buttressed by moral and religious imperatives. Original sin was inextricably linked with the sexual act. Virginity was seen as heroic virtue, far more impressive than, say, the avoidance of idleness or greed. Monasticism, the cultural institution that dominated medieval Europe for centuries, was grounded in the renunciation of the flesh. The Catholic reform of the eleventh century imposed a similar standard on all the clergy and a heightened awareness of sexual requirements on all the laity. Although men were asked to be chaste, female unchastity was much worse: it led to the devil, as Eve had led mankind to sin.

To such requirements, women and their defenders protested their innocence. Furthermore, following the example of holy women who had escaped the requirements of family and sought the religious life, some women began to conceive of female communities as alternatives both to family and to the cloister. Christine de Pizan's city of ladies was such a community. Moderata Fonte and Mary Astell envisioned others. The luxurious salons of the French *précieuses* of the seventeenth century, or the comfortable English drawing rooms of the next, may have been born of the same impulse. Here women might not only escape, if briefly, the subordinate position that life in the family entailed, but they might make claims to power, exercise their capacity for speech, and display their knowledge.

THE PROBLEM OF POWER. Women were excluded from power: the whole cultural tradition insisted on it. Only men were citizens, only men bore arms, only men could be chiefs or lords or kings. There were exceptions, which did not disprove the rule, when wives or widows or mothers took the place of men, awaiting their return or the maturation of a male heir. A woman who attempted to rule in her own right was perceived as an anomaly, a monster, at once a deformed woman and an insufficient male, sexually confused and, consequently, unsafe.

The association of such images with women who held or sought power explains some otherwise odd features of early modern culture. Queen Elizabeth I of England, one of the few women to hold full regal authority in European history, played with such male/female images—positive ones, of course—in representing herself to her subjects. She was a prince, and manly, even though she was female. She was also (she claimed) virginal, a condition absolutely essential if she was to avoid the attacks of her opponents. Catherine de' Medici, who ruled France as widow and regent for her sons, also adopted such imagery in defining her position. She chose as one symbol the figure of Artemisia, an androgynous ancient warrior-heroine, who combined a female persona with masculine powers.

Power in a woman, without such sexual imagery, seems to have been indigestible by the culture. A rare note was struck by the Englishman Sir Thomas Elyot in his *Defence of Good Women* (1540), justifying both women's participation in civic life and prowess in arms. The old tune was sung by the Scots reformer John Knox in his *First Blast of the Trumpet against the Monstrous Regiment of Women* (1558), for whom rule by women, defects in nature, was a hideous contradiction in terms.

The confused sexuality of the imagery of female potency was not reserved for rulers. Any woman who excelled was likely to be called an Amazon, recalling the self-mutilated warrior women of antiquity who repudiated all men, gave up their sons, and raised only their daughters. She was often said to have "exceeded her sex" or to have possessed "masculine virtue"—as the very fact of conspicuous excellence conferred masculinity, even on the female subject. The catalogs of notable women often showed those female heroes dressed in armor, armed to the teeth, like men. Amazonian heroines romp through the epics of the age—Ariosto's *Orlando Furioso* (1532) and

Spenser's *Faerie Queene* (1590–1609). Excellence in a woman was perceived as a claim for power, and power was reserved for the masculine realm. A woman who possessed either was masculinized and lost title to her own female identity.

THE PROBLEM OF SPEECH. Just as power had a sexual dimension when it was claimed by women, so did speech. A good woman spoke little. Excessive speech was an indication of unchastity. By speech, women seduced men. Eve had lured Adam into sin by her speech. Accused witches were commonly accused of having spoken abusively, or irrationally, or simply too much. As enlightened a figure as Francesco Barbaro insisted on silence in a woman, which he linked to her perfect unanimity with her husband's will and her unblemished virtue (i.e., her chastity). Another Italian humanist, Leonardo Bruni, in advising a noblewoman on her studies, barred her not from speech but from public speaking. That was reserved for men.

Related to the problem of speech was that of costume—another, if silent, form of self-expression. Assigned the task of pleasing men as their primary occupation, elite women often tended toward elaborate costume, hairdressing, and the use of cosmetics. Clergy and secular moralists alike condemned these practices. The appropriate function of costume and adornment was to announce the status of a woman's husband or father. Any further indulgence in adornment was akin to unchastity.

THE PROBLEM OF KNOWLEDGE. When the Italian noblewoman Isotta Nogarola had begun to attain a reputation as a humanist, she was accused of incest—a telling instance of the association of learning in women with unchastity. That chilling association inclined any woman who was educated to deny that she was or to make exaggerated claims of heroic chastity.

If educated women were pursued with suspicions of sexual misconduct, women seeking an education faced an even more daunting obstacle: the assumption that women were by nature incapable of learning, that reason was a particularly masculine ability. Just as they proclaimed their chastity, women and their defenders insisted on their capacity for learning. The major work by a male writer on female education—that by Juan Luis Vives, *On the Education of a Christian Woman* (1523)—granted female capacity for intellection but still argued that a woman's whole education was to be shaped around the requirement of chastity and a future within the household. Female writers of the next generations—Marie de Gournay in France, Anna

Maria van Schurman in Holland, Mary Astell in England—began to envision other possibilities.

The pioneers of female education were the Italian women humanists who managed to attain a Latin literacy and knowledge of classic and Christian literature equivalent to that of prominent men. Their works implicitly and explicitly raise questions about women's social roles, defining problems that beset women attempting to break out of the cultural limits that had bound them. Like Christine de Pizan, who achieved an advanced education through her father's tutoring and her own devices, their bold questioning makes clear the importance of training. Only when women were educated to the same standard as male leaders would they be able to raise that other voice and insist on their dignity as human beings morally, intellectually, and legally equal to men.

THE OTHER VOICE. The other voice, a voice of protest, was mostly female, but it was also male. It spoke in the vernaculars and in Latin, in treatises and dialogues, in plays and poetry, in letters and diaries, and in pamphlets. It battered at the wall of prejudice that encircled women and raised a banner announcing its claims. The female was equal to (or even superior to) the male in essential nature—moral, spiritual, intellectual. Women were capable of higher education, of holding positions of power and influence in the public realm, and of speaking and writing persuasively. The last bastion of masculine supremacy, centered on the notions of a woman's primary domestic responsibility and the requirement of female chastity, was not as yet assaulted—although visions of productive female communities as alternatives to the family indicated an awareness of the problem.

During the period 1300–1700, the other voice remained only a voice, and one only dimly heard. It did not result—yet—in an alteration of social patterns. Indeed, to this day, they have not entirely been altered. Yet the call for justice issued as long as six centuries ago by those writing in the tradition of the other voice must be recognized as the source and origin of the mature feminist tradition and of the realignment of social institutions accomplished in the modern age.

We would like to thank the volume editors in this series, who responded with many suggestions to an earlier draft of this introduction, making it a collaborative enterprise. Many of their suggestions and criticisms have resulted in revisions of this introduction, though we remain responsible for the final product.

PROJECTED TITLES IN THE SERIES

Isabella Andreini, *Mirtilla,* edited and translated by Laura Stortoni

Tullia d'Aragona, *Complete Poems and Letters,* edited and translated by Julia Hairston

Tullia d'Aragona, *The Wretch, Otherwise Known as Guerrino,* edited and translated by Julia Hairston and John McLucas

Giuseppa Eleonora Barbapiccola and Diamante Medaglia Faini, *The Education of Women,* edited and translated by Rebecca Messbarger

Francesco Barbaro et al., *On Marriage and the Family,* edited and translated by Margaret L. King

Laura Battiferra, *Selected Poetry, Prose, and Letters,* edited and translated by Victoria Kirkham

Giulia Bigolina, *Urania,* edited and translated by Valeria Finucci

Elisabetta Caminer Turra, *Writings on and about Women,* edited and translated by Catherine Sama

Maddalena Campiglia, *Flori,* edited and translated by Virginia Cox with Lisa Sampson

Rosalba Carriera, *Letters, Diaries, and Art,* edited and translated by Shearer West

Madame du Chatelet, *Selected Works,* edited by Judith Zinsser

Christine de Pizan et al., *Debate over the "Romance of the Rose,"* edited and translated by Tom Conley with Elisabeth Hodges

Christine de Pizan, *Life of Charles V,* edited and translated by Charity Cannon Willard

Christine de Pizan, *The Long Road of Learning,* edited and translated by Andrea Tarnowski

Gabrielle de Coignard, *Spiritual Sonnets,* edited and translated by Melanie E. Gregg

Vittoria Colonna, *Sonnets for Michelangelo,* edited and translated by Abigail Brundin

Vittoria Colonna, Chiara Matraini, and Lucrezia Marinella, *Marian Writings,* edited and translated by Susan Haskins

Marie Dentière, *Epistles,* edited and translated by Mary B. McKinley

Marie-Catherine Desjardins (Madame de Villedieu), *Memoirs of the Life of Henriette-Sylvie de Molière,* edited and translated by Donna Kuizenga

Princess Elizabeth of Bohemia, *Correspondence with Descartes,* edited and translated by Lisa Shapiro

Fairy-Tales by Seventeenth-Century French Women Writers, edited and translated by Lewis Seifert and Domna C. Stanton

Isabella d'Este, *Selected Letters,* edited and translated by Deanna Shemek

Moderata Fonte, *Floridoro,* edited and translated by Valeria Finucci

Moderata Fonte and Lucrezia Marinella, *Religious Narratives,* edited and translated by Virginia Cox

Justine Siegemund, *The Court Midwife of the Electorate of Brandenburg* (1690), edited and translated by Lynne Tatlock

Gabrielle Suchon, *"On Philosophy" and "On Morality,"* edited and translated by Domna Stanton with Rebecca Wilkin

Sara Copio Sullam, *Sara Copio Sullam: Jewish Poet and Intellectual in Early Seventeenth-Century Venice,* edited and translated by Don Harrán

Arcangela Tarabotti, *Convent Life as Inferno: A Report,* introduction and notes by Francesca Medioli, translated by Letizia Panizza

Francesco Buoninsegni and Arcangela Tarabotti, *Menippean Satire: "Against Feminine Extravagance" and "Antisatire,"* edited and translated by Elissa Weaver

Arcangela Tarabotti, *Paternal Tyranny,* edited and translated by Letizia Panizza

Laura Terracina, *Works,* edited and translated by Michael Sherberg

Katharina Schütz Zell, *Selected Writings,* edited and translated by Elsie McKee

APOLOGY

FOR THE WOMAN WRITING

and other works

INTRODUCTION
TO MARIE LE JARS DE GOURNAY
(1 5 6 5 – 1 6 4 5)

THE OTHER VOICE

Among that distinct, but often distinguished, minority who spoke with the "other voice" in early modern Europe—that is, in opposition to the dominant discourse of misogyny—one would be hard-pressed to identify another figure at once as versatile, as prolific, and as thoroughly committed to her particular sense of mission as Marie le Jars de Gournay, whose voice was insistently heard on the French literary scene over a period of roughly fifty years (from the early 1590s to the early 1640s). Hers is a case in which the rubric "woman of letters," which today risks sounding bland and quaint, acquires a radical luster. It also virtually imposes itself, as the most succinct way of conveying her precocious professionalism together with the sheer scope of her endeavors. In a milieu where literary pursuits were largely the privilege of those with independent means, where making a living from writing depended on patronage, where the intellectual education of women was hardly a priority, and where women of even modest standing in "society" were excluded from remunerative labor altogether, Gournay succeeded in fashioning something like what we would term a "career" as an independent intellectual.

Her "business" was letters of all sorts—classical and contemporary, secular and religious, poetic and philosophical. Hence, her contribution covered a wide variety of activities and genres: Gournay was by turns an editor, a translator, an activist on behalf of (and against) controversial literary movements and ideas; as a producer of texts in her own right she was formidably prolific, publishing one novel, a substantial corpus of poetry, and, especially, numerous essays on a broad gamut of subjects. She also corresponded with a number of eminent persons, although few of her letters survive. The final edition of her collected works, published in 1641, when she was in her mid-seventies, runs to roughly a thousand pages. Moreover, many of those pieces, notably including her only work of fiction, *The Promenade of Monsieur de Montaigne* (which appears in English for the first time in the present volume), were continually rewritten, so that they exist in multiple versions—a fact that students of her work need to consider, as, of course, do editors and translators.

Taken all in all, and especially with regard to her disadvantaged position as an intellectually ambitious woman in a masculine world, Gournay's literary achievement, however sprawling and fragmented, stands as a monumental challenge to patriarchal attitudes and structures—hence Élyane Dezon-Jones's title for her edition of selected works: *Fragments d'un discours féminin* (Fragments of a feminine discourse). Further, as even the small sample of Gournay's work included in the present volume will demonstrate, within her oeuvre are to be found explicit subversions and challenges, which are often tightly focused, highly articulate, and dauntingly indignant. Nevertheless, the nature and extent of Gournay's "feminism" are still not a matter of universal agreement. It is true that one cannot responsibly apply the term without allowing for certain contrary cultural biases, which were clearly reinforced in her case by personal circumstances. Thus Gournay's religious and moral conservatism—including her unquestioned acceptance of the value of female chastity—needs acknowledging, as does her general endorsement of class distinctions (despite her frequent critique of the morals and behavior of the highly placed).

At the same time, both of these positions may be recognized as essentially defensive—indispensable to her social survival as a single woman, and one of precarious means. In her position, it was equally inevitable that the author regularly styled herself "la damoiselle [maiden] de Gournay" and that she clung to the notion of her (modestly) noble birth. Also to the point is the grounding of much of her thought in tenets associated with Neoplatonism and Christian humanism—most notably, the interdependence of classical education and moral superiority, of wisdom and right conduct, that often went by the name of "sufficiency" (*suffisance*). Gournay was hardly exceptional among early feminists in this regard. Indeed, the same attitude can be traced into later times—at least to Mary Wollstonecraft (*A Vindication of the Rights of Women* [1792]) and, arguably, to Virginia Woolf in the early twentieth century. The fact remains that Gournay's role as an important feminist forerunner is very much a discovery of recent scholarship. It is a discovery still in process.

LIFE AND WORKS

Gournay's material and psychological struggles began early—at least from the death of her father (whom she apparently loved and admired) in 1577, when she was twelve.[1] Guillaume le Jars was a member of the minor nobility who held a series of increasingly responsible and profitable offices during the reigns of Charles IX (d. 1574) and Henri III (d. 1589). By 1568 he was in a position to purchase the ancient estate of Gournay-sur-Aronde, in Picardy, and the title that went with it.[2] The family initially resided in Paris, where Marie was born on 6 October 1565, the first of six children, four of whom were daughters. Several years after Guillaume's death, however, the ensuing financial difficulties, compounded by the ruinous effect of the civil Wars of Religion then raging, impelled his widow to move with her children to the provincial estate, where it would be possible to live more economically. Still, the financial strain was by no means eliminated, and it was to persist for the rest of Gournay's life. In addition, as she recounts in vivid detail in her most substantial autobiographical piece, *Apology for the Woman Writing*, after the death of her mother in 1591 it was she, as the eldest, who incurred the burden of managing her siblings' precarious affairs.

What Gournay leaves unsaid in that account, but makes unmistakable elsewhere, is that her relation with her mother was by no means an easy one. One of the few ways of improving such a family's fortunes, at that period, was by arranging advantageous marriages. Daughters had to be provided with dowries but might well make alliances that would be profitable socially, if not materially. Apart from the religious life, which was indeed chosen by one of Marie's sisters, there was simply no alternative to such marriage, and Marie was first in line. Already, however, she had independent leanings—and, in particular, literary aspirations, nourished by the celebrated models of learned noblewomen that France had produced, however sparingly. (Prominent among these was Marguerite de Valois, sister to Henri III and wife to the future Henri IV, under whose auspices Gournay was eventually to mingle in

---

1. Marjorie Henry Ilsley, *A Daughter of the Renaissance: Marie le Jars de Gournay: Her Life and Works* (The Hague, 1963), 15. For this part of my discussion, I have relied chiefly on Ilsley's thorough modern biography of Gournay; future citations of this work will appear parenthetically in the text. See also the brief but useful account in English (complementing the same author's extensive treatment in French in *Fragments d'un discours féminin* [Paris, 1988]) by Élyane Dezon-Jones, "Marie le Jars de Gournay (1565–1645)," in *French Women Writers: A Bio-bibliographical Source Book*, ed. Eva M. Sartori and Dorothy Wynne Zimmerman (New York, 1991), 203.

2. It sheds a provocative (if not necessarily equitable) light on the family's position that Pierre de L'Estoile cites some satirical verses dating from 1576 in which a certain "le Jars" is named in a collection of upstart nobles forming part of a corrupt court (*Registre-Journal du regne de Henri III*, ed. Madeleine Lazard and Gilbert Schrenck, 3 vols. [Geneva, 1992–97], 2: 20); the point holds even if the reference is not to Guillaume, as seems likely, but to Louis le Jars, probably his brother, who was also at court (and who, incidentally, was a minor literary figure). See Ilsley, *A Daughter of the Renaissance*, 18, 18 n. 21.

intellectual circles for about a ten-year period, between the queen's return to Paris in 1605, after her divorce from the king, and her death in 1615.) Gournay's mother had no sympathy with such notions, still less with the resistance to her own projects that they engendered.

Given her mother's distaste, and the dearth of educational resources at their country estate, Gournay resorted to a challenging strategy for educating herself—one that manifested the determination and self-discipline she displayed throughout her life. Over a period of years, largely in secret, she managed to teach herself Latin by comparing original texts with French translations. Eventually, she graduated to doing her own translations, especially of Virgil. Greek followed in due course (apparently with some help from a tutor), although she never became fully confident in it (Ilsley, 19). The authors Gournay preferred—prominent among them Seneca and Plutarch—generally matched the taste of the time, as did her humanist assumption, maintained throughout her life, that the raison d'être of reading the classics was that they conduced to virtue. For this reason, too, the Greek philosophers, especially Plato, held a privileged position in her imaginative hierarchy, and it is clear, from her recurrent citation of the *Lives of the Philosophers* by Diogenes Laertius, whose life of Socrates she is known to have translated, that it was at least as much their supposed examples as their writings that attracted her. But if she was a humanist, she was also very much a Christian humanist—specifically, a Roman Catholic one (this mattered vitally in the religiously torn France of her earlier years)—and her devotion to the canonical pantheon of ancient writers and thinkers went hand in hand with a frequently professed respect for the Church Fathers, in whom she also read extensively.

Around 1584, when Gournay was eighteen or nineteen—just at the point when the prospect of marriage would have been most pressing, and oppressive—an event occurred that, in her own subsequent account of it, changed her life. In fact, it offered her, in what must have been her despondent restlessness, a virtual lifeline, by which she was able, it seems, to pull herself to a precarious safety, psychologically if not practically. The event was her reading of the *Essays* of Michel de Montaigne, of which the second edition had recently been published (in 1582). The *Essays* were a radically innovative work in their time, not least for their author's complex self-portrayal, which makes him a fascinating presence within his own work; they also apply abundant classical learning to a wide variety of moral, political, and philosophical questions of contemporary concern, which are often treated in a manner at once iconoclastic and profound. To judge from the *Preface* she wrote to the *Essays* some ten years later, it was this combination of qualities, together with the attraction of Montaigne's vivid style—always a point of sensitivity for Gournay—that instantly led her to cast the author imaginatively in the role of a spiritual and intellectual "father."

The language in which Gournay recounts her discovery has a heady air of intellectual "love at first sight": "They were ready to give me hellebore [traditionally, a remedy against madness], sent into ecstasy as I was when the *Essays* were fortuitously put into my hands at the point when I was leaving childhood behind."[3] In Montaigne she found the reincarnation of the ancient sages (whom he himself abundantly cites)—the third member of a "triumvirate" formed with Plutarch and Seneca (see the *Promenade*, below, 35, and the *Equality*, below, 82). Here was an impeccable patriarchal authority to sponsor her own interests against those of her mother—even, pretty clearly, a safely inaccessible substitute for the husband her mother would have chosen for her. Four years later she visited Montaigne when he was in Paris, expressed her admiration, and invited him to spend time with her in Picardy. The visit lasted three months, and the result was an informal adoptive arrangement, or alliance, such as was not uncommon in intellectual circles at that time. According to her own account—which, however, may well be a fabrication (see below, 25)—it was during this period, during a stroll near her home, that Gournay told Montaigne the tragic story of love gone wrong that became the *Promenade*, the manuscript of which she sent to him after his departure. The slim volume containing the novel, some miscellaneous verses, and translated extracts from the *Aeneid* comprised her first publication, in 1594.

Gournay's mother died in 1591, Montaigne in the following year, leaving Gournay doubly orphaned. She was now free to marry or not—though she was hardly a particularly attractive match from the prevailing practical point of view. Moreover, she was also, in a sense, widowed, and as loyal to Montaigne's memory as she praises his actual widow for being; after all, "there is no lady of merit and worth who would not rather have had her husband that have any other, whoever he might be" (*Preface*, 29). Indeed, she participated in the widow's own loyalty, claiming that Madame de Montaigne sought "to rekindle and rewarm in me the ashes of her husband" (*Preface*, 31).[4] From this point on, Gournay's struggle for a place in the intellectual community was inextricable from her self-appointed role as custodian

---

3. *Preface to the* Essays of Michel de Montaigne by His Adoptive Daughter, Marie le Jars de Gournay, trans. with supplementary annotation by Richard Hillman and Colette Quesnel from the edition prepared by François Rigolot (Tempe, Ariz., 1998), 27. This work will henceforth be cited parenthetically in the text as *Preface*.

4. This image is worth putting in context so as to give a sense of the tangled politics of loyalty and identity at stake in Gournay's relations with Montaigne's widow: "Everyone owes her, if not so much gratitude, at least as much praise as I accord her for having wished to rekindle and re-

of Montaigne's intellectual legacy; in practice, this meant overseeing a succession of reissues of the *Essays*, as she did with an editorial acumen that has been increasingly treated with respect by modern scholars.

These reissues began with her monumental edition of 1595, published with a flamboyant *Preface* defending Montaigne against his critics. The latter piece, which she subsequently retracted under a storm of criticism, remains one of the best introductions to Gournay's preoccupations, both intellectual and social, as well as to her often uneasy mixture of styles and attitudes. For in the course of justifying her "father," as she regularly termed him, she engages equally in self-justification, largely in angry feminist terms that do not necessarily serve her argument (or square with Montaigne's own views, for that matter). She was widely viewed as having impertinently mingled her own interests with those of Montaigne—a veritable usurpation of the "father" by the "daughter." It was a charge she had anticipated and seems to have half-welcomed: "I cannot take a step, whether in writing or speaking, without finding myself in his footsteps; and I believe that I am often supposed to usurp him" (*Preface*, 85). None of the several versions of the *Preface* produced during her lifetime, not to mention the original one, saw the light again before the late twentieth century. But it says even more about dominant attitudes from her own time to ours that the numerous editions of the *Essays* published after her death neglect or obscure her scholarly contribution. Apart from the pains she took with the text itself (not always productively, by modern standards), she provided an index of subjects and authors cited (1611); for a still later edition (1617), she finished tracking down Montaigne's classical citations (with the assistance of several collaborators) and produced French translations, which formed an appendix of nearly a hundred pages. (Editors of her own work, as our notes bear witness, may reasonably suspect her of mischievously imposing the same sort of labor on them.)

After her mother's death, Gournay traveled to Cambrai with her younger brother and a sister, who were generously received into the household of the governor, the Maréchal de Balagny; as she recounts in the *Apology* (see below, 137), she too might have had a place there, but she had chosen to build a far more difficult life for herself in Paris, the center of French cultural activity. She paid a much different visit to Montaigne's widow and family in Périgord, where she began dealing with the literary inheritance of

---

warm in me the ashes of her husband, and, not to marry him, but to make of herself another him—reviving in herself at his death an affection in which she had never participated except by hearing of it—and so truly to restore to him a new appearance of life by the continuation of the friendship that he bore me" (*Preface*, 31).

her "father," and in 1597 she voyaged to Brussels and Antwerp, where she was actually treated as a celebrity by local dignitaries—a highly gratifying experience for her (see below, 144). But she definitively settled into a Parisian existence of genteel poverty, mitigated by the company of a single loyal servant, Nicole Jamyn, but also relieved by regular intellectual stimulation. In her reduced and anomalous circumstances, the opportunities open to her for fulfilling her aspirations as a woman of letters were decidedly limited. Yet she succeeded to a surprising degree. She gained the respect and friendship of a select group of intellectual men. She frequented the literary "salons" of Queen Marguerite and others, where sophisticated conversation was de rigueur, and established one of her own on a more modest scale. Despite her often-expressed scorn for the shallow but pretentious intellects flourishing in high society, she even won some influential friends at court, although the 1610 assassination of Henri IV, whose personal favor she had just obtained, was a particular blow to her. The blow was doubled, moreover, when she ill-advisedly wrote a defense of the Jesuits, on whom the attack was widely blamed, thereby incurring both a social stigma and a satirical attack in print.[5] Nevertheless, she was eventually granted a modest pension by Henri's son and successor, Louis XIII, and still later another by the powerful Cardinal Richelieu.

Above all, Gournay continued to pursue her career as a woman of letters. Apart from her ongoing editorial labors, she produced several new versions of the *Promenade*, which had met with considerable success. She continued composing and publishing her poetry, which appeared in a number of anthologies between 1613 and 1644, as well as translating from the classics. Especially notable is a 1619 collection of excerpts from Virgil, Tacitus, and Sallust, but there were separately published versions of Ovid, Cicero, and, again, Tacitus and Sallust. She worked continually on the essays that form the bulk of her oeuvre. Through them, and otherwise, she plunged headlong into controversies regarding prosody and the French language. This was a subject guaranteed to engage Gournay's passionate idealism about poetry—even to lead her into excesses. Thus, in 1624, she chose to defend Ronsard, the outstanding poet of the previous century, then under attack as old-fashioned, by pretending to have discovered a more "modern" authorial revision of one of his pieces, which she proceeded to publish with a dedication to the king. In fact, the "revision" was her own work (and not particularly distinguished at that).

In more substantial ways, and from our primary perspective today, the

5. See Ilsley, *A Daughter of the Renaissance*, 114–21, who also gives the known facts surrounding Gournay's apparent foreknowledge of the assassination and attempt to alert the king.

1620s, as she approached and entered her sixties, were Gournay's most fruitful period. There is a sense that, while fully retaining her intellectual vigor
and commitment, she was determined to begin shaping a conclusion to her
career. This meant preparing the first collection of her complete works,
which came out in 1626 under the multiply suggestive title of *L'Ombre de la
Damoiselle de Gournay* (The shadow of Miss de Gournay).[6] It also meant having
a particularly frank (if hardly final, as it turned out) say on two interrelated
subjects that had been less directly handled in earlier work. This is the period
when she turned her concentrated and indignant attention to the status of
women, producing the first versions of the two essays for which she is best
known today and which inevitably stand at the center of the present volume:
The Equality of Men and Women, first published separately in 1622, and *The Ladies'
Complaint*, which originally appeared in the collection of 1626. The second
major subject that came to the fore was Montaigne's pervasive one—herself.
L'Ombre saw the first appearance of a moral self-analysis in verse (*Peincture de
moeurs* [Character portrait]), as well as the original version of the *Apology for
the Woman Writing*. The latter text, strenuous and distressed as it is in its account of her personal past and present, should serve as a caveat against the
temptation to view her later years in a calm and gentle light.[7] Special mention may also be made here of Gournay's earliest explicitly autobiographical
text, which was apparently occasioned by one of the practical jokes to which
she was increasingly subjected. She was tricked into writing the *Copie de la vie
de la Demoiselle de Gournay* (Representation of the life of Miss de Gournay),
which is dated 1616, on the pretext that King James I of England wished to
read about her (Ilsley, 126). Her revenge, in a sense, was to publish the piece
anyway, though she did so only in 1641.[8]

The latter date, four years before her death at the age of almost eighty,
is that of Gournay's last edition of her collected works, *Les Advis; ou, Les Presens
de la Demoiselle de Gournay.*[9] A previous version of the *Advis* had appeared in
1634, for which she added several pieces to the first collection of 1626—including her translation of the sixth book of the *Aeneid*—and revised others.

6. The metaphorical suggestions include the "shadowy" presence of her identity throughout the
text, the still-present shadow of Montaigne, and even her defiant ill humor with regard to her
critics. As for the term *damoiselle*, "Miss" comes reasonably close, for a modern English-speaker,
to conveying the claim to genteel celibacy (accompanied, in effect, by an invitation to ridicule)
that belongs to Gournay's use of it in the mid-seventeenth century.
7. See Ilsley's chap. 17, "The Golden Years," in *A Daughter of the Renaissance* (243–65).
8. A similar point is made by Dezon-Jones in *Fragments*, 103.
9. This title, too, is richly suggestive, with multiple puns, and difficult to translate: *Advis* combines "notice," "caution," and "opinions"; *presens* combines "gifts" and "presence"—the latter an especially significant term, given her designation of her first collection as her "shadow."

The 1641 volume further adds and revises, so that it is longer again by over a hundred quarto pages. Not only, then, did she publish a collection in each of her final three decades, but she remained continuously productive virtually until the end of her life. That end, when it finally arrived on 13 July 1645, seems to have come peacefully, piously, and in the company of several close male friends. Also present, naturally, was the ever-devoted Nicole Jamyn, who had actually made provision in her own will, to the best of her ability, for the support of her mistress, should the latter survive her.

THE OEUVRE

The themes of Gournay's work, by contrast with her varied presentation of them from genre to genre, and from revision to revision, remained remarkably constant throughout her career. The subjects of her essays, and of essay-like interpolations in other works (including the *Promenade*), mostly fall into three broad categories: literary theory, moral and social commentary, and autobiography. Further, in her hands these categories overlap to a surprising extent, and especially on common ground that, in a broad sense (and with the qualifications stipulated earlier), may reasonably be termed "feminist." For even where she is not overtly concerned with the general undervaluation and frequent mistreatment of women by men, she regularly manifests her resentment of the injustice dealt to her personally, as an independent woman and intellectual, by an oppressively patriarchal society. Such resentment is a pervasive presence, if often in the background, when Gournay deploys an argument on virtually any subject; it makes itself felt in her tendency to defend herself excessively—that is, against something more than rational counterargument. It also underlies her regular—to the point of nearly obsessive—attacks on calumny, from which she deemed herself to have suffered for most of her life. Finally, it issues in what must be termed a vindictive streak. Indeed, vengeance actually figures as a motif from her earliest work—the suicide of her romance heroine in the *Promenade* has a distinct tinge of revenge extending to patriarchy itself—and surfaces as the subject of an essay that first appeared in 1626. The question posed by the latter's title—"Si la vangeance [sic] est licite" (Whether revenge is legitimate)—is answered, with due qualification, in the affirmative.

Gournay's angry side, however, is conspicuously counterpointed by the emotional generosity she evinces toward those figures, present or past (or indeed mythical), whom she admires. Not all of them are female, by any means, and of course Montaigne occupies a privileged position. The women she celebrates range from those chiefly notable for suffering and endurance to models of intellectual, spiritual, and physical heroism. Dido and Ariadne, who suffered betrayal in love, are invoked throughout the *Promenade;* else-where, classical figures of stoic endurance, such as Porcia, are ranged with Christian saints.[10] Not surprisingly, learned women make frequent points of reference; they are enumerated at length in the *Equality*—from the legendary inventor of the Latin alphabet to her own admiring correspondent Anna Maria van Schurman (1607–78), the outstanding Dutch scholar. Perhaps the most revealing expressions of Gournay's fascination with female strength and achievement are her allusions to the Amazons, who make multiple appear-ances throughout her oeuvre, and to Jeanne d'Arc, whose contemporary glo-rification as the savior of France, as well as the champion of pure morality and religion, impelled Gournay to write several poems in her praise. The writer's ultimate figurations of female triumph, then, are women who excelled in the ultimate masculine sphere, epitomizing the fulfillment of her aspiration to beat men at their own game. For while she liked to envisage herself, in terms redolent of Neoplatonic idealism, as a collaborator in a noble human enter-prise, she was also, at a practical level, a fierce and irascible competitor.

Even in a volume devoted to recording the other voice, it seems impor-tant to conclude this survey by returning to Gournay's major contribution in a field that is not directly gender-related. The essence of her attraction to let-ters was her love of language, hence of poetry, where she considered lan-guage to be most richly developed and deployed. Prominent in her oeuvre are essays on prosody, translation—not surprisingly, given her method of learning the classical languages—and the evolution of the vernacular. All of these, but particularly the last, were contentious topics at the time, and the evidence is clear that her interventions in such debates excited greater con-temporary interest, and controversy, than did her feminist writings. Gournay was not a greatly gifted poet, as she herself acknowledged, but her style in both verse and prose displays a decided talent, besides a pervasive penchant, for vivid diction and imagery. Accordingly, she continued in her maturity to value those aspects of vocabulary and syntax that, in her view, had imparted vividness to the writing she loved in her youth—not least, that of her "father." She also considered metaphors to be essential to imaginative expression, and her own are often strikingly original.[11] These opinions were antipathetic to

10. Dido was the legendary queen of Carthage and lover of Aeneas, who abandoned her; the story of their love affair and of her death by suicide is recounted in Virgil, *Aeneid*, bk. 4. Ariadne fell in love with Theseus and provided him the thread of wool to escape from the Labyrinth af-ter Theseus had killed the Minotaur. The two fled together to Naxos, where Theseus abandoned her (see Ovid, *Heroides* 10). On Porcia, see below, *Equality*, n. 62.

11. See Peggy P. Holmes, "Mlle de Gournay's Defence of Baroque Imagery," *French Studies* 8 (1954): 122–31.

the self-appointed reformers of poetry, and of the French language generally, in early seventeenth-century France, who were led by the court poet François de Malherbe (1555–1628) (see below, *Complaint*, 104 and n. 8). Gournay had some prominent allies in her cause, but she attracted particular ridicule for espousing it, ridicule that increasingly delighted in dismissing her, not just as old-fashioned but as an "old maid" (*vieille fille*) as well. In the end, therefore, the struggle associated with this accomplishment also calls for a reading in feminist terms, as is indeed adumbrated in Ilsley's tribute to her innovation: "She is the only women of her time who has left an analytical and critical work on the French language" (131).

CONTEMPORARY VIEWS

We may usefully begin by reconstructing the intellectual context for Gournay's arguments concerning the female sex, for that context also explains, at least in part, the paucity of recorded response to those arguments. The tradition of public debate about the merits of women that most immediately situates Gournay is that of the *querelle des femmes* (woman controversy), which ramified in the Renaissance throughout European culture but developed with particular vigor in France.[12] Although defenses of women in religious terms may be found even among the early Church Fathers—notably Jerome and Clement of Alexandria—the protracted series of arguments and counterarguments that developed in the early modern period had its immediate roots in late medieval culture, where it was intertwined with issues of courtly love.[13] It is only superficially paradoxical that the latter subject offered plenty of occasions for negative treatments of women—hence, for instance, the misogynist discourse of the thirteenth-century *Roman de la Rose*, as extended by Jean de Meun, which was countered by Christine de Pizan in *The Book of the City of Ladies* (1405).[14]

Now Gournay was certainly aware of the *Roman de la Rose*, since she cites

12. This phenomenon has been much documented and analyzed. See, e.g., Ian Maclean, *Woman Triumphant: Feminism in French Literature, 1610–1652* (Oxford, 1977); Marc Angenot, *Les Champions des femmes: Examen du discours sur la supériorité des femmes, 1400–1800* (Montreal, 1977); and Ruth Kelso, *Doctrine for the Lady of the Renaissance* (Urbana, Ill., 1956).

13. Gournay draws heavily on Jerome, as her own statements and our notes make clear; she obviously finds it useful to enlist his impeccable authority. On Clement's more obscure text, which more closely—even remarkably—anticipates aspects of Boccaccio and Agrippa, see below, *Equality*, n. 24.

14. See the series editors' introduction, above, xiii and xvi–xvii, for a general view of the relation and significance of these works.

it as an example of freedom in the use of language (*Preface*, 41), but it does not figure in her explicitly feminist arguments. Neither does Christine de Pizan.[15] On the other hand, Gournay does, in the *Equality*, include Boccaccio in a list of writers "thoroughly opposed to the disdainers of the female sex and . . . partisans of its advantages, aptitude, and readiness for all praiseworthy functions and practices and for great undertakings" (see below, 83). This is so far from describing most of Boccaccio's work, and especially his general treatment of love matters, that the reference can only be to the series of positive female portraits, *Concerning Famous Women* (ca. 1365), which indeed includes a number of the same figures cited by Gournay. As often, however, she was reading selectively, given the conspicuous conventional prejudices of her precursor. In fact, of the writers she cites, the only one who really fills her laudatory bill is Henricus Cornelius Agrippa, whose *Declamation on the Nobility and Preeminence of the Female Sex* (first published in 1529, twenty years after its delivery as a oration) energized the *querelle des femmes* and exercised an enormous influence on subsequent feminist advocates.[16] These included Gournay, especially in the *Equality*, where, as our notes demonstrate, she redeploys a number of Agrippa's arguments and exempla. She also adopts his basic strategy (which itself has ample precedent in medieval and early modern argumentation) of appealing both to secular instances and to the divine will, the latter as illustrated through biblical citations and illustrations.

Apart from the texts of Boccaccio and Agrippa, there are few definitive points of contact between Gournay's feminist writing and the *querelle des femmes*, although her arguments often run parallel with other works in that tradition. One intriguing case of simultaneous parallelism and divergence involves Claude de Taillemont, the author of the mid-sixteenth-century novel from which she derived the basic plot, and in part the feminist tendency, of the *Promenade*. This issue will be outlined in the introduction to that work. For the moment, a cursory comparison with Boccaccio and Agrippa will suffice to highlight Gournay's shifting of the ground in a personal direction: her autobiographical allusions and bitter commentary confirm that her advocacy of women was no mere exercise; unlike Boccaccio and Agrippa, she writes very much from within the disadvantaged position she deplores. And the position, as she defiantly occupies it, is doubly disadvantaged, for she self-

---

15. Jean-Claude Arnould considers it likely that Gournay was influenced by Christine de Pizan, although this cannot be proved (Arnould, letter to Richard Hillman, 26 January 2000).

16. See the concise summary of Albert Rabil, Jr., introduction to *Declamation on the Nobility and Preeminence of the Female Sex*, by Henricus Cornelius Agrippa, trans. and ed. Albert Rabil, Jr., The Other Voice in Early Modern Europe (Chicago, 1996), 27–29. It is especially pertinent to the case of Gournay that Agrippa strongly influenced Taillemont, whose work also lies behind hers.

consciously engages her subject as an anomalous woman—a woman scholar. Her secular references tend to be less anecdotal, more fully developed in relation to literary and philosophical sources. Her religious arguments, even while evincing greater devotional fervor, go well beyond the more usual biblical references to reveal an extensive and thoughtful acquaintance with the Old and New Testaments, as well as with the Church Fathers. The overall effect is to fold her feminist arguments back into her usurpation of male prerogatives in her professional life as a whole.

This point bears on both the elements sometimes identified as original in Gournay's feminism: first, the fact that she chose, as the *Equality* states and demonstrates, to argue for simple parity between the sexes, not for the superiority of her own; second, the way in which she communicates, through the evolution of her work, "a sense of the history of her protest."[17] She challenges the male establishment on its own ground yet remains outside it; this is also, however, to remain—painfully, often pessimistically, yet also productively— within a psychological version of what Virginia Woolf would term, speaking of a woman writer's necessary private space, "a room of one's own." When she reports, in the *Equality,* that she has learned about Saint Catherine of Siena by reading Saint Francis of Sales (see below, 90 and n. 71), she may have had particularly in mind this passage—from the most extended discussion of Catherine to be found in Francis's two books: "When St. Catherine of Siena's parents deprived her of the time and place for prayer and meditation, our Lord inspired her to make her soul a shrine to which she could retire with him in spirit in the midst of her exterior occupations. Worldly criticism caused her no inconvenience for the same reason; she merely shut herself in this interior shrine, she said, and found consolation with her heavenly spouse."[18] All in all, it is not surprising that the abundant "worldly criticism" attracted by Gournay focused less on her feminist declarations, which after all fit within the familiar framework of the *querelle,* than on her impressive success in using

17. Constance Jordan, *Renaissance Feminism: Literary Texts and Political Models* (Ithaca, N.Y., 1990), 286. On Gournay's attitude toward parity of the sexes, see Lula McDowell Richardson, *The Forerunners of Feminism in French Literature of the Renaissance from Christine of Pisa to Marie de Gournay,* Johns Hopkins Studies in Romance Literatures and Languages, 12 (Baltimore, Md., 1929; reprinted, New York, 1973), 155. On the other hand, Kelso, *Doctrine for the Lady of the Renaissance,* 20–21, demonstrates that this position was widespread within the *querelle des femmes* and cites, among others, Taillemont. She, in her turn, may go rather too far in categorizing those who argued for female superiority (including Agrippa) as "extremists" (284), although the view seems to be shared by Gournay in the *Equality* (see below, 75). It is perhaps best to evaluate Gournay's stance in terms of her development of the idea of *mediocritas*—see Jordan, 281–82.

18. Saint Francis de Sales, *Introduction to the Devout Life,* trans. Michael Day, Everyman's Library (London and New York, 1961), 66.

masculine materials and tools to "make her soul a shrine." In engaging the feminist issue, as she did all issues, specifically as a woman scholar, she received what was ultimately the compliment, however inadvertent, of being engaged as such in return.

Similarly, it was a backhanded tribute to her growing eminence on the cultural scene that she increasingly attracted the hostility and satirical scorn of her (overwhelmingly male) intellectual adversaries. The literary circles of the capital were notoriously fractious in the period, and her taste and talent for controversy seem to have been particularly provocative. As she aged, moreover, it became easier not only to stamp her as a holdover from a remote era but to make fun of her eccentricities. These were real enough, running the gamut from rashness—of tongue, temper, and judgment—to a shameless thirst for praise and a fascination with alchemy. Humorous stories were recounted at her expense; she was the object of practical jokes, the target of satire in print, even of caricature on the stage.

Yet derision was by no means the universal attitude toward Gournay. In her early years, besides the special favor she received from Montaigne, Gournay also sought—and to some extent gained—as a mentor the eminent Flemish humanist scholar Justus Lipsius, equally an admirer of Montaigne. A substantial correspondence developed between them, and his praise of her was echoed in other quarters.[19] Much later in her career, as Ilsley has demonstrated (217–31), she was influential enough to contribute significantly to the founding of the Académie française in 1634. (That institution, ironically, was itself at first subjected to satirical critique for its monitoring of the French language, only to develop subsequently into the epitome of establishment culture.) Gournay had numerous friends and admirers among devotees of learning and literature. And she attracted the explicit praise of two younger feminist scholars.[20] The more noteworthy of these was Anna Maria van Schurman, whom Gournay praises in the *Equality* (see below, 78). Formidably multilingual, Schurman enjoyed a wide reputation throughout Europe and was seen by some as Gournay's successor. The two women were in essential sympathy— witness Schurman's 1641 *Dissertatio de ingenii muliebris ad doctrinam et meliores litteras aptitudine* (Treatise on the suitability of women's nature for learning and higher literary studies). They were also in contact—Gournay actually advised Schurman at one point to devote less energy to studying languages!—and Schurman offers several published compliments to her predecessor. The second

---

19. See *Fragments*, ed. Dezon-Jones, 186–93; *Preface*, 25–29, 25 n. 11; and below, *Promenade*, n. 15.
20. For fuller information, see Ilsely, *A Daughter of the Renaissance*, 211–15, to whom my account is indebted.

feminist voice to be heard in praise of Gournay was that of Marguerite Buffet, writing in 1668, who not only adapted Gournay's arguments—though her case was for the superiority rather than the equality of women—but also included Gournay in her own list of exceptional women.

As a measure of the esteem she had earned from at least some male contemporaries, it is worth mentioning that "epitaphs" were composed for her by a number of prominent intellectuals, who pay tribute to her learning, hence effectively to her life and work. That of François Ogier testifies that in his view she had justified not only her literary paternity but also her claim to be considered on a par with distinguished men of letters: "Marie de Gournay, whom the renowned Montaigne acknowledged as a daughter, Justus Lipsius—and indeed all learned men—as a sister."[21] Finally, the favorable attitude evident here was supported by one serious assessment of her career, with special attention to her ideas about language, that appeared near the turn of the seventeenth century in the *Dictionnaire historique et critique* of Pierre Bayle (1696).

LATER RECEPTION AND INFLUENCE

The salient fact about Gournay's reception and influence is that, after the seventeenth century, not one of her works appeared in print again until the edition of the *Equality* and *The Ladies' Complaint* by Mario Schiff in 1910.[22] Between the seventeenth and the nineteenth centuries she seems to have been virtually forgotten by readers and literary historians alike, except for a few notices dismissing her as old-fashioned and unreadable.[23] Her feminist views seem to have attracted no more attention than did her editorial labors with respect to Montaigne. The revival of interest in her work began with Charles-Augustin Sainte-Beuve's essay on earlier poetry in 1828. There Gournay's position on language once again received respectful attention, as did her own style. Still, it was only toward the end of the nineteenth century that her rehabilitation began on a large scale in major articles and books, the first of the latter being Paul Bonnefon's *Montaigne et ses amis* (1898).[24]

This title, like that of Schiff some twelve years later (*La Fille d'alliance de Montaigne*), points to the fact that Gournay was again being viewed as an adjunct

---

21. "Maria Gornacensis, quam Montanus / ille filiam Justus Lipsius adeoque omnes / docti sororem agnoverunt" (cited in Ilsley, *A Daughter of the Renaissance*, 262).

22. In *La Fille d'alliance de Montaigne, Marie de Gournay* (1910; reprinted, Geneva, 1978).

23. See the survey by Dezon-Jones, "Marie le Jars de Gournay," 204–5; cf. Ilsley, *A Daughter of the Renaissance*, 269–77.

24. Paul Bonnefon, *Montaigne et ses amis: La Boétie, Charron, Mlle de Gournay*, 2 vols. (1898; reprinted, Geneva, 1969).

to Montaigne, who was himself now coming into vogue after relative neglect. And although Schiff chose to print her two most explicitly feminist pieces, his editorial attitude, like that of most commentators, was largely disparaging. From Bonnefon to Pierre Villey, the eminent Montaigne scholar who discusses Gournay in *Montaigne devant la postérité* (1935), and even Alan M. Boase, largely responsible for introducing her to an English-speaking readership in the same year (*The Fortunes of Montaigne*), the name of the "father" dominates, while Gournay comes in for more or less subtle depreciation: her emotionalism, faulty judgment, and lack of self-discipline are recurrently blamed for subverting her intellectual potential.[25] (Boase, however, does take Gournay seriously as a thinker on the philosophical level, as well as with regard to literary theory.)

Given the gender stereotyping of the negative qualities regularly attributed to Gournay, it is hard to resist putting such critiques in her own category of "strokes of contempt" delivered by "doctors with moustaches" (see below, *Complaint*, 103). And the persistence of highly personal scorn into even more recent times makes the same point: there is finally little to choose between the attitude of a 1634 satirical dialogue, in which she is addressed as "Pucelle de mille ans, vieille Muse authentique" (Thousand-year-old maiden, authentic old Muse) (cited Ilsley, 236), and the commentary of Maurice Rat, in the introduction to his major scholarly edition of Montaigne's *Essais* (1962): "Avec son enthousiasme de vieille fille à cheveux blancs, Mlle de Gournay, qui eut le tort de vivre trop longtemps, paraissait un peu ridicule . . . ; elle avait toujours été pédante, mais elle l'était devenue terriblement, et son attitude agressive ou grognon nuisait fort à son 'père.'" [With her enthusiasm of a white-haired old maid, Mademoiselle de Gournay, who made the mistake of living too long, seemed a bit ridiculous . . . ; she had always been a pedant, but she had become one in the extreme, and her aggressive or grumpy attitude did great harm to her "father."][26]

It was largely thanks to women scholars that Gournay began to be taken seriously in her own right and from all points of view even before the advent of late twentieth-century feminism. Lula McDowell Richardson, with *The Forerunners of Feminism in French Literature of the Renaissance* (1929), was an important pioneer, as, in the 1950s, were Holmes and especially Ilsley, who produced a still-unsurpassed (if not always thoroughly reliable) literary biogra-

---

25. Pierre Villey, *Montaigne devant la postérité* (Paris, 1935); Alan M. Boase, *The Fortunes of Montaigne: A History of the* Essais *in France, 1580–1669* (1935; reprinted New York, 1970).

26. Maurice Rat, introduction to *Essais*, by Michel de Montaigne, 3 vols. (Paris, 1962), 1:xiii.

phy. It was, however, the subsequent feminist movement that brought Gournay to the attention of readers apart from scholars of French Renaissance literature and that further induced a number of such scholars to undertake reevaluations, as well as to make available—indispensably—further editions and translations. Even the useful editions and commentaries of Constant Venesoen, resistant to feminist readings as they generally are, show a debt to this new orientation. The resulting climate has also been favorable to two major editorial projects from which we have been privileged to benefit prior to publication: an edition by Jean-Philippe Beaulieu and Hannah Fournier of Gournay's final collected works, the *Advis* of 1641, and a truly mammoth undertaking, a variorum edition of the complete writings under the general editorship of Jean-Claude Arnould.[27]

Milestones along the route of feminist criticism include articles by Domna C. Stanton and Patricia Francis Cholakian; the latter's facsimile edition, with introduction, of the first edition of the *Promenade*; and the innovative combined edition and commentary of Dezon-Jones. Dezon-Jones and Stanton, particularly, have developed an approach to Gournay's life and works in terms of the postmodern theory of *écriture féminine*, emphasizing, respectively, her "kaleidoscopic" mixture of voices and "the problem of the constitution of the subject."[28] These are clearly ideas whose time has come, to judge from their currency and influence: they increasingly inform conference presentations on Gournay, which have been proliferating in recent years; they have encouraged François Rigolot and Philippe Desan valuably to revisit her relation with Montaigne from a discursive point of view.[29]

As for English versions, finally, the original editions of the *Equality* (1622) and *The Ladies' Complaint* (1626) were the first of her few works to be

---

27. Marie le Jars de Gournay, *Oeuvres complètes*, ed. J.-C. Arnould, E. Berriot, C. Blum, A.-L. Franchetti, M.-C. Thomine, and V. Worth, under the direction of J.-C. Arnould (Paris: Champion, 2002), in press.

28. Dezon-Jones in *Fragments*, ed. Dezon-Jones, 80; Domna C. Stanton, "Autogynography: The Case of Marie de Gournay's *Apologie pour celle qui escrit*," in *Autobiography in French Literature*, French Literature Series, vol. 12 (Columbia, S.C., 1985), 22. See also Domna C. Stanton, "Woman as Object and Subject of Exchange: Marie de Gournay's *Le Proumenoir* (1594)," *L'Esprit créateur* 23, no. 2 (1983): 9–25.

29. See François Rigolot, introduction to "Préface à l'édition des *Essais* de Montaigne (Paris: Abel L'Angelier, 1595)," by Marie de Gournay, ed. François Rigolot, *Montaigne Studies: An Interdisciplinary Forum* 1 (1989): 8–20; and Philippe Desan, "The Book, the Friend, the Woman: Montaigne's Circular Exchanges," trans. Brad Bassler, in *Contending Kingdoms: Historical, Psychological, and Feminist Approaches to the Literature of Sixteenth-Century England and France*, ed. Marie-Rose Logan and Peter L. Rudnytsky (Detroit, Mich., 1991), 225–62.

translated—indeed, twice, by Eva M. Sartori and Maja Bijvoet in 1987 and 1989, respectively.[30] In choosing to present here Gournay's latest revised versions of these two central feminist texts—those of the *Advis* of 1641—we have sought to provide readers not only with the author's "last word" (likewise the case with the 1641 *Apology*) but also with the material for a comparative study, so that her practice of revision, so important throughout her career, may be at least roughly grasped. With regard to the *Promenade*, by contrast, we have responded to that practice by recuperating the first published version, which contains a long "digression," subsequently eliminated, on the subject of male-female relations—a particularly forceful manifestation, even a cri du coeur, of the other voice.

30. Marie de Gournay, "Of the Equality of Men and Women" and "The Complaint of the Ladies," trans. Eva M. Sartori, *Alligorica* 9 (Winter 1987): 135–63, and "The Equality of Men and Women" and "The Ladies' Grievance," trans. with a biographical introduction by Maja Bijvoet, in *Women Writers of the Seventeenth Century*, ed. Katharina M. Wilson and Frank J. Warnke (Athens, Ga., 1989), 3–29. The translations of Bijvoet are readily accessible, those of Sartori less so. To our knowledge, the only other translations published prior to the present volume are our own of the 1595 *Preface* and "Imitation of the Life of Damoiselle de Gournay," a rendition by Élyane Dezon-Jones of *La Copie de la vie de la Demoiselle de Gournay*, in *Writings by Pre-Revolutionary French Women: From Marie de France to Élisabeth Vigée-Le Brun*, ed. Anne R. Larsen and Colette H. Winn (New York, 2000), 237–41.

THE PROMENADE OF
MONSIEUR DE MONTAIGNE
(1594)

INTRODUCTION

Gournay's only work of fiction, the raison d'être of her first published volume, falls under the generic rubric of *histoire tragique*. The forerunner of the Gothic form, the *histoire tragique* had for some decades been a popular kind of romantic and sensational narrative, typically involving tangled erotic relations and invariably ending in disaster. The *Promenade* delivers the standard elements in profusion, beginning with an exotic setting (ancient Persia) and a beautiful princess (Alinda) menaced with arranged marriage. The main action then gets underway with a desperate love affair, an elopement, and a shipwreck on the shores of barbarous Thrace. After passing through a complex amorous intrigue involving a lustful Thracian lord and his unscrupulous sister, the tale concludes with the bloody suicides of both the heroine and the husband who has betrayed her (Leontin). This is, then, raw material that is especially raw. In processing it, however, Gournay makes several provocative contributions—much against the grain of the genre, which tended to wallow in standard female (and male) stereotypes—so as to produce a text that may fairly be labeled feminist in its broad trajectory, as well as in significant particulars.

Gournay's most distinctive contributions bear on the movement of the narrative and on the representation of the characters. In the first category, there are two main effects, which attest a determination to guide the reader's reception of the romance plot: at numerous points, the author either comments directly on the story or interpolates classical citations within it— equally a form of commentary. The most notable of the former instances is a "digression" that not only interrupts the action at its most dramatic moment (as Alinda is preparing for her death) but even threatens to eclipse it by extending to about a quarter of the entire text. Gournay's commentary here, which is hardly digressive in thematic terms, consists of reflections on

21

the inconstancy of men, its potentially tragic consequences, and the consequent necessity for women to guard against false promises and superficial attractions.

Her reflections are occasioned by one of her citations, and indeed the same note of female vulnerability resounds through the great majority of the latter, most of which are taken from the portrayal of the tragic fate of the abandoned Dido in Virgil's *Aeneid* or from the so-called *Epithalamium* of Catullus (number sixty-four in Catullus's oeuvre)—a poem that backhandedly celebrates the mythical marriage of Peleus with the nymph Thetis by recounting the abandonment of Ariadne by Theseus. It should be noted that in subsequent versions of the *Promenade* Gournay not only omitted the major digression—a principal reason for our choice of the 1594 edition for translation—but also rendered the classical quotations into French. These she had at first incorporated in the original, as if to demonstrate that a woman, however painfully her acquaintance with the classics might have been acquired, could move comfortably in scholarly territory normally reserved for men.[1]

Gournay's most decided innovation, however, takes place on the level of characterization and is linked with various elements of plot. As it happens, it is possible to gauge her originality with precision, because the basic elements of her story, as she allows in the dedicatory epistle, are derived from "a little book that I happened to read about a year ago" (30), whose title and author, she affirms, have slipped her mind; but then even if she still had the book in hand, she continues, "I would wish just as much as at present to borrow nothing from it, because I would make it a point of honor not to sully its inventions with an admixture of my own and because I have not learnt the example of Aesop's crow—except for the sake of shunning it" (30). It is highly likely that Gournay is merely pretending to "forget" Claude de Taillemont's popular work of 1553, *Discours des champs faëz* (Discourses of the enchanted fields), since she retains not just the basic plot but even the name of the central male character of one of the narratives contained within it. She all but gives the game away when she affirms her originality by citing the same Aesopian fable (it concerns the crow's vain attempt to beautify himself with the feathers of other birds) that is invoked in her source-text for the same purpose.[2] The effect, for an astute contemporary reader, would have been to call attention

1. Hence it has seemed to us especially important to present the original texts in our notes. They have been regularized according to standard modern scholarly editions.

2. See *Le Promenoir de Monsieur de Montaigne: Texte de 1641, avec les variantes des éditions de 1594, 1595, 1598, 1599, 1607, 1623, 1626, 1627, 1634,* ed. Jean-Claude Arnould, Études montaignistes, 26 (Paris, 1996), 51 n. A; and Claude de Taillemont, *Discours des champs faëz,* ed. Jean-Claude Arnould, Textes littéraires français (Geneva, 1991), 168 n. 165. Even the assumed memory lapse has its counterpart in the source (Arnould, introduction to *Le Promenoir,* 2).

to the complex (even ambivalent) dynamic of borrowing and subversion that marks Gournay's text.

It must be stipulated that, in adapting the *histoire tragique* to the cause of women, Gournay is, up to a point, taking her cue from her predecessor, who dedicated his *Discours* as a whole "À l'honneur, et exaltation de l'Amour et des Dames" [To the honor and exaltation of love and ladies]. This subtitle Gournay might well have found contradictory in itself, however, and the contradictions in Taillemont's work hardly stop there, as Patricia Francis Cholakian has shown in her comparative analysis of the two novels.[3] Rather, they lead to a conclusion that Gournay appears to have shared with modern feminism—namely, that to celebrate women in the context of courtly love, as after all was regularly done, is a very different matter from promoting their interests as human beings. Certainly, Taillemont closely anticipates some of Gournay's own arguments in both the *Promenade* and the *Equality*, including her case for educating women, yet his celebration of romantic love never lets one forget that he writes from outside the position he advocates. And the male narrator who tells the story that furnishes the *Promenade* with its plot actually purports to teach "Mes-demoiselles assez subjettes à mutation" [young ladies susceptible to fickleness] to remain "constantes et loyales en amitié" [constant and loyal in friendship]—that is, in conformity with the courtly love ideal, even if their lovers are not worthy of them (or even, presumably, drive them treacherously to their deaths).[4]

Although the endurance and courage of Gournay's heroine are themselves largely anticipated in the precursor narrative, the lack of a psychological dynamic in the characters of Taillemont finally fosters a view of Laurine (the counterpart of Alinda) not as sacrificed on the altar of patriarchal values but, on the contrary, as justly punished for having disobeyed her father. Gournay richly supplies such a dynamic and makes changes to plot and structure accordingly. In Taillemont, the causes of the tragic effects are largely external, if not arbitrary. Gournay eliminates the mysterious aunt of the heroine—the equivalent of the wicked witch of fairytale—and supplies her place with an important psychological presence, a living mother, of whom Alinda thinks intensely in her pathetic last moments. Gournay turns the unworthy Leontin from a cynical illicit lover into a feckless husband and makes him less calculating, less conscious even of his treachery. Instead, he is the conspicuous dupe of his own passions and egotism, and when he is

3. See Patricia Francis Cholakian, introduction to *Le Proumenoir de Monsieur de Montaigne* (1594), by Marie le Jars de Gournay, facsimile reprint, ed. Patricia Francis Cholakian (Delmar, N.Y., 1985), 8–18.

4. Taillemont, *Discours*, 270.

confronted with the consequences of his actions, his intense remorse renders him worthy, if hardly of the living Alinda, at least of a noble suicide whereby he can mingle his blood and ashes with hers and share in the self-accusing pity of the "barbarian" who is the immediate author of their destruction.[5] His belated recuperation of loyalty makes for a significant difference from the Leontin of Taillemont, who, though he comes to pay lip service to his guilt, never ceases to think of himself first and meets death at sea in an attempt to flee the wrath of his frustrated rival. The love-stricken Thracian Othalcus is less crude, more sympathetic, than his counterpart Sador, while his sister—and here Gournay pointedly refuses to endorse a simplistic distinction between admirable women and despicable men—is no longer the innocent friend of the heroine but blinded by her own passion for Leontin. Alinda herself is at the outset less conscious than Laurine of the practical attractions and advantages that complicate her emotions; it is therefore fitting that she discovers the treachery of Leontin not from his self-interested rival but on her own—by involuntarily eavesdropping, as if she were at last compelled to listen to an inner voice. And instead of being punished, she punishes herself—and the patriarchal world in the process—for not having paid attention to that voice sooner.

Neither the story itself nor Gournay's development of it would necessarily have made the *Promenade* a natural candidate for dedication to Montaigne, who disapproved of romantic fiction and whose attitude to women is generally taken to have been equivocal, at best. Nevertheless, the very title, supported by various direct addresses to Montaigne throughout the text, resoundingly proclaims the *Promenade* to be his, even as the dedicatory epistle explains the attribution in terms hinting at an ambivalence within their relation unknown to Gournay herself. According to the epistle, the *Promenade* derives directly from an idyllic moment: while walking with Montaigne during

---

5. Several elements suggest (however inconclusively, given the commonplaces involved) that Gournay's adaptation of Taillemont may have been influenced by an intermediary text, the *histoire tragique* of Perside, Eraste, and Soliman by Jacques Yver, first published in 1574 in *Le Printemps d'Yver contenant cinq histoires discourues par cinq journées en une noble compagnie au château du Printemps* [The springtime of Yver ("winter"), containing five stories related over five days in a noble assembly at the château of spring], ed. Paul Lacroix (1841; reprinted, Geneva, 1970), 532–48. Yver's tale of lovers driven to their deaths by the jealous sultan Soliman shows numerous reminiscences of Taillemont's *Discours* but makes the couple a faithful husband and wife, whose noble constancy is acknowledged when their remains are united in the elaborate tomb raised by the guilt-stricken Turk. The narrator comments, "Voilà comment ce pauvre barbare, par un dernier honneur digne d'une somptuosité persique, voulut réparer la faute commise, de laquelle s'accusant soi-même, protesta d'en faire deuil toute sa vie" [Lo, how that wretched barbarian, by a last honor worthy of Persian sumptuousness, sought to redeem the fault he had committed, accusing himself of

his visit to the family estate, Gournay was able to recount the tale, which she subsequently wrote out for him, of the "vicissitudes of love" (below, 29) in an atmosphere of perfect intellectual and spiritual complicity. The adoptive "father" and "daughter" shared a consummate "good will" that "nevertheless surpasses that of real fathers and children" (29).

This is Gournay's heavily Neoplatonic version of "true love," an intellectual bond uniting like spirits—potentially across time and space, not to mention "accidental" differences such as gender and age. In fact—and the fact is telling in itself—the gap in this case may well have been wider than Gournay allows: Arnould has convincingly shown that her account of the origins of the *Promenade* is probably as fictional as the tale itself and that the work may well have been composed, not merely recovered, after she learned of Montaigne's death.[6] In any case, Gournay's putative transformation of speech into writing palpably enacts the encroachment of "better knowledge"—an Eve-like fall from the imagined purity of the originating experience into an acute sense of the barriers between them, and of her own identity as not merely subordinate but precariously contingent: "The reason that impels me to put it [the story] in writing now and send it, following your departure, to run after you, is so that you may have a greater opportunity to recognize in it the faults of my style than you would have had in my recounting, which went by quickly. . . . I do not know if I am not willingly taking pleasure in committing some foolishness on purpose, so as to put you, in chastising me, my father, to the exercise of the power you have over me" (30).

The "identity politics" couched playfully, perhaps quite fancifully, here are painfully played out in tragic and erotic terms within the fiction itself, in which the daughter, princess though she is—and clearly fit for exalted undertakings—is betrayed to base destruction by her female condition, at once disappointing her noble father and incurring humiliation from the unworthy lover she allows to take his place. These are the "vicissitudes of love" with a vengeance. It would be fascinating to know what Montaigne might have made of this highly charged and conflicted act of homage; as solicitous of his good opinion as Gournay professes to be in the epistle, she did not venture—

---

which, he vowed to remain in mourning all his life] (548). Similarly, Gournay's Thracian and his sister "firent vn long & grand deuil, apres auoir posé l'orne de leur commune cendre en vn sepulcre qu'ils feirent eriger expres" [went into long and deep mourning, after having placed the urn with the common ashes in a tomb that they had erected for the purpose] (Cholakian, ed., fol. 65r; below, 67).

6. Arnould, introduction to *Le Promenoir*, 3–4. The evidence includes changes made in subsequent editions to the dating of the epistle and to the amount of time she claims to have elapsed between the narration and the writing down of the story.

presuming that the circumstances of composition are invented—to supply him with a response.

If the *Promenade* has never before been translated into English, it also remained unpublished in French from the seventeenth century until the very late twentieth. Yet beginning in 1986, with the facsimile reprint of the original version edited by Cholakian (the basis of our translation), the novel's modern publication history recalls that of its own era, when its popularity resulted in nine editions after the first in 1594 (counting its appearances in Gournay's successive collected works). Its current interest for students and scholars of Gournay is reflected in its inclusion in Constant Venesoen's 1993 anthology and, especially, in the monumental variorum edition, expertly annotated, that was produced by Jean-Claude Arnould in 1996. As the latter volume vividly demonstrates, in the case of the *Promenade*, Gournay's layers of revision form fascinating narratives of their own, telling several stories at the same time: one of the evolution of her style, another of her assimilation of classical allusions into the vernacular, a third of her moderation of overt feminist declaration—perhaps coexisting, paradoxically, with a broader and more thoroughly integrated critique of power relations—and even a fourth of the transition from the Renaissance to the baroque era.[7] These are all finally, in some measure, stories about the other voice. Yet it is arguably in the original version, most vividly illuminated by the afterglow—and tinged by the shadow—of the richly imagined presence of Montaigne, that Gournay most powerfully releases, by an innovative route, the symbolic power inherent in the fantastic romance as a genre and that the *Promenade* comes closest to justifying the claim of Domna C. Stanton that it constitutes the "'embryon' of the modern novel."[8]

7. On Gournay as engaging in a critique of power relations, see Cathleen M. Bauschatz, "'Les Puissances de Vostre Empire': Changing Power Relations in Marie de Gournay's *Le Proumenoir de Monsieur de Montaigne* from 1594 to 1626," in *Renaissance Women Writers: French Texts/American Contexts*, ed. Anne R. Larsen and Colette H. Winn (Detroit, Mich., 1994), 197–99.

8. Domna C. Stanton, "Woman as Object and Subject of Exchange," 13.

THE PRINTER TO THE READER[1]

It was several years ago that this little book was sent to the late Monsieur de Montaigne by his adoptive daughter. It has been found among his papers since his death, and Messieurs his relations had it brought to me because they thought it worthy of seeing the light and capable of doing honor to the deceased—if anything can be added to the glory of such a great and divine personage. So have a look for yourself, Reader.

1. This note of the "printer," which was varied revealingly in subsequent editions, is certainly by Marie de Gournay herself—see Jean-Claude Arnould, introduction to *Le Promenoir,* 2–3.

DEDICATORY EPISTLE

To Michel, Lord Montaigne

You well understand, Father, that I name this your promenade[2] because, when we were strolling only three days ago, I told you the story that follows, as suggested to me by the reading that we had just done of a variation on the same theme (it was the vicissitudes of love, in Plutarch). The reason that impels me now to put it in writing and send it, following your departure, to run after you, is to give you a greater opportunity to recognize in it the faults of my style than you would have had in my recounting, which went by quickly. Sample it, therefore, and correct me; but I fear lest, if I charge you to note its defects, you may say to me that it would be more difficult to perceive its graces. That can't be helped. If you do not excuse me, you will excuse my age, and the good will you bear me will grant its pardon, if reason refuses. In truth, if someone is surprised that, although we are not father and daughter except in title, the good will that allies us nevertheless surpasses that of real fathers and children—the first and closest of all the natural ties— let that person try one day to lodge virtue within himself and to meet with it in another; then he will scarcely marvel that it has had more strength and power to harmonize souls than nature has. Natural affections have often failed; brothers have made war on each other, even fathers and children, but the most sacred love of Pythias and Damon, whom reason (nature appropriates the scepter among beasts—among men, reason must wield it) had joined together by the merit of their sufficiency and their virtue, was inviolable.[3] It is necessary to enter into friendships by the gates of virtue, for one who

---

2. In French, a *promenoir* unambiguously designates a place, not an activity.

3. The mutual devotion of Damon and Pythias, Pythagorean philosophers, was a legendary type of ideal friendship, even if the friend in question was really called Phintias; see *Preface*, 97. Gournay here is establishing her relation with Montaigne in terms that are recognizably Neoplatonic

would be well assured of not leaving except by those of death. Now, finally, do not be offended that I have dared to adorn such a worthless toy with your name, for I mingle it there only like that of Jupiter among the sacrifices offered him.

I derive the plot of this tale from a little book that I happened to read about a year ago, and inasmuch as I have never been able to see it again since then, I have even forgotten its name and that of its author as well. Yet, were I to have it in hand, I would wish just as much as at present to borrow nothing from it, because I would make it a point of honor not to sully its inventions with an admixture of my own and because I have not learned the example of Aesop's crow—except for the sake of shunning it.[4] I prefer to be empty rather than full of debts. But it remains an annoyance that a female pen is always constrained, in such subjects as this one, to flow in flaccid strokes. Those strokes bear in recompense, however, the utility of warning women to be on their guard. What is more, your opinion having borne honorable witness that my understanding was more apt for solid than for light matters, you will judge at once that, if I share with you certain verses, which are at the end of this work, it is not a stroke of ambition but of conscience—that is, to ensure that you do not deceive yourself by misjudging me to be subtler than I am. It is all one, although I do not know if I am not willingly taking pleasure in committing some foolishness on purpose, so as to put you, in chastising me, my father, to the exercise of the power you have over me.

(though not necessarily un-Aristotelian—see the *Eudemian Ethics* 1245a[7.12]). Compare in the *Preface*, 87–97, Gournay's adaptation to their relation of the terms employed by Montaigne in his essay "De L'Amitié" [On friendship], in *Les Essais de Michel de Montaigne*, ed. Pierre Villey (Paris, 1965), 1.28.183–95. All subsequent citations of Montaigne are to this edition and are by book, chapter, and page numbers, with the letters A, B, and C referring, respectively, to the versions of 1580, 1588, and subsequent manuscript additions; any translations are our own.

We have chosen in this text to translate literally the word *suffisance*—Gournay's favorite term of praise at this period—where its connotations appear so thoroughly contingent on cultural and personal values that alternatives would be unduly restrictive. Compare *Preface*, 27 and 27 n. 12. In the latest editions, suggestively, she speaks instead of *sagesse* (wisdom).

4. Gournay refers to the famous fable widely known as "De Graculo" (usually translated as "The Vain Jackdaw" or "The Jackdaw and the Birds"); see Aesop, *The Complete Fables*, trans. Olivia and Robert Temple (London, 1998), 119 (no. 162); and Erasmus, *Adages* (no. 2591). The fable had long lent itself to the question of literary originality, since it concerns the ugly bird's vain attempt to beautify himself with the feathers of other birds, so that he might be chosen king. It is highly ironic—to the point where the irony must be deliberate—that, as Arnould observes (*Le Promenoir*, 51 n. A), Taillemont had himself invoked the fable in support of the originality of his *Discours*.

As for the translation from the *Aeneid,* which you will also see, since the noble Du Bellay himself has engaged himself in this before me, the others who have taken part in that enterprise with him must not accuse me of impugning him with the idea of gaining the prize.[5] On the contrary, they ought to wish for companions in the race, from whom they would glean honor; for competition is the essence of victory. It is a highly laborious and ticklish business to render such poets. Convey the intelligence without the beauty, or the beauty without the intelligence, and you make a fool of yourself. Take care to convey one as well as the other, and, apart from the extreme difficulty involved, you cannot help adding something to them, in the choosing of which, so as not to diminish the poem, one normally gets worn out; and inevitably, in the end, do as well as you please, they lose out in the exchange of languages. And as for the fact that the rhyme will sometimes appear a bit freer than in the compositions of our poets, one slavish version will excuse me for this only too well in the eyes of the clear-sighted. Now I would like to be able to give you two or three hours of my reading, so as to make you laugh at the futile use I have made here of a few evenings, but a page-boy will be charged with that function in my place, so as to keep you, on one of those evenings after supper, from exercising your soul in more serious occupations.

I kiss the hands of Madame de Montaigne and my sister Mademoiselle de Montaigne, as well as of your brothers, Messieurs de la Brousse and de Mattecoulon, who do me the honor of declaring themselves also members of my family (as for Monsieur d'Arsat, I believe that he is not with you)[6] that they will not make fun of the worthlessness of this work—if Monsieur de Mattecoulon does not wish me to complain that he has by no means made use of the credit that his well-known valor has

---

5. The author refers to her translation of book 2, included in the same volume as the *Promenoir,* together with miscellaneous verses. Joachim du Bellay (1522–60) had published several excerpts from Virgil's work, and, since 1560, there had been a complete French version by Louis des Masures (Arnould, ed., *Le Promenoir,* 52 n. A). Ilsley, *A Daughter of the Renaissance,* 193 n. 26, counts seven French renderings in the sixteenth century and comments (193–96) on translation from the *Aeneid* as a significant activity throughout Gournay's career. Martine Debaisieux provides a stimulating feminist analysis of some of Marie de Gournay's translations in "Marie de Gournay cont(r)e la tradition: Du *Proumenoir de Monsieur de Montaigne* aux versions de l'*Énéide,*" *Renaissance and Reformation/Renaissance et Réforme,* n.s., 21, no. 2 (1997): 45–58.

6. The "family" here referred to included Montaigne's wife, Françoise de la Chassaigne, his only surviving daughter Léonor, and his three brothers: Pierre, seigneur de la Brousse; Bertrand, seigneur de Mattecoulon; and Thomas, seigneur d'Arsac. As the remainder of the sentence implies, Bertrand was indeed known for his military prowess.

lent him with Minerva to induce her to give me a pen as good as the sword she gives to him.[7] Father, receive here the adieu of your daughter, glorified and beatified by that title.

> Nor is there any fear that our descendants will grudge to enroll our name among those renowned for friendship, if only the fates are willing.[8]

At Gournay the 26th of November, 1588.

7. Minerva, the Roman goddess corresponding to the Greek Athena, presided over warfare as well as the arts of peace, including letters and learning. She appears in a dream-vision to initiate at once the action and the ethos of Taillemont's *Discours*.

8. "Nec metus, in celebres ne nostrum nomen amicos / Invideant inferre, sinant modo fata, nepotes." Arnould has informed us (conversation with R. Hillman, May 2000) of his discovery, since his initial edition of *Le Promenoir*, that these verses are taken from Estienne de la Boétie, "Ad Michaëlem Montanum," 10–11 (*Oeuvres complètes d'Estienne de la Boétie*, ed. Paul Bonnefon [1892; reprinted, Geneva, 1967], *Poemata* 20 [p. 225]). Gournay is thus implicitly appropriating for herself and Montaigne the latter's intimacy with La Boétie, as she does elsewhere—see *Preface*, 95–99 and nn. 98 and 100 there.

THE PROMENADE OF MONSIEUR DE MONTAIGNE—
FOR HIMSELF

Father:

The king of Persia having been captured by another potent king—that of the Parthians—in the final battle of a long war, the Persians, laid prostrate by that blow, knew no other course than to try to make good fortune out of patience and went to offer the victor carte blanche, in order to obtain peace for their miseries and deliverance for their Prince. Now, whatever his true reason may have been, he settled for conditions that were far from ruinous to the state. Yet, having demanded, as one article, marriage with a beautiful and well-born princess, the daughter of a Satrap who was the uncle of the King himself, it was supposed that he treated Persia so mildly for her sake, wishing to oblige her by making a present of the safety of her country, as if in advance of a splendid and magnificent settlement, and how much he must love her was judged by his offering her straightaway, to purchase her favor, a prize of victory, and one that depended wholly on his will.

The father of the lady—

> . . . a royal maiden, whose chaste little bed, breathing forth sweet odors, nurtured her in a soft maternal embrace, as the streams of Eurotas beget the myrtles, or the spring breeze brings forth the flowers in varied colors[9]—

---

9. Virgo Regia, quam suavis expirans castus odores
    Lectulus, in molli complexu matris alebat
    Quales Eurotae progignunt flumina myrtos
    Aurave distinctos educit verna colores.

    (*The Poems of Gaius Valerius Catullus*, trans. and ed. F. W. Cornish, in *Catullus, Tibullus and Pervigilium Veneris*, rev. ed., Loeb Classical Library [London and New York, 1924], 64.86–90)

33

a wise old man and the second in rank of Persia, found the prospect of a foreign marriage disturbing, inasmuch as he saw himself thereby deprived of the future reign of his daughter's children, to whom the realm would descend, the King having no hope at all of issue.[10] Nevertheless, he let himself be bound by the desire of the country, and of the Prince, and betrothed her to him by means of the Persian ambassadors, whom he dispatched to him shortly afterward.

Now the princess, who was named Alinda, found it very hard that she would have to renounce her sweet native air, the bosom of her mother and company of family and friends, to cast herself, as a spoil of the right of victory, upon the mercy of a man unknown to her, and of a proud and barbarous nation, where the only sweetness left to her[11] would be to weep and miss Persia to her heart's content.

But her father remonstrated with her, saying, "Remember your condition, my daughter: considerations of personal welfare are for private persons, who have none but individual interests; but princes, who have charge of the public sphere, should be moved only by regard for the public. So if we suppose ourselves to have been born at once kings and free persons,[12] true, every man is subject to only one Prince, but a Prince is subject to all men: he is the sole person in a state who can refuse nothing for its welfare, and the sole whom all can reproach for its ruin when it arrives, if he has not anticipated it with his own. If we command many, it is to do good to many, for we are superiors only to be protectors, and what we can impose on the common people we should employ on their behalf; those who say that heaven showed it cherished us, and was declaring us its eldest sons in making us kings, say true, but this is not (as they suppose) that we may be set up to rule the rest of mankind (for that privilege costs us too dearly), but because, in the greatness of our power, heaven suggests to us the means of doing more

---

We have regularized Marie de Gournay's citations of Catullus according to Cornish's text but have preferred to supply our own translations. As part of the process of ongoing revision, Gournay eventually either eliminated the *Promenade*'s Latin and Greek quotations or translated them (freely) into French. Her rendering of this passage from Catullus, which first appeared in 1626, stresses the maternal element. She completed a translation of book 4 of the *Aeneid*, from which there are a number of excerpts in *Le Proumenoir*, in 1634 (Ilsley, *A Daughter of the Renaissance*, 193).

10. This appears to qualify as a low-key contribution to the controversy, fueled by the religious question, over France's Salic Law, which barred claims to the throne by way of the female line. See *Equality*, below, 84.

11. *Leur* (them) in the 1594 text does not seem right, and we have translated according to post-1599 editions, which substitute *lui* (her).

12. Later editions more naturally make this a question: "Do we suppose ourselves therefore to have been born at the same time kings and free persons?"

good than others and, by lending us the means of doing evil, renders our good deeds more meritorious and more worthy.

"We are given to men so that we may be to them as the nurse is to the child, and the prince who thinks that men are given to him as his own must no longer threaten them with the sword, if they offend him, but rather with thunderbolts, for he has made himself God, inasmuch as the gods cannot attribute to themselves anything more advantageous or sublime than to be owners and masters of the animal for which they created all things. When someone comes to me preaching that we have such an absolute right of ownership over the people—age and experience having taught me that poverty would be less miserable to us great ones than is wealth, which renders our favor so desirable to flatterers of that ilk—I smilingly ask that person to enlighten me as to who has been able to move the gods to abrogate their justice and their providence, their dominion over the human species, in order to substitute the injustice and blindness of a man: how are they henceforth to be rulers, since they are no longer rulers of men? Who wrongfully attributes to them the privilege of punishing human beings for their faults, since they have placed that function in the hands of kings? For what consideration consistent with the order and equity that reside in them have they handed over so many honorable and wise men to a leader who will often be the most wicked and ignorant man of the country he rules? What new inconstancy has provoked them to strip peoples of the liberty allotted to them by nature, in order to give it to a prince, and, for that praiseworthy pleasure of rendering one among them a usurper, to dispossess all the others? And finally, why have they not preferred to construct the universe for so many thousands of human souls rather than for only four, who are to rule it? For if nations are the exclusive property of monarchs, the world, heavens, earth, moon and sun are made for them alone, as the sheepfold is for the shepherd, given that the possession is dependent on the possessor. And surely, my dearest, even if you should leave aside these considerations, it would still not be permissible ungratefully to cheat your fatherland, which, because it always hoped for a great and happy benefit from your marriage, can attribute those favors accorded you by the gods to the merit of the benedictions it bestowed upon you, embracing you from an early age with a tenderness of love equal to that with which your mother and I embraced you as our only child."

In your *Essays*, father (which amount to the third member of the Triumvirate that includes Plutarch and Seneca),[13] you express the wish that our

---

13. Montaigne had singled out Plutarch and Seneca as his two essential authors (*Essais*, 1.26.146C).

Justus Lipsius would undertake a certain useful and noble work;[14] I have often wished for him the undertaking of another still, in which he should instruct us regarding the mutual duty of princes and peoples,[15] and how far the
privileges of the one extend toward the others. The foregoing discourse of
the Satrap reminded me of this. If that mind, which, following your lead, I
more than justly call highly refined, judicious, and the most learned that remains to us,[16] had taken up the task of deciding the perpetual disagreement
between the two parties on those points, surely it seems that, by the credit
that he has earned in all of Europe, each of them would incur more shame in
not acquiescing in his judgment than in that of another judge who might
wish to become involved. And therefore one must believe that such a book
would teach the art of living, not to the kings and subjects of our age only,
but also to as many as shall be born after, because, having been composed by
such a good and great hand, it could not perish so long as the muses had
power of speech.

The Satrap (to return to my subject) did indeed, by these remonstrances,
bring his daughter to give her consent, but she gave it only under the duress
of duty, still regarding this plan with a mournful eye, which filled with tears
whenever she pictured to herself the happiness and the benefits that they
were taking from her in banishing her from her country. In short, an ample
and royal train was prepared, which, apart from her own rank, respected the
honor of the captive king, and she was sent on her way, suffused with anguish
and tears at the farewell of her mother. The Satrap himself, out of respect for
his prince, chose to head the expedition. They arrived for their first stopover
at the home of an elderly lord of the country, who had recently retired from

14. Montaigne had hoped (*Essais*, 2.12.578B) that Lipsius might compile an encyclopedia of ancient philosophy.

15. Editions from 1594 to 1607 contain this marginal note: "It appears that in this she gives
a certain presage of the *Politics* which he has since written." In fact, Lipsius had in 1589 published his *Politicorum sive Civilis doctrinae libri sex qui ad Principatum maxime spectant* (Six books of
politics or civil doctrine, chiefly regarding sovereign power), which is, moreover, cited by
Montaigne. Arnould, introduction to *Le Promenoir*, 3 n. 3, sees Gournay as covering her tracks
with regard to the novel's pretended date of composition; cf. *Le Promenoir*, 67 n. B. See also Patricia Francis Cholakian, "The Identity of the Reader in Marie de Gournay's *Le Proumenoir de
Monsieur de Montaigne* (1594)," in *Seeking the Woman in Late Medieval and Renaissance Writings*, ed.
Sheila Fisher and Janet E. Halley (Knoxville, Tenn., 1989), 214–15, who discerns an attempt
by the author to interpose, via the Satrap's political speech, between the two learned men,
Lipsius and Montaigne. It is worth noting that ancient Persia was sometimes treated, in the
period, as a source for political lessons; thus, e.g., Pierre Matthieu's politically charged
tragedy *Vashti* (1589) was published along with an *Abregé de l'histoire des Roys de Perse* (Digest of
the history of the kings of Persia).

16. In terming Lipsius "trespolly, iudicieux, & le plus sçauant qui nous reste" (*Le Proumenoir*, ed.
Cholakian, fol. 11r), she is indeed following Montaigne almost verbatim: "le plus savant homme
qui nous reste, dun esprit trespoly et judicieux" (*Essais*, 2.12.578B).

the court, and who had with him a son whose graces rendered his youth and beauty so dangerous that the wisest ladies were not those who frowned at him, but rather those who fled from him; and he had a Greek name: Leontin. Beauty of a crude and simple kind is made to be looked at; that which comes with the graces in its train is to be feared. So that, had it been permitted to bestow a suitable gift on each of the two, I have seen some people who would have given the comb and mirror to the first, the mask to the second, judging that, if one wishes to profit from them, it is necessary to paint and embellish one, but to hide the other: indeed, if one observes their particular courses, one will find that affectation without beauty has actually wrought more miracles than beauty without affectation.

So, I say, the Satrap was received there according to his dignity: great honors were rendered, great preparations made for feasting them. The elderly lord himself served the Satrap at supper as cupbearer and assigned his son to the same office for the princess. Now the young Leontin, contemplating the decorous behavior and the elegance of that lady, supposed that the gods, opening the sky on the spot, had revealed the goddess Juno to the eyes of men, and wondered at the happiness of him who would possess her, as at a companion of Jupiter. But afterward that imagining of another's felicity was transformed, if not to outright jealousy, at least to an unhappiness that the supper lasted too briefly to allow him to consider her at his ease, and then that she was leaving the following day: and that unhappiness, little by little, became thorough misery and torment. Yet he did not yet dare to admit to himself that what was hurting him was an attack of love, because of the terrible error it was to become enamored in this fashion, so that he exerted himself all evening to deny his own emotion, in order to convince himself that he had no idea where the languid and mild fever was coming from that troubled his rest all that night, after having fixed his eyes on that face as long as they could eagerly breathe in the sight of it.

> He seems to me the equal of a god—to exceed the gods, if it is lawful to say so—the man who, sitting across from you, constantly watches and hears you.[17]

At this point, Fortune played a trick on him that he had not hoped for, for the following morning at the time of departure, the ancient Satrap found himself unwell, with the result that he had to remain. But as the ambitious say

17. Catullus, 51.1–4: "Ille mi par esse deo videtur, / Ille, si fas est, superare divos, / Qui sedens adversus identidem te / Spectat et audit." It sheds interesting light on Gournay's practice of revision that, in editions after that of 1623, she substituted for these lines a verse-translation of a different portion of Catullus's lyric (itself adapted from Sappho)—the same portion that Montaigne had cited (1.2.13A); see Arnould, ed., *Le Promenoir*, 82 nn. 6 and A.

that acquiring one advantage is but the prick of desire for another, so, having gained this point of her presence, his fire, strengthened by the continual sight of its object, then began to cause him greater torment over not being able to speak than it had done at first over her leaving. A number of things impeded his access: the Princess always surrounded by a legion of ladies, the chastity, coldness, and gravity inscribed on her forehead, and, no less, that timidity of which lovers complain.

He begins to speak and in midspeech stops short.[18]

For while he was scarcely so mad as to venture so soon to say anything to her that would convey his amorous condition, it was in this manner that conscience, which penetrates into secret motives, denied him more boldness than he had good intentions. Now one afternoon, when the invalid wished to sleep, she retired to a chair drawn back into a corner of the room, where, resting her head on her hand, she fell into deep reverie. Leontin found the courage to approach her, but as, on his knees, he sought to begin to speak, Alinda, who saw him hesitating, anticipated him in a gentle and friendly manner: "Since fortune would have it that we see my father ill, she could not have detained him in a more convenient place than this, nor among people to whom we would rather be obliged than to your father and yourself, Leontin."

With these words, she inflamed with love the enkindled soul.[19]

He, reassured by these words, said, "And fortune, O Princess, will always give Leontin cause to complain of her, as long as she denies him the means to employ, not these petty services, but his very life for the sake of the most noble blood of Cyrus.[20] But if I were permitted to choose, at my desire, one occasion out of others to devote it to that sacred duty, I would immediately choose to pour forth my blood and my soul at the base of the altar of the gods, in order to expiate the ire (such as they could have conceived) by which they have condemned Persia to allow itself to be deprived of you. What have we gained from offering so many vows to heaven that you might be brought into the world, so that we might see issue from your womb that child whose power should be such that the human race would henceforth

18. "Incipit effari, mediaque in voce resistit" (*Aeneid* 4.76)—the first of several allusions to the story of Dido and Aeneas. The text of Virgil's *Aeneid* used to regularize Gournay's citations is that of H. Rushton Fairclough, Loeb Classical Library, rev. ed., 2 vols. (Cambridge, Mass., and London, 1934), although we have supplied our own translations.

19. "His dictis incensum animum inflammavit amore" (*Aeneid* 4.54); the line describes Dido's response to her sister Anna's urging that she pursue her love for Aeneas.

20. Cyrus (559–529 B.C.E.) was the heroic founder of the enormous Achaemenid Persian Empire.

have to seek his good will instead of good fortune, and to despise bad fortune when he would have it favorable? That child, I say, whose reign would relieve us of hoping and fearing? Wretches that we are, a foreigner will now teach us that we have gained you only in order to lose you! But what of that? Can your homeland cease to enjoy your virtue while memory lasts? Shall some other land be accounted worthy for carrying you off from the one sufficiently blessed by fortune to produce you? Happy are the base-born daughters of the common people, who, without ever leaving the bosom of their country, one day hear her whom they have called mother instruct their little creatures[21] (who are beginning to untie their tongues) to greet them in turn with the sweetness of that name. Alinda would be happy like them if that unfortunate title of Royal Maiden were not an obstacle, and if being such a one, the lady and mistress of others, did not forbid her the common pleasures of human life, instead of lending her particular benefits. Surely, anyone having the heart to deprive us of your graces and favors, and you of our services, would be willing also, if he could, to ravish from men the beneficence of the gods, and from the gods the sacrifices of men.

"But what sudden madness has come upon the Persians?[22] Among all those alive, they did not manage to find in twenty years a husband worthy of engendering, in their Princess, the heir of the most lofty and imperial state on earth. And that state having now been made captive through recklessness, they are going to throw her to it as a prey, her and her most happy fecundity, and, what is more, in a place where all the remedy they can henceforth apply to her ills will be pity. If they say that a conqueror has so wished it, shall we not answer them that he is no conqueror of our virtue, nor of our destiny, as long as he finds our swords at home with us, together with our submission? The enemy shall lose his victory if we lose our fear. His advantage cannot permit him to go higher, nor the natural inconstancy of fortune to remain in one place. The last stage of the ascent on that ladder of happiness is the first on the way down. Of what use, therefore, are our youth and strength? We can at least gain the point of dying in combat when we may not prevail. And, thanks be to the gods, I have to this point seen none of us who has fallen into weakness, none who would not sooner fight his enemy than serve him, and who does not blame and condemn the decree to give such a ransom as you

---

21. We have been true here to Gournay's slippery pronoun usage, which shifts from *celle* to *leurs*, although we cannot reproduce (or explain) her shift to the masculine pronoun (*ils*) in speaking of the daughters.

22. We here follow later editions in clarifying the syntax so as to set off the first part of Gournay's sentence as a question.

as being the decision of people more fearful of failing to save themselves than of failing to recover the King."

No doubt, with the speaker of the words inducing Alinda to hear this pretty spell-binding, she failed to observe that Leontin was pitying her troubles only so as to multiply them, and was making her swallow the poison of love in the cup of adulation. She was moved to weep with bitterness over her calamity, again placing her head on her hand, but the new struggle of love against that grief disturbed and diverted its flow, and a secret storm that began to gather in the bosom of her misery dispersed and dissipated her tears in midcourse, allowing nothing to come to her eyes but a little burning drop, which, instead of softening them, seemed to kindle them,[23] and modesty could not so prevail but that they let slip some inviting glances—

> Nor did she turn her burning eyes from him before she received a flame through her entire body and, from below and within, wholly took fire in her marrow.[24]

Leontin, who in truth had too much art and intelligence for the simple goodness of that young woman, at once felt that she had been wounded, and from this he took a redoubled courage: "And indeed, it is not only, then, to our homeland's detriment but to its scorn (saying this through his tears) that they are tearing her from us! What are we Persians waiting for? To take up arms when the infamy of not having dared to do so now will render us unworthy of doing so forever?" He reloaded in this way, and was about to go too far, when a crowd of ladies arrived, ranging themselves round the Princess, and cut him short. He got up to leave, and went away so much altered that he found himself almost someone else. Thus he could not tell himself how much the emotion of those beautiful eyes had increased his flame, for displays of shared resentment inflame lovers not only through hope but also through gratitude, whose least atom is a world to them, inasmuch as they never measure it by its own value but by that of the person who confers it.

Alinda, for her part, to try to compose herself after the thrill that Leontin had given her, and to put him out of her head, diverted her soul as much as she could by dwelling on her misfortune. But she had no sooner placed this thought uppermost than, despite all her efforts, she felt herself once more

23. Gournay continually retouched this image in subsequent editions, finally clairifying it by adding, "de mesme qu'une goutte d'eau sur le fer chaut irrite son ardeur en la fournaise" [just as a drop of water on the hot iron arouses its heat in the furnace] (*Le Promenoir,* 90 and 90 n. 12).

24. Non prius ex illo flagrantia declinavit
    Lumina, quam cuncto concepit corpore flammam
    Funditus atque imis exarsit tota medullis.
       (Catullus, 64.91–93)

putting in its place the affected plaints with which the young man had represented such disaster to her, protesting against it to gods and men; and then his form, gestures, spirit, and valor flooded into her imagination.

But it is not my aim to describe the progression of this poor woman's love, father; it is enough for me to pity it:

> Alas, unhappily rousing frenzies in the agonized heart, Sacred Boy, you who mingle human joys with cares, and you who are queen over Golgi and fern-shaded Idalium, with what waves you toss the girl, her heart enkindled, sighing again and again over the flaxen-haired guest.[25]

Still less could my simplicity divine with what persuasions Leontin was able to bring to a head the monstrous design that he effected with Alinda. Suffice it to say that, within fifteen days, while the illness of the Satrap lasted, Love and he so skillfully hunted down a naïve soul that he reduced her to agreeing to follow him, as her new husband, wherever he might wish to lead her in disguise. However, it is certain that she did not yield without great opposition and resistance, as much against herself as against her pursuer.

"Shall it be said that I betrayed my father—I, his daughter, I, Alinda? That I betrayed the King's expectation of liberty—I, so honored as to be elected to serve as his ransom, when the mighty Empire of Persia itself was seen to be rejected, as one of the things unworthy of doing him this service, by a prince to whom victory accorded everything it might have pleased him to choose! Shall it be said that forever, out of horror at the example I set, mothers shall teach their daughters to shun evil? Must it be that I render myself the most hateful and harmful thing in all the world to the father and mother who brought me up so dearly and tenderly? And what pushes me to it? Is it the cruel torments that my soul endures? This face pale and wasted? This blood and spirit drained from my veins, which threaten soon to pour forth life itself by the power of such affliction? As if it had not been commanded, not merely to let oneself die, but to kill oneself intentionally, so as not to transgress one's duty! O great Oromasdes,[26] come to my aid, and I call death itself an aid and cure, provided that you grant it to me in my innocence."

She spoke in this way, and these considerations at times restored her to

---

25. Heu misere exagitans immiti corde furores
    Sancte puer, curis hominum qui gaudia misces,
    Quaeque regis Golgos quaeque Idalium frondosum,
    Qualibus incensam iactastis mente puellam
    Fluctibus in flavo saepe hospite suspirantem!
        (Catullus, 64.94–98)

26. The first person (equivalent of God the Father) in the divine trinity of the Zoroastrian religion.

a good state. But to what avail? The more she applied all her strength to rend Leontin from her fantasy, the more deeply she engraved him there again; for the more vividly she feared him, and the more vividly she pictured him to herself,

She hung on his lips again as he told it.[27]

The wound bloodying itself the more she probed it, she fled, insofar as she could, but she carried her hurt with her—

> like an incautious doe amid the Cretan groves, pierced from afar with a shaft sped by a shepherd hunting with arrows, who, unknowingly, has left the flying steel behind; in her flight she covers the Dictaean forests and wooded pastures; the deadly rod is fixed in her side.[28]

At last, then, as I said, the love and the lover forced her reason and evicted her from herself, so that she had no refuge but her eyes only, which, for want of ability to do anything better, she drowned with tears. And so Alinda prepared herself with the help of one of her ladies, whom they had won over. Then, the night before the morning when the Court was due to depart, Leontin stole them away disguised and, by secret doors and detours, managed their escape to the closest port in Anatolia, where he embarked himself, the women, and a certain servant of his on a ship appointed for the purpose, together with an enormous treasure in rings, which the Princess caused to be carried with them to serve their need. At liberty, then, as they were on the high seas,

We have prevailed, he exclaims, my wishes are carried with me.[29]

Leontin, the new husband, would not have shrunk from affirming that the Elysian fields had been translated to the sea.

---

27. "Pendetque iterum narrantis ab ore" (*Aeneid* 4.79).

28. Qualis coniecta cerva sagitta,
    Quam procul incautam nemora inter Cresia fixit
    Pastor agens telis liquitque volatile ferrum
    Nescius; illa fuga silvas saltusque peragrat
    Dictaeos; haeret lateri letalis harundo.
       (*Aeneid* 4.69–73)

29. "Vicimus, exclamat, mecum mea vota feruntur" (Ovid, *Metamorphoses*, trans. and ed. Frank Justus Miller, 2 vols. Loeb Classical Library [London and Cambridge, Mass., 1960], 6.513). The inauspicious context is the carrying off of Philomela by Tereus, who is about to rape her and cut out her tongue. This citation disappears from editions after 1623.

Neither Juno, the marriage goddess, nor Hymen, nor any blessing was
present at that marriage bed.[30]

She too, for her part, was so intoxicated and entranced in her pitiful love that
she would not have exchanged her little boat for any great empire, reckoning that to be Queen could not at all outweigh the felicity of holding that
man in a place where she could not lose him from her sight for a moment,
dart a glance that he would not garner up, or breathe out a sigh that would
not fall upon his ears.

Meanwhile, when morning came, the Satrap arose. He sent to see how
his daughter was, and whether she was going to keep the Persians, who were
all mounted at the gate already, waiting much longer. But when it was reported
to him that her chamber and her bed were empty, her women all unknowing
where she was, then he went there in person, with the sinister presage of a sudden pounding of the heart. He caused her to be searched for on all sides, and
there was no corner or hiding place in the house where an army of people, intent on their task, did not look high and low. After that, the gardens, and finally the grounds and the neighboring fields were gone through, and all the
air was filled with the calling of her name. Now up to this point the minds of
those ages—as you know, father—were capable, in keeping with what they
had been taught, of believing that some god might have carried her off; but
when Leontin was found to be missing, the truth was thereby clearly seen. Nevertheless, as great as the misfortune was, the Satrap's constancy was equal to it,
so that he could have taken it in stride, knowing that patience is a remedy for
hopeless things; but, his despair being aggravated by such weighty circumstances—a conqueror offended, the King still unsuccored,[31] and the state in
new confusion—he had great difficulty in keeping it in check.

By this time, the newlyweds, driven by a favorable wind, had already
measured an infinite space of ocean, when a tempest, arising all of a sudden,
first astonished them, then, gradually strengthening, overcame them, so that,
sometimes twisting the vessel and sometimes hurling it in all directions, after

---

30. —non pronuba Juno,
    Non Hymenaeus adest, illi non gratia lecto.
    (*Metamorphoses* 6.428–29)

The reference is to the wedding of Tereus and Procne, the sister of Philomela (see n. 29 above).
The verses are absent from editions after 1607.

31. A case where the cryptic original text ("demeure court") will be clarified in future editions:
"le Roy demeuré court en sa prison" [the King still deprived in his prison] (Arnould, ed., *Le
Promenoir*, 106).

some days it cast them upon a beach in wildest Thrace, contrary to their intentions. For Alinda was insistent that they should go to live in some region of Italy, in order to be further from recognition, waiting in case some good fortune might mollify her father toward her and reopen to her the sweet road home to her country, desire for which nourished her hope. So they remained on that shore, disconcerted, deserted, having neither knowledge of the place nor any direction, and the Princess still in the chill grip of her former fear, which moved everyone to compassion, to see her so patiently endure the exchange of her accustomed pleasures for those coarse inconveniences.

But a certain lord of that country, rich and well enough born for that region, happened upon them, who, when he saw them in such poor condition, yet judging they had issued from good stock (by I know not what animation in their faces and by their bearing), offered to lodge them until they had put themselves and their boat in a condition to complete the voyage they intended. "Since it pleases you, my lord," said Leontin, "to take in these poor strangers, I would hope that we will have suffered no loss in being shipwrecked. Moreover, no benefit ever offered to me will oblige me more than that which grants me the means of taking this poor lady out of her present misery, and we will go, under your favor and that of the sheltering gods of hospitality: may they be pleased always to maintain in your home the happiness that you know how to employ so courteously." Thus they followed the Thracian, who was named Othalcus, to his nearby country house, where they were well and cordially welcomed, as much by himself as by a sister of his, who had recently come there from the city for diversion. But they had not yet enjoyed that respite for eight days when the same eyes that had vanquished Leontin, having neither dissipated their power in that first effort nor quenched their lively flames in the sea, began to kindle little by little the coarse breast of the Thracian, who had previously been accustomed only to war and hunting savage beasts. At the first assaults of his pain, he restrained himself, inasmuch as he found it repugnant to injure his guest through her, whom he saw to be so precious to him. However, in the end his passion tormented him so greatly that one day, when Leontin had gone to see the nearby town, he disclosed himself in ardent prayers. Alinda, who, on the one hand, held her duty in the highest regard, and, on the other, was wholly immersed in her love for Leontin, faced the dilemma, not of deciding between yes and no for her answer, but of seeking some form of refusal calculated to flow gently from her, so as not to offend one who had them wholly in his power. Thus, then, she repulsed him gently—and if it had not been supposed, although the common opinion contradicts it, that other women would have impugned their honor by saying no both gently and even laughingly, would that they had never ceased to laugh like that!—and excused herself in the most skillful way allowed her by the perturbation in which the apprehension of her peril put her, and a new pity for the desolation of her fortune, which brought great tears to her eyes. Yet it must be acknowledged that neither this weeping nor this difficulty made Othalcus despair of the conquest so much as they made it appear more glorious and desirable to him, and he at once withdrew without otherwise pressing it, because he had proposed to gain it by gentle means, so as not to lose the pleasure of acquiescence, in which consisted, he firmly believed, the tenderest of love's delights. Now, as soon as the Princess became aware of these new circumstances, she set about devising a complete escape from his power, and in fact she would have got out of that house at all hazards if the storms of a rough winter had not served as a civil pretext, in Thrace, for stopping them.

> Indulge him with hospitality and spin out reasons for delaying, while winter rages on the sea, and Orion stirs up the waves, and boats are shaken, and the sky cannot be tamed.[32]

If only she could have disclosed these things to Leontin, he might perhaps have hit upon a means of gaining safety, but out of fear that his fury would drive him to some dangerous course, the wretched woman suffered without complaining, unable to do anything to prevent the disaster that threatened, except to avoid, as much as possible, the sight of the amorous Othalcus and to try to diminish her own attractions when she was forced to let herself be seen. All of this did nothing to hinder the continual assault of Othalcus's importuning, which resistance, no less than conversation, caused to grow warmer from day to day. And that battering did not fail also to reinforce the constancy of Alinda. Truly, someone wishing to conquer her should not have entered into combat against the interest of Leontin. For not only, in consideration of the wrong offered to him, did she love him more out of pity; but, further, the more she was tormented, the more she was drawn, from a certain proud satisfaction, to suffer for the sake of his love. Whoever wishes to put invincible arms into the hands of a true friend—it suffices to attack what he loves.

Thus the Thracian, so enamored, at last, that he was wasting away, developed the obsessive idea that he had to remove Leontin from this woman,

---

32. Indulge hospitio causasque innecte morandi,
    Dum pelago desaevit hyems et aquosus Orion,
    Quassataeque rates, et non tractabile caelum.

    (*Aeneid* 4.51–53)

This is Anna's advice to the love-stricken Dido. The setting of the constellation Orion in November was associated with stormy weather.

however it might be done, and that, since it was love that fed her stubborn resistance, he would tame it (as he supposed) by the loss of its object—if, as a point of honor, he would vanquish it by marriage. On top of this, it came to him that he had perceived his sister to have fallen in love with Leontin, and from this he considered that by means of her—for she was a pretty girl—he might insensibly draw Leontin away from the one who was causing him pain. His intention was to get Alinda out of her marriage through one between Leontin and his sister, with the assistance of the free trade in marriages obtaining at that time. Having drawn up these plans, he took aside his sister, named Ortalde, who was quite pleased at this disclosure, as one who, through her brother's plot, felt hope arising in herself, where there had earlier been only desire. Thus she promised him to move heaven and earth to deliver him from his rival, adding, "You could not, my brother, have chosen for your sister a husband worthier of the benefit you wish for him, and it has not come to pass without some blessing of the fates upon our fraternal friendship that I could not serve myself in this pursuit without equally serving you." At this, Ortalde deployed all the attractions she possessed and set herself to hunting this prey, emboldened by extreme love and by the pretext of a marriage. But would you believe that there might be an effort to batter him sufficiently to make a breach in the loyalty of that most committed of men, and one so excellently provided?

Certainly, we shall be capable of freeing ourselves from evils, when we know how to remain constant in our benefits. Perseverance in general is the perfection and the consummation of the virtues, and no one can ever truly be what he is not always. It is the virtue of the virtues, for one can indeed have justice without courage, courage without justice, and so with the others; but a person could not consider justice or courage as his rightful possession unless he had them constantly. A tranquil existence, whatever other virtue—or indeed several together—may belong to it, may still have some vice attached, but not a tranquil existence that is constant: for the inherited wisdom of our reason[33] teaches that, to denote a perfect action, it suffices to say that it is a constant one, since vice cannot remain fixed. He who has one virtue will not always have another, but he who has this one has them all, inasmuch as it is never to be found except in the perfection of will and capability. It is never set in place except upon the entire body of the virtues, as the pinnacle of the ed-

33. Marie de Gournay's phrase is "la caballe [kabbala] de la raison" (Cholakian, ed., *Le Proumenoir*, fol. 29v), with *caballe* apparently used in the sense (documented elsewhere in the period) of our translation; post-1607 editions substitute the less colorful but clearer "la Philosophie" (Arnould, ed. *Le Promenoir*, 118). Marie de Gournay's interest in the arcane found expression in the practice of alchemy for a certain period (see *Apology*, below, 127–29).

ifice, and whoever thinks to arrive there must not allow any intelligence to remain above his own, any more than it allows any virtues above itself.

Therefore, ladies are quite wrong to accuse men generally of deceit, when they find their promises of love broken. Indeed, there are some who promise like cheaters, having no desire to keep faith, but there are still more of those who promise like fools, without, I say, being aware to what degree the weakness of their minds is incapable of that great virtue of constancy. They were genuinely in love, ardent and burning, when they pledged their souls, and heaven and earth besides, to carry out their words, but they should have been told: "My friends, in order to make us believe that you are constant, it will serve no better to show us that you are passionate to excess, than if you caused us to see that you have strong arms so as to gain the reputation of running well. On the contrary, this amorous violence is the enemy of perseverance.[34] But make it apparent to us that you have the sufficiency of Epaminondas and Xenophon, and then we shall believe you capable of steadfastness."[35]

But to leave off this speech, father, neither, I say, his indebtedness, nor his faith, nor the ardent love of Alinda, nor the ruin to which his treachery was pushing her could prevent Leontin, not from abandoning her outright, but from making an inferior choice.[36] And so he at once turned to Ortalde, with the same heat of affection and pursuit in which Alinda had seen him a while before. Nevertheless, Ortalde, who was shrewd, was far from putting herself at risk of stopping that lover halfway to the refuge—that is, the marriage that she wanted and had been promised her—by a concession made in advance. Furthermore, she was aware how many women have been deceived by promises of marriage and also knew that thousands and thousands of women, who had initially been lured deceptively by those promises, would

34. In the 1594 text, this sentence is joined to the preceding one by a comma and ends with a question mark. We here follow the more logical punctuation of later editions.

35. Epaminondas, the fourth-century Theban general and statesman, received Montaigne's highest praise (*Essais*, 3.1.801B, 2.36.756A), which Gournay echoes in the *Preface* (63). Montaigne likewise admired Xenophon, the Athenian philosopher and soldier (ca. 428–ca. 354 B.C.E.), and considered him one of the few authors worthy of writing about himself—again, a point taken up by Gournay in the *Preface* (79). Still, in her final edition, Xenophon's place as an emblem of constancy is taken by the clearer instance of Cato. See Arnould, ed., *Le Promenoir*, 120 n. B.

36. The French is elusive here: "ne sceurent empescher Leontin qu'il n'aimast mieux choisir pis, que ne la point abandonner" (Cholakian, ed., *Le Proumenoir*, fol. 31r). In translating, we have been guided by a subsequent reading—"ne sceurent empescher Leontin, qu'il n'aymast mieux choisir une pire dame que de ne la point abandonner" (Arnold, ed., *Le Promenoir*, 122 n. 5)—although the final edition of 1641 reverts to the first version of the phrase.

in the end have successfully constrained their men to keep them by the force of love, had they not surrendered eight days too soon. What more is there to say? This Thracian would have instructed ladies that if he who plays the love-struck part does not perform such promises the first day he is able, that means that he does not want to (notwithstanding all the pretty colors he lends his delay, as Leontin did his), and might have warned them that if desire for what he wanted could not compel him to expedite the marriage, satiety would force him to it just as little, once he had triumphed.

But in any case, in proportion as the ancient flame weakened in Leontin through the increase in the new one, the countenance and the treatment that the Princess had been accustomed to receive also grew much colder. He was no longer continually at her side and became far less gentle in consoling her and calming the commotion in her soul when she wept in his presence concerning the danger that threatened her, which she had been constrained, at long last, to disclose to him by a necessity all too urgent. And yet he seemed to take up that cause in no more than a casual way: "Refusal will deter him," he said; "some other object will divert him; don't worry—I know him." But how far did this cooling-off have to go for a poor blind woman, enchanted with love, to become aware of it? If he had once given her, out of pity, some feeble remnant of a pleasant look, he would have raised her up to paradise, and his ordinary meager cheer she would have attributed to the trouble that uneasiness over her fortune put into his mind, as it seemed to her. In short, she would not have been sensible of the alienation if his excessive confidence had not finally rendered these new lovers so nonchalant about pretending that they scarcely concealed themselves any longer from her, any more than from others.

Souls that are good and well composed are difficult to rouse to mistrust, because they think of others as they know themselves to be. She was beginning, therefore, to regard herself in a pitiful light, when, one day as she was bound up in this cruel anxiety, seated in a chair against a wall where she was resting her sorrowful head, she heard in her vicinity a secret murmur like the voice of her Leontin. For this reason she suddenly cast her glance all round, but, not seeing anything there but emptiness, she supposed that it must be in the adjoining room. Therefore, turning to face where she had her shoulders, she began to peer through a fairly wide crack. This was the stark truth: Leontin with Ortalde in close conversation, mingled with all the courting behavior that he could purloin from Alinda, so ardent and so passionate that he had never appeared to her so love-sick on her account. Exclamations regarding the future marriage ran through the midst of this mystery, and he was begging her to advance it because she sought to prolong his protracted hardship until then.

At this blow, Alinda thought she was collapsing as if struck dead, stifling a great cry that pierced her stomach with burning need to express her pain. But, steadying herself on her legs as best she could, she gained enough time to seat herself again. As soon as she was back in her chair and her spirits began to recover from the icy weight of the chill, since the betrayal of Leontin had pronounced her mortal end, she pronounced her testament in a word: "Wait only ten hours more, O Leontin, and I will set your hand free to engage your faith again, but what a pity you did not set your sights on marriage with a mere citizen of Thrace after you had become the widower of the heir of Persia, instead of hastening that event!" She said only these words, then, after remaining there for about half an hour with her arms folded and her sad eyes gazing upward, she composed her visage and commanded the Persian woman, whom she summoned, to put her to bed and not to let anyone speak with her, unless it were the lord of the house, when he came to visit her, according to his custom. And if Leontin himself came to see her, she was to beg him, on Alinda's behalf, to let her rest and by no means to return to sleep there that night, on account of a certain indisposition with which she did not wish to trouble him, and in the morning he would see her cured. All this she did deliberately, for she recognized that, as thoroughly intoxicated as she was with the man's love, the slightest feeble excuse he might wish to offer would be capable of making her take pleasure in life once more, so that she could possess him again. This she by no means desired, knowing well that the only way she had of being sure of him was through death. Ortalde, meanwhile, who felt sure of Leontin, went to inform her brother, who had no sooner heard than, boiling with desire to realize the fruit of such good news, he climbed to the Princess's chamber, where he seated himself in a chair near the bed and became most tenderly anxious on account of her indisposition.

He remained there some while without speaking, lost in contemplation of her face. Then he blurted out to her in ten words (for those nations have little skill in speaking) her sister's intention to marry, Leontin's agreement, and his own warm desires, followed by a promise of better treatment than woman had ever received. The wretched lady, hearing this harangue, could never have held back two floods of tears, if the feeling of death close at hand had not aided her, already half dulling her senses and functions. But while she contained her tears by this means, she summoned, on the tip of her tongue, in a deep sigh, all that remained to her of her thwarted life: "While fortune has permitted, I have been the wife of Leontin, and while I have been his wife, I have been his loyal wife," she said, "—loyalty that, besides enabling me to keep myself pure for Othalcus, also lends me this benefit—that it will serve him as some pledge of my future fidelity to him. I yield, my lord, disarmed by the gods, for since they have brought it about, by the divorce of Leontin, that I may satisfy you without guilt, I well recognize that they are enjoining me to recompense your sincere affections. And I yield also to that humanity with which you indulged my weakness, which you could have compelled, when I fought against your desire out of strict observance of my moral teaching, which indeed I held in high esteem, however reduced you see me now. But before going farther, I implore you, do me a service."

Othalcus, so overwhelmed with joy at this stroke that he all but jumped out of his skin, begged her to command whatever she pleased, and she continued thus: "That meddling old woman (and she named one of the household) has been by speaking so shamefully about the familiarity that exists between us that, until you have granted me her death, I shall never be out of distress and will deplore my injured honor, which carries yours along with it. Therefore, I ask that you have her killed when she is asleep in her chamber at midnight, choosing that hour to avoid noise." The Thracian cheerfully accorded her request and strongly pressed her to grant that he marry her at once, or that if, doubting his promise, she wished to reserve that benefit for after the execution, she would allow him to have the old woman killed instantly. "It isn't that," she replied, "I would have only too much faith in your word, but give me the rest of this day and tonight, I beg of you, to recover somewhat from the indisposition that keeps me here. Besides, I confess to the goodness in you that, having had that close union with Leontin, and having loved him so much, I feel a strong need for some small interval in order to put his love behind me, together with my marriage to him. For, considering how much I owe to you, my lord, I would have great scruples about coming to a marriage with you, my soul still fettered, and like an adulteress in another bed. Once this is so done, I will no longer deny you any of your rights, and you will not begrudge four or five hours of waiting, since by this means I must needs render you, in the place of this distracted and dull woman, Alinda healthy and lively in agreeing to your pleasure." Thus, I say, she extricated herself from the urgent importunity to which victory and advantage had just consigned Othalcus. And when she had endured him, sitting on the edge of her bed, for another hour or so, she finally begged him to let her rest, which she obtained with great difficulty.

Then, seeing herself alone and night approaching, she asked the Persian lady for writing-tablets; after which, having remained motionless some while looking at them, she wrote these words: "To my marriage with you I gave the first fruits of my body; to it, O Leontin, I still give my dying breath. Thus the end of my life and marriage approaches, and also of my birth—far, along with my marriage and myself, from all good fortune. I turn away from this world still a child—from this world, I say, which I would never have had to enter if, before birth, I had not deserved torment. If my eyes had not seen, my ears would not have believed what they heard this afternoon, and my eyes would have disavowed what they beheld if my ears had not heard. My youthful simplicity was easy indeed to deceive, Leontin, and my weakness to tread underfoot, but if they do not deserve justice, at least they deserve pity. Alas, I do not at all complain that I must die, after having so offended my good father; I complain only that, having ruined so many people—ah, wretched Persians, who will relieve you after my flight?—I still could find no murderer but the person for whose advantage I ruined them. No doubt, if you so well knew an art for changing love, you equally knew one for resisting it; O that you did not, for pity's sake, teach me that formula, when you summoned death to help me defend myself against love's force—for you knew that she who yields her bed obliges her lover to grant her death in recompense.

"I dispatch myself before your new wife compels me to. I fly before Leontin has the trouble of begging Ortalde to forgive wretched Alinda for having once given up the Empire of Persia for a little boat, and power for servitude, in order to call herself his wife. Moreover, I will leave you no issue to trouble you in the future with my memory by representing my image to you, and those gods be praised from whom the germ beginning to come alive in my womb obtains such favor that it perishes before being born, lest it have the heartache of being told one day the wretched destiny of its mother. Adieu, I say, Leontin—I can no more. It seems that the power of grief seeks to anticipate in me the blow of the sword I dedicate to curing my miseries. Yet I will not allow my life to escape except with my blood, for it must honor the new rites of Hymen with a thoroughly solemn sacrifice. But if you still remember at all that I have been yours, have a bit of earth thrown on my body after it has rendered up its soul: such a funeral will do for a poor exile. Alinda I am no more; I left my name where I left my diadem. And you, the new bride, do not refuse to let that trifling benefit be done for her who did not refuse to go to her grave a young woman to yield you a marriage-bed.[37] At least I will have something to console my sorrowing mother with, when grief for my misfortune has driven her among the dead with me—namely, that I will not have lost everything with my marriage, for from it I will gain a tomb."

---

37. With this part of Alinda's speech, cf. the inscription that Alexander caused to be placed on the tomb of Cyrus: "I am Cyrus, and I won for the Persians their empire. Do not, therefore, begrudge me this little earth which covers my body" (Plutarch, *Plutarch's Lives*, trans. and ed. Bernadette Perrin, 11 vols., Loeb Classical Library [London and New York, 1919], 7:417 [Alexander, 69.2]).

This letter having been well sealed, and those tears somewhat allayed that she had aroused, she give it to the Persian lady, commanding her to carry it to Leontin the next morning before waking her, because it was a message he had to consider when he got up, and not before. After this she threw herself down miserably upon her pillow, and upon her painful thoughts, for the last time.

> Could nothing change the intent of your cruel mind? Was there no mercy at hand to move your adamant heart with compassion? This was not what you promised me once with coaxing words, nor what you led me, miserable women, to hope for. . . . From now on, let no woman believe a man when he swears; let none hope that the words of a man are trustworthy. While the desiring spirit is keen to get something, they do not shrink from vows or spare their promises. But as soon as the hunger of passion is satiated, they cannot be bothered to hold in awe their words or their perjuries.[38]

These verses of the wretched Ariadne should be written everywhere in women's Books of Hours, and whoever he was who first forbade them learning, as the kindling of lasciviousness, I believe, father, that it was because he knew so little of letters that he feared they would consign him to the spinning wheel on the second day of their studies.[39] The vulgar say that a women, if she is to be chaste, should not be so finely discerning; truly, it says little for chastity to suppose that its beauty could be perceived only by the blind. On the contrary,

38. Nullane res potuit crudelis flectere mentis
Consilium? tibi nulla fuit clementia praesto
Immite ut nostri vellet miserescere pectus?
At non haec quondam blanda promissa dedisti
Voce mihi; non haec miseram sperare jubebas. . . .
Iam iam nulla viro juranti femina credat,
Nulla viri speret sermones esse fideles;
Quis dum aliquid cupiens animus praegestit apisci,
Nil metuunt iurare, nil promittere parcunt:
Sed simul ac cupidae mentis satiata libido est,
Dicta nihil metuere, nihil perjuria curant.
(Catullus, 64.136–40, 143–48)
The lines omitted by Gournay refer to Theseus's promise of marriage and so would not suit Alinda's case.

39. Arnould, in his edition of the *Le Promenoir*, 142 n. A, points out the resemblance at this point to Taillemont, *Discours*, 118–19. Compare especially this sentence, which follows the argument that women inclined to vice (like similar men) can be improved by learning, and which precedes the point that custom alone is to blame for depriving women of intellectual opportunity and consigning them to spinning and housework: "Mais . . . n'a esté jusques aujourd'huy le vouloir et consentement de nos ancestres et predecesseurs tant miserable et pervers, que meuz des erreurs

one should render it as subtle as possible, so that if anyone is wicked enough to wish to deceive it, nobody will be clever enough to be able to.

Stroke the steed clumsily and back he kicks, at every point on his guard.[40]

Most of the offenses against modesty that women commit today stem not from wantonness but from foolishness. And I less readily believe what I am told about the most sublime than about the least. If some woman should yield to Xenophon, in whom the physical and spiritual graces were combined together with honesty, that would be called a lapse in chastity. But to entrust oneself to the men of the present age, who do not come close to his qualities (as handsome and gallant as they may be) and who make it so plain that they get less pleasure from possessing women than from betraying them—that I call ineptitude. And I consider that she who does herself such a turn has greater need of hellebore[41] than of penitence. Perhaps it was feared[42] that if ladies studied ancient philosophy it might lead them to believe, in keeping with it, that continence is not commanded by reason but rather by civil law. Yet when it had persuaded them of this point, it would nevertheless not absolve indecency, for it everywhere preaches lawfulness as much as reason. To identify a virtue is not to disdain it. On the contrary, philosophy, professing chiefly the keeping of the soul at home, once it recognized that pleasure carries it outside, has forbidden pleasure, if not to the wise, at least to the generality of men. Do we not find this feature among its lessons—that it prefers to be enchained by pain rather than by pleasure?

Ladies, in the final analysis, will discover in books that whoever knows men better distrusts them more and that the most trustworthy of those who promise constancy is the one who cannot keep his promise because of the

---

d'autruy, ou de leur proper ignorance, n'ont permis aux esprits femenins gouster ce doux fruict de science et doctrine?" [But have not the will and consent of our ancestors been to this day so worthless and perverse that, whether moved by others' errors or out of their own ignorance, they have not allowed female minds to taste of that sweet fruit of knowledge and learning?] (118).

Gournay's reference to the spinning wheel brings to mind Omphale's domination of Hercules, while Taillemont has also just cited Hercules as having been, despite his strength, "bien souvent vaincu par ses propres affections et voluptez" [very often vanquished by his own affections and pleasures] (116–17). Gournay also uses the figure of Hercules below, 59 (as in the *Preface*, 37), to mock falsely heroic men and further cites the defeat of Hercules by women in the *Equality* (below, 88).

40. "Cui male si palpere recalcitrate, undique tuta" (Horace, *Satires*, in *Satires, Epistles, Ars Poetica*, trans. and ed. H. Rushton Fairclough, rev. ed., Loeb Classical Library [Cambridge, Mass., and London, 1929], 2.1.20). Horace's point is the need for tact and subtlety in approaching Caesar.

41. Hellebore: a remedy for "madness" dating back to ancient times; cf. *Preface*, 27 and n. 13.

42. With Arnould, ed., *Le Promenoir*, 142, we correct our text's *peu* to *peur* ("A l'aduanture a-on eu peu[r]" [Cholakian, ed., *Le Proumenoir*, fol. 42v]).

instability of human nature. They will derive from books a contempt for thousands and thousands of lovers whom ignorant women would admire, and the sort that would be bliss for the latter would be a penance to them. So, if their misfortune will have it that they meet someone capable of wounding them, the resolution and austerity they have acquired in their dealings with those admirable ancient intellects will thereby prevent that passion from tyrannizing over them as strongly as it would tyrannize over another. Moreover, if they should hold continence in contempt, then prudence itself would keep them from giving someone for whom they have a warm affection what they know he wants from them, lest he either stop loving them or, at least, take his leave of them when he pleases; and so it would amply prevent them from casting themselves into the baneful plight of depending on another. In such writings, they will see so many examples of women betrayed that finally they will learn that those who have made the best bargain in loving have still lost their freedom. Besides, a woman who has been able to furnish herself wisely with sufficiency and virtue could never meet a man, as great as he might be, whom she would judge too good to require marriage of. And while the ordinary sort of woman would not refuse a would-be lover of higher rank than herself, except as an enemy to her modesty, she will repulse him as an enemy of her chastity, and thus will hate him as a scorner of those praiseworthy qualities that reside in her, when he thinks that another woman, for whom he reserves marriage, deserves it more, on account of her titles, than she does for her worth.

Which is not to say, however, that she would automatically wish to accept such a marriage, if it were offered her, for the gifts that God has bestowed on her are of such value that advantage, for her, consists in making choice, not of him who is above her, but of him who most closely resembles her. Whoever possesses wisdom possesses particles of the unique excellence that God has reserved for himself above men; and God plainly shows how far he prefers it to greatness and power, since he has judged men worthy of power and greatness, but wisdom worthy of himself. It follows that such a woman, who cannot be, in truth, the choice of any but the shrewdest, nor the lot of any but the happiest, knows no man in the world to whom she would not consider herself to be doing as much honor, by giving him her understanding and her virtue in marriage, as he would be doing her by giving his wealth and rank. His fortune can give her what her suitor has; the suitor's fortune cannot give him what she has. So, if he is more visible from a distance than she, the same goes for a house on fire.

The remarkable thing is that every lover supposes that he, too, has understanding and virtue; but when one is encountered who could rightfully boast of having these two perfections, and, on top of them, exalted rank, which would justify him in considering the lady unworthy to be his equal because he betters her in one respect, she will then inform him that he does himself wrong to be seeking a mere bed and that he must ask for an altar. Now everyone will say afterward that such a women does ill, because she does not behave like others, neither in choosing her activities nor in regulating her actions. Let them talk; the worst I see in this is that we have to live in an age when a person who wishes to follow the right road must quit the well-worn one. Great intellects always stray from the beaten path, the more so because they have persuaded themselves that what is straying, according to custom, is submission to reason. And one should not be surprised if noble and staunch souls can so poorly subject themselves to the rules of common understandings—no more than at the fact that one cannot manage a jennet with the bridle of an ass. In a time of bad example, it is glorious to incur reproof for one's way of living. Approbation is for the ambitious, duty for persons of honor; to do what is praised is the integrity of those who cannot do what should be done. He who holds back from performing a good action out of fear that he will be blamed would do something evil if he were praised for it.

The common people are quite content to have no touchstone for good behavior other than conformity to example. Yet superiority itself exists only in difference, and God is not God except insofar as he differs from us. Because we have not known how to arrive at true virtue, we have set up an imaginary one, and, sensing that doing well was not what we were capable of, we ordained that doing what we were capable of would be doing well. Nevertheless, if holy scripture says true that there is not one good in a thousand,[43] the praises of the multitude are hardly to be desired, inasmuch as each praises only his likeness, being unable to praise someone different without accusing himself. Never did Phocion fear that he had failed except on the first day when he saw himself applauded by the common people.[44] The vulgar crowd is far from praising lives that possess some extraordinary excellence, for nature, which

43. A particularly interesting case of selective reading on Gournay's part, since the scriptural source is Eccles. 7:28: "One man among a thousand have I found; but a woman among all those have I not found." Her sentence seems to have been modeled on Montaigne, *Essais*, 1.39.237–38A: "Toutefois, si le mot de Bias est vray, que la pire part c'est la plus grande, ou ce que dit l'Ecclesiastique, que de mille il n'en est pas un bon" [Still, if what Bias says is true, that the worse part is the larger one, or what Ecclesiastes says, that out of a thousand there is not one good man]. (The apophthegm of Bias, the sixth-century [B.C.E.] Greek "sage," was, "Most men are bad," according to Diogenes Laertius, 1.88).

44. See *Plutarch's Lives*, vol. 8, from the biography of Phocion, the Athenian military and political leader (fourth century B.C.E.): "And when, as he was once delivering an opinion to the people, he met with their approval, and saw that all alike accepted his argument, he turned to his friends and said: 'Can it possibly be that I am making a bad argument without knowing it?'" (162–63 [8.3]).

denies it the capacity to lead such lives, likewise denies it the sufficiency to appreciate them; and whoever is far from emulation is far from understanding. Testimony of this is those sublime *Essays* of ours,[45] about which Pindar seems to have written these verses several thousand years earlier by poetic prophecy:

> Full many a swift arrow have I beneath mine arm, within my quiver, many an arrow that is vocal to the wise; but for the crowd they need interpreters.[46]

Still, it will be said, it is a risky business to aspire to render oneself wiser than one's fellows—Socrates died for doing it. But in this respect women, in particular, incur a double misfortune. For only wise actions are attacked in men; in women, the very name of wisdom is mocked, and when an able woman has no other title, they will speak ill of her. Is there any person so wicked as to dare to think, contrary to the testimony of the whole church, that it was any other cause that led those great Roman ladies to slander the saintly Paula and Melania?[47] Not to mention a million others that abound in books and memory. We would not believe that they had had their chastity impugned, if Saint Jerome had not told us the story in order to make us pity their misery, and we would believe still less that they were accused of lapsing in chastity with Saint Jerome, if he himself, in publishing it, had not forgotten his patience and penitent humility to rail against the poison of tongues.

Women themselves will be the first to slander this woman—some out of envy, others because, if they had qualities with which they might so please an admirer, they would not pass up the occasion to profit by them. And finally, revive for them the wise Theano and, when they consider her grace, her conversation, the moderation of her humors, and the spice that she could lend to love if she pleased, they will indeed feel that, if they were as strongly

---

45. "Ours" (*nos*) became "yours" (*vos*) in the edition of 1598 (Arnould, ed., *Le Promenoir*, 144).

46. ... πολλά μοι ὑπ'
   ἀγκῶνος ὠκέα βέλη
   ἔνδον ἐντὶ φαρέτρας
   φωνάεντα συνετοῖσιν· ἐς δὲ τὸ πᾶν ἑρμανέων
   χατίζει.

   (Pindar, *Olympian Odes* 2.82–86, in *The Odes of Pindar including the Principal Fragments*, ed. and trans. William H. Race, Loeb Classical Library [London and New York, 1997])

47. Gournay's text uniformly has "Menalia" for "Melania." Jerome recounts this episode, and angrily deplores the malice of the slanderers, in his letter to Asella (*Letters*, in *The Principal Works of St. Jerome*, trans. W. H. Fremantle, G. Lewis, and W. G. Martley, Select Library of Nicene and Post-Nicene Fathers of the Christian Church, 2d ser., vol. 6 [1893; facsimile reprint, Grand Rapids, Mich., 1989], 58–60 [no. 45]).

desired as such advantages must make her desired, they would not have enough strength to resist the advances, and thereupon they will speak ill of their companion, all the more because they cannot do well.[48] Further, whoever is a strong enemy of vice will not lightly believe that another person is giving way to it. And when someone willingly believes of others the ill that he hears told of them, it is a sign that others should believe the ill spoken about him. That, I say, is cited to women as admonishment. But why would great women and great men not suffer detraction coming from those minds that have persuaded themselves that they cannot speak any folly or wickedness unworthy of them, since Jesus Christ himself was put on the cross for nothing but calumnies?

Now, father, in your *Essays*—so is called the thrice-happy gift that God bestows on our age from the deep reserve and store of all human wisdom that He amassed for fourteen hundred years—you defend Plutarch and Seneca against certain reproaches laid to their charges.[49] I too wish, in your *Promenade*, to defend and console Paula and Melania.[50] May it suffice you, poor Roman ladies, that if Socrates had been a woman, he would not have been spoken well of any more than you. Use a bit of imagination and envisage in a female role the vigor of his soul, his frankness in chastising common opinions where they injure truth, his aptness in conversing naturally on all matters, as well as in perceiving and considering them, his freedom in coming and going everywhere where someone's need or indeed his duty summons him: you will find, in the end, that precisely the actions that make him Socrates would make him[51] the most slandered woman in Athens. And that even after you have added to that perfection of virtue he possesses the

48. On Theano of Crotona, the wife of Pythagoras, see Diogenes Laertius, 8.42–43, and Agrippa, *Declamation*, 81. Gournay's explicit allusion to this Theano in *Equality* (see below, 77) makes it probable that she is the person meant, rather than the later philosopher of the same name; so, for that matter, does the allusion to her sexuality—see Mary Ellen Waithe, ed., *A History of Women Philosophers*, vol. 1, *Ancient Women Philosophers, 600 B.C.–A.D. 500*, and vol. 2, *Medieval, Renaissance, and Enlightenment Women Philosophers, 500–1600* (Dordrecht, 1987–89), 1:12–15 and 41–48. On the commentaries that made the name of Theano a byword for female wisdom, see Gilles Ménage, *The History of Women Philosophers*, trans. with an introduction by Beatrice H. Zedler (Lanham, Md., 1984), 48–51. (It is important to note that the learned Ménage, who modeled his work on Diogenes Laertius, was an acquaintance and admirer of Gournay—see Zedler, introduction, xi.) Finally, in one of his letters to Gournay, Lipsius paid her the compliment of comparing her to Theano (*Fragments*, ed. Dezon-Jones, 25). See also *Preface*, 95.

49. Montaigne devotes a brief essay to the defense of Plutarch and Seneca (*Essais*, 2.32.721–27).

50. Melania lost her husband and two sons at the same time. Like defense, consolation was a conventional rhetorical function—see Cicero, *De Oratore* 3.211; and Quintilian, *Institutia Oratoria* 10.1.47.

51. The pronoun is pointedly masculine.

chastity of Saint Margaret.[52] For to be a modest woman, in the world's view, means not preserving modesty but rather putting off candor, renouncing freedom of speech, of conduct, and even of judgment, giving strict religious observance to the myriad ceremonies that human fantasy is capable of inventing to this end, and not having any other rule for living well but popular opinion (even though it imposes vices and forbids virtues), nor other happiness than its approbation. Now in such a soul as that woman's, one can indeed readily imagine continence, but not the practice of such laws. Moreover, console yourself with the fact that, if Saint Paul had been of your sex, he could never have remained a woman of reputation while establishing the Christian Church and opening the gates of Paradise to the human race. For he needed to proceed in his design by travel, conversation, public meetings, which in truth are quite worthy of Saint Paul, and of an instrument of human salvation, but not of a proper woman.

Further, provided that a censure is false, he who spews it avenges those he accuses as much as he injures them. For if he makes things up, he reveals himself as a nasty villain; if he passes on gossip, he declares himself a poseur, since the only essential difference between a poseur and a clever man is that one speaks of what he understands, the other of what he does not, and gossip, properly speaking, is what one does not understand. For what ineptitude is it to believe that one knows something because people who may be lying, or deceived, to their hearts' content have said it? The ear is the crucible where one puts to the proof the fool and the man of sufficiency. Everyone sees him who talks, yet Democritus, Pyrrho, Socrates deny ever having seen him who knows, and the great Montaigne bears as his motto, "What do I know?"[53] One of two things holds: either you are indeed laughably stupid, you the reseller of news, to believe report, given that it has lied to you ten thousand times; or if you maintain that it is no liar, assuredly you admit to us that your life

---

52. Saint Margaret of Antioch, who suffered martyrdom, accompanied by the usual miracles, in order to preserve her chastity, was a popular exemplum of that virtue in the Middle Ages, thanks largely to the thirteenth-century compilation of saints' lives by Jacobus de Voragine known as the *Legenda Aurea* (*Golden Legend*).

53. Democritus (ca. 460–357 B.C.E.), who believed that all reality (except for atoms and empty space) was illusory, and Pyrrho (ca. 360–270 B.C.E.), the founder of the Sceptic school, are featured in Diogenes Laertius, 9.34–49 and 9.61–108. Montaigne, for whom Pyrrho was a particularly important figure, makes a point about both similar to Gournay's in his "Apology of Raimond Sebond" (*Essais*, 2.12.502C). Elsewhere he cites Socrates to the same effect (3.13.1075B), and the instance was a familiar one—cf. Jerome, *Letters*, 101 (no. 53)—grounded in Plato (see Plato's *Apology*, 21D). Montaigne adopted his famous sceptical motto, accompanied by the symbol of a scale, in 1576—see 2.12.527B.

and actions are in a most pitiful state. For they are saying of you what you are saying about someone else; and if you were to think that, by burdening your conscience with calumny, you could relieve your honor of that burden, you would be excessively fooling yourself.

But what is more, besides the fact that the slanderer incurs the reproach of being either a fool or a villain, O Roman ladies, if he does not outrage those who are greatest and strongest, he plentifully accuses himself of being a coward. For if any other person refrains from wounding with his tongue a great personage or some belligerent young man, and one with a sword that cuts well, one cannot say that it is on account of fear, inasmuch as he maintains the same respect for those whom he might offend with impunity; one says that it is on account of temperance and reason, which govern him. In a case where the slanderer thus spares such a man, it must needs be because he fears and dreads him, since he is well known for so delighting in slander as to manifest, with regard to the weak, that neither temperance nor reason nor conscience could deter him from it. How it must enrage him, then, that he does not dare to scratch that itch that he feels on the tip of his tongue for fear of giving somebody itchy fingers! And fear all the more pressing because it has greater force here in holding him back than either duty or a concern not to make a fool of himself has had elsewhere. But I am wrong to say that it is fear that cools him in this circumstance: rather, it is conscience. Because he knows that almighty God "hath put down the mighty and exalted them of low degree,"[54] he is afraid that he might be supposed desirous of familiarity with Him if he did not, contrariwise, flatter the powerful and put down the humble. And then, having heard it preached that murder is prohibited, he prefers to pass his time spinning yarns instead of fighting with Hercules.[55] Helen had overturned Asia by her inappropriate marriage—was anything more justifiable than detesting and stoning her? Nevertheless, we see that when she weeps for Hector at his death, she says, among other praises, that he was the only person in Troy from whom she had never heard an angry word—nay, many consolations for those of others:

> But never yet have I heard an ill word or a rash one from you;
> rather, indeed, if any other in the palace reproved me

54. "Deposuit potentes de sede et exaltavit humiles" (Luke 1:52, omitting "de sede" [from their seats]).
55. "°Pelotter des contes": we attempt to keep the image by way of the double meaning of "yarn." Another oblique allusion, seemingly, to Omphale.

among my brothers by marriage, or sisters, or those brothers'
   elegant wives,
or your mother—though your father was always as kind as my own—
then you checked them with words of persuasion,
and with your gentleness and your gentle speeches.
Therefore, with heart-felt grief, I lament for you along with myself,
   bereft as I am,
for I no longer have anyone in the wide reaches of Troy
who is kind or loving to me, and all of them shudder at me.[56]

One sees by this to what degree Homer and antiquity believed that this
alacrity of tongue, and harming of those who cannot defend themselves, belonged to temperaments far removed from a soldier of great accomplishment. The ancient motto of heroes was

Spare the vanquished and subdue the proud.[57]

It must be added here that whoever offends one more feeble than himself gives a just privilege to someone stronger than himself to offend him.
Moreover, take from among the slanderers (I do not include him who speaks
well-known truth, where there is need) those who slander in order to cover
their shame, and calumny will remain without its supporters. The reason for
this is that by dint of putting forward numerous offenders, they will hide
themselves in the crowd, and that in order to have themselves deemed ex-
empt from a vice with which their conscience reproaches them, to their
perpetual alarm, there is no better formula than to speak a good deal of ill

---

56. ἀλλ᾿ οὐ πω σεῦ ἄκουσα κακὸν ἔπος οὐδ᾿ ἀσύφηλον·
    ἀλλ᾿ εἴ τίς με καὶ ἄλλος ἐνὶ μεγάροισιν ἐνίπτοι
    δαέρων ἢ γαλόων ἢ εἰνατέρων εὐπέπλων,
    ἢ ἑκυρή—ἑκυρὸς δὲ πατὴρ ὡς ἤπιος αἰεί—,
    ἀλλὰ σὺ τὸν ἐπέεσσι παραιφάμενος κατέρυκες,
    σῇ τ᾿ ἀγανοφροσύνῃ καὶ σοῖς ἀγανοῖς ἐπέεσσι.
    τῶ σέ θ᾿ ἅμα κλαίω καὶ ἔμ᾿ ἄμμορον ἀχνυμένη κῆρ·
    οὐ γάρ τίς μοι ἔτ᾿ ἄλλος ἐνὶ Τροίῃ εὐρείῃ
    ἤπιος οὐδὲ φίλος, πάντες δέ με πεφρίκασιν.
       (*Iliad* 24.767–75, ed. A. T. Murry, Loeb Classical Library, 2 vols. [London and
    New York, 1925)

57. "Parcere subiectis et debellare superbos" (*Aeneid* 6.853, slightly varied)—from the prophecy
of Roman destiny delivered by the shade of Anchises. The saying (again, in varied form) also figures as a traditional motto of the Romans—one which they no longer live up to—in Antonio
de Guevara, *The Diall of Princes*, trans. Thomas Norton, select passages edited and with an introduction and a bibliography by Kenneth Newton Colvile (London, 1919), 106. Gournay cites
this work in *Equality*—see below, 85 and n. 41.

about it,[58] since one would not suppose that they would wish to decry it if they had been tainted by it. That is why salacious women, or the illegitimately born, never stop cackling about the honor of women. The thief seeks to make us mistrust everyone's hands, and someone whose foolish recklessness has ruined affairs of peace or war will always mock the administrative and military skill of his companions. Hence, the perspicacious embrace the suspicion stemming from such notable slanderers and say that leprosy of the soul reveals itself by the tongue, as does that of the body.[59]

It is true that, apart from their hope of masking their infamy behind the profession of slanderer by their manner of speaking, they have learned the trick of making themselves esteemed and valued in the eyes of the world. But what is that art based on, if they are so hungry to gain reputation and credit that they do not follow the tracks by which Caesar and Xenophon mounted to the heaven of glory? Or indeed, if they scorn those men as stupid and judge the deeds too slight for their own praises to be founded upon emulation of them, why do they not, as the lesser of two evils, make use of the role they have been playing to free themselves from repudiation by a prince, and from the lack of money that their insults so often cause them? Certainly the paltriest fishwife would have beaten them in the fencing-match of babbling about others, for they were just as content as lumpish peasants to use their tongue alone to establish for themselves a perpetual rule over the obedience of men, to make a scepter of their voice, to make the destiny of kings and nations hang on their speech, when they harangued their people against them, or for them, and to give ten thousand soldiers the courage to vanquish a hundred thousand in battle. And Caesar, who even by doing miracles could not subdue the Gauls except in eight years with the sword, thoroughly subdued all the great Roman Empire by his eloquence in that single day when authority over it was granted to him.

Finally, Paula and Melania, sort out the most gallant and perfect character from all these storytellers, entrust him with the least of the exploits of Themistocles and Scipio:[60] he may well and truly go look elsewhere for someone to perform it; and no wonder, since they have never said that one was a more able person for saving one's country and for triumphing over one's

---

58. "Dire bien du mal de lui" (*Le Proumenoir*, ed. Cholakian, fol. 54v): as strange a turn of phrase as its English equivalent. The text of 1598 gives the variant, "dire bien ou mal de luy" [speak well or ill of it] (*Le Promenois*, ed. Arnould, 148).

59. The term *lèpre* ("leprosy") was formerly applied to a variety of contagious diseases affecting the flesh.

60. Themistocles (ca. 528–462 B.C.E.) was an outstanding but controversial Athenian leader, hero of the struggle against the Persians under Xerxes; his fame in the Renaissance owed much

enemies, nor a less able one for doing nothing and ruining everything—but yes, indeed, for not blathering. After all, do not account them so stupid that they are not keenly sensible of the advantage that the activities of Caesar and Xenophon possess over their own, but they resemble the ape, who, not being able to be admired for his beauty, tries to be so by making faces, and the suitors of Penelope, who contented themselves with chambermaids when they saw that the mistress was not to be caught by them.[61] They do not do what they prefer but what they are able. And truly, whoever has the stomach to try to distinguish himself by a thing of little weight (and there is nothing slighter and more vain than babbling) shows well enough that he has nothing of great worth to boast about. And he who adorns and prettifies himself with copper makes it only too apparent that he has no gold. As the man is, so is his occupation, and you make a judgment about the feebleness or the beauty of intellects according to the things they amuse themselves with; for each of them, by natural instinct, in this chooses the measure of his sufficiency, and of his powers. And you could not bring it about that a god would take pleasure in feeding on barley or a hog on nectar. Now, whatever the case, worthy persons have been so generally vilified in all ages, as is apparent by their books, that to endure calumny has since become a sign of worthy persons. Still, they have always consoled themselves by that nobleness of heart conferred by integrity of conscience and with the fact that they would not wish, for the life of them, to resemble those whose tongue was injuring them. They too much prefer to receive the detractions of those souls rather than their persuasions or their examples. What is more, truth regains its luster with time, no matter what the price:

but the days that are still to come are the wisest witnesses.[62]

And the reproaches that were spewed upon Cato, Seneca, Plato, and Socrates serve now merely to bring contempt upon those from whom they came.

But father, who could pardon my long-winded chattering in this digression but you, who take me to task for usually being, on the contrary, too taciturn. All this while Othalcus (to bring our tragedy to an end), sending ten times to see how Alinda was doing in her illness, applied himself to having

---

to the account in *Plutarch's Lives.* There were several notable Romans called Scipio, but the reference is certainly to Scipio Africanus Major (236–183 B.C.E.), the hero of the Second Punic War (against Carthage).

61. According to the final books of the *Odyssey* (and, for that matter, Boccaccio in *Concerning Famous Women,* trans. and ed. Guido R. Guarino [Rutgers, N.J., 1963], 81–83 [chap. 38]), this was, rather, part of the suitors' depraved behavior while they waited for Penelope's much-deferred decision.

62. "ἁμέραι δ'ἐπίλοιποι / μάρτυρες σοφώτατοι" (Pindar, *Olympics* 1.33–34).

the house done over in new splendor, so as to beguile the impatience of that day, which, for him, lasted a thousand years. Everything gleamed as in the palace of Jupiter:

> it is resplendent with shining gold and silver, ivory gleaming on the chairs, cups glinting on the tables; all the house is gay.[63]

He had given charge to two of his servants to go and kill the supposed old woman in her bed, and their daggers were sharpened for that enterprise. The night being already well advanced, therefore, with everyone at rest and Leontin sent away, with no great difficulty, from the funeral chamber, Alinda, all trembling with horror, rose from the bed.

She sought to go straight to the door, but she went round the chamber almost three times before finding it. At once,

> with blotches interspersed on her trembling cheeks and pallid at the approach of death,[64]

she drew toward that of the old women, where, having gently awakened her, she gave her to understand that, because she was said to have spoken ill of Or-talde and Leontin, her master had given order that, in an hour, she should be killed while she slept, and that she had come out of compassion to warn her of this, so that she might be hidden somewhere while she restored her to favor, which she hoped she would soon succeed in doing. At this news, the poor old woman fled, wholly seized with fright, and Alinda remained alone—

> all things show forth death[65]—

and put herself in place, where, raising her eyes, and crossing her arms on her breast,

> she lay down on the bed and uttered her final words.[66]

---

63. Fulgenti splendent auro atque argento.
    Candet ebur soliis, collucent pocula mensae,
    Tota domus gaudet.
       (Catullus, 64.44–46).

64. Maculisque trementis
    Interfusa genas, et pallida morte futura.
       (*Aeneid* 4.643–44)

The lines describe Dido shortly before she falls on the sword.

65. "Ostentant omnia letum" (Catullus, 64.187).

66. "Incubuitque toro dixitque novissima verba" (*Aeneid* 4.650). Again, the reference is to Dido at the point of suicide; her final words provide the model for Alinda's.

"It is I," she said, "O gods, whom you caused to be born in such a high and happy estate, who now render you my life here amid exile, abandonment, servitude, and massacre—not complaining of it, however, except that it cannot be called guiltless. Nevertheless, ye gods, grant me pardon, or if my fault does not deserve grace, please bestow it upon my penitence. Forgive me, my father: you are not yet wholly a wretched one, if no one ever happens to relate to you what punishment the gods have today judged your child worthy of for the offense she did to you. Accept this adieu, which goes forth with my last breath—or, rather, after it, for already there is no longer any difference between me and the dead, except that they have passed over the pain of dying, and I await it. All the glorious blood of Cyrus will fall at that instant at the feet of a barbarian, and through the wound of a woman, and through the wound of your daughter.[67] O cruel fortune, if I had to die, why did I not die a queen? Or if I had to die a slave, why did I not at least die pitied? Adieu, my sweet mother, adieu; I regret nothing in the world but your old age in need of consolation. Your daughter will never see you more; you will never more see your daughter, unless some unhoped-for good fortune causes her one day to return to you in ashes. You never had of me anything but a painful childhood and tears. But do not shed all of them for my guilt; some of them must be reserved for my grave."

As soon as she had finished this speech, she drew down in the bed, where she prepared to await the blow without further stirring hand or foot, turned with her face buried in the pillow, for fear that the gleam of her complexion, too different from that of the old women, would give away the deception in the dim moonlight:

> So she spoke, and with her mouth pressed on the bed, "We shall die unavenged, but let us die," she said. "Thus, thus willingly we descend to the shades."[68]

And she seemed soundly asleep, with her weeping, and even her breathing, stifled in the bedding. Shortly thereafter the henchmen arrived, and, when they had approached the bed in silence, one put his hands on her to stay her, and she cried out in her soul, "Ah, my friend, do not touch me except with your sword," but the other thrust a sharp dagger into her neck, then gave a second blow in the body to finish her off. At all of this she let out neither cry

---

67. Alinda's reference to the blood of Cyrus ironically recalls the seduction speech of Leontin (above, 38).

68. "Dixit et os impressa toro, 'moriemur inultae! / Sed moriamur,' ait. 'sic, sic iuvat ire sub umbras'" (*Aeneid* 4.659–60). With these lines, much echoed by early modern authors, Gournay continues to follow the thread of Dido's suicide, which also, incidentally, involved deception (of her sister Anna).

nor yell—only a single pitiful groan at the painful drawing out of the dagger, which, by the violence of the blow, had penetrated into the mattress, soon bathed in the blood disgorged from those two wounds, which from there spread even to the floor.

And so Alinda thereby consummated, in so few years as she had lived, all that the histories of many ages can report and pity in the way of misery. There was no tender mother there, who, by the warmth of her kisses, might seem to wish to inspire a new soul:

—And, if any final breath strays from her, may she catch it with her
mouth.[69]

No maternal hand to close those gentle eyes and to anoint that beautiful body with balm and tears.[70] Nothing at all, but the horrid defilement of two strong blows of the knife, which stained her, as it happened, for a long while as she lay motionless.

Now, morning having come, the henchmen returned to the body, which they were going to throw in some ditch out of the way, as their lord had commanded. But even as they turned it over, behold them pale and stricken as if the sky had fallen on them; and they knew no other course but to flee in order to avoid the fury of their master. He—who for his part was waiting for them, when he arose, so as to go and impart the news of their exploit to the princess—sent to have them searched for everywhere, and, impatient of waiting any longer, he finally climbed himself up to the chamber of the massacre. One can imagine what a furious Thracian did and said at such an astounding encounter—in love to the point of madness, and a lover from whose hands the victory had been snatched that had cost him so much. But as he was tormenting himself and crying out with all his might, Leontin came in hurriedly from the other side,

rolling his bloodshot eyes.[71]

---

69. "—Et extremus si quis super halitus errat / Ore legat"—an adaptation of the words spoken in the first person by Anna in kissing her expiring sister: "Et, extremus si quis super halitus errat, / ore legam" (*Aeneid* 4.684–85). These lines disappear after the edition of 1598, only to reappear in French with that of 1626 in connection with Leontin's reaction (see *Le Promenoir*, ed. Arnould, 162).

70. This detail, which suits Gournay's development of Alinda's psychological preoccupation with her mother (the mother of Taillemont's heroine has died before the story begins), confirms that the author also drew on Ovid, *Heroides* 10 (Ariadne's lament), esp. 119–20: "Ergo ego nec lacrimas matris moritura videbo, / nec, mea qui digitis lumina condat, erit?" [Am I, then, to die, and dying, not behold my mother's tears; and shall there be no one's finger to close my eyes?] (Ovid, *Heroides and Amores*, trans. and ed. Grant Showerman, Loeb Classical Library [London and Cambridge, Mass., 1921], 130–31).

And it must be understood that, when the Persian lady, fulfilling her charge, came to show him that miserable letter, he made it quite apparent what force is exerted by the realization of his wrong in a soul who has something of generosity and good birth in him. For, suddenly taking on the countenance and color of the dead, with an outburst of piteous cries, he left his chamber in such a fury that, nearly mistaking the precipice for the way out, he ran out of it into that of the princess, where he thought that she must have killed herself in her bed. But the tumult of the disaster, raised during these events by the whole household, turned him toward the other side. There, then, pale and trembling with despair, with the remorse of love, and with pity all together, he went and threw himself outstretched on the body through the blood and the press of people. At first he seemed in a trance, showing no sign of a man awake but a sort of dull and agonized groaning, which one would not have known whether to attribute more to rage, to affection, or to pity. But when the little blood that still remained in her, flowing out under that intense pressure, came to spurt in his face, then he recoiled sharply: "Ah, innocent blood," he said, "you may wash me but cannot efface the stain of my crime. Such a pestilence should not be anointed but ripped out, the part and the whole, and the soul and the entrails with it. Die boldly, Leontin, die boldly; your victories are achieved and perfect: you have had the virginity of Alinda; you have had her life. O earth, O heavens—what monster is like you in cruelty? The embraces of their females mollify the tiger and the lion, but you, quite the contrary, you made that delicate woman cross the seas, you made her abandon father and mother, the purple and the royal honors, the empire, and almost the very altar and sacrifices, only to drag her to be massacred in your bed. Alinda would weigh her greatness against the gods if she had not loved Leontin; Leontin would not have committed parricide in Alinda if he had not received her favors. Truly, I should not die so quickly but reserve myself a long while in the torment caused me by the horror of the sight I have before me, for it alone is sufficient to punish me: hell has no punishment terrible enough. But, alas, grant that I may escape its rigor, O sweet and dear companion, so that I may come to you, not to obtain pardon (I am too unworthy of that) but only to beg you for mercy."

At that instant, the sight of that beautiful face, so pale and ravaged, led him to descend from his fury to languor and compassion, and to kiss those extinguished eyes like a lost man. "Will you shine for me no longer?" he said,

---

71. "Sanguineam voluens aciem." (*Aeneid* 4.643)—an interesting transfer to Leontin of part of the description of Dido quoted earlier (4.643–44), in anticipation of the union of his fate with Alinda's.

with a plaintive voice; he kissed her pale mouth: "Will you no longer breathe
life into my veins?" Then her ear: "Will you not hear the voice of my penitence? Will I not see you again? Have I lost you? Have I killed you, Alinda?"
But having two or three times wavered in this way, now furious, now in col-
lapse, finally he hurled a cry, "Ah, thus I will rejoin you!" After which, having
got up on his knees, he drew his dagger, and, looking askance at Ortalde, who
was present there, he struck himself violently in the heart and with one blow
sent his soul to join that of his lady. The body fell at Alinda's side; the wounds,
joining, seemed lovingly to welcome each other, and this new blood, hot and
steaming, seemed to wish to reanimate the other by its infusion.[72]

Now the pity of such a sight drew tears from all onlookers, and since
then has done so from many whom it touched only by hearing of it. As for
the Thracian Othalcus and his sister, they went into long and deep mourning, after having placed the urn with the common ashes in a tomb that they
had erected for the purpose.

Go in peace, holy couple, sprinkled with our tears.
There is no longer any sword a fair neck to pierce;
To steal away a lover, there remains no stratagem.
Love, a tyrant in the world, is God in Elysium.

72. Arnould, in his edition of *Le Promenoir* (168 n. B), points out the echo of Montaigne
1.25.222B, where, in a dramatic conclusion to an essay, the mutual destruction of a Roman father
and son facing execution is recounted; they rush on each other's swords and die in a close embrace, their blood mingling *amoureusement* (lovingly).

THE EQUALITY
OF MEN AND WOMEN
(1 6 4 1)

INTRODUCTION

With this explicitly feminist essay, we move into more familiar territory (if any portion of Gournay's oeuvre may be so described). As previously mentioned, the *Equality* was (together with the much shorter *The Ladies' Complaint* of a few years later) not only the first of her works to be translated into English but also the first to be reprinted in modern times. After Schiff's initial edition, moreover, and latterly with the encouragement of feminist trends in literary scholarship, these two texts have been regularly included in collections and featured in critical discussions. The result is that, at least for many non-specialists, they now virtually epitomize Gournay's intellectual identity.

Such a picture would necessarily be imprecise, given that these works comprise a small fraction of her literary production and originally appeared during the 1620s, when she was about sixty, thirty years or so after she began to publish (with the *Promenade*). Further, as essays devoted to the cause of women, they are unique within the canon: such advocacy was not, at least avowedly, Gournay's primary project as a writer. For that matter, the essay in general is not self-evidently her "essential" genre, despite her prolixity as an essayist—and, of course, the towering precedent of Montaigne. (In fact, Gournay's generic practices and preferences are intriguingly consistent with the other evidence of a profound ambivalence regarding her "father.")

At the same time, a strong case can be made that the *Equality* and the *Complaint* are, if not representative of Gournay's achievement as a "woman of letters," unavoidably central to her position as one—hence essential to a volume documenting the other voice. In them, but particularly in the former, the intellectual underpinnings of attitudes expressed throughout her career are revealed in detail—and, equally to the point, revealed as coherent. The ultimate result, therefore, of restoring these texts to their less than dominant position within the oeuvre—an effect approximated here by juxtaposing them with the *Promenade* and the *Apology*—is to highlight their multiple connection with works that are less explicitly (indeed more equivocally) feminist. Gournay herself attached particular importance to the *Equality.* She first published it on its own, and with a dedication to the queen (Anne of Austria) that remarkably combines the typical deferential flattery, redolent of hope for the patronage of which Gournay was always in need, with an audacious insistence that the queen educate herself so as to set an example to other women. Gournay further drew attention to the essay in introducing her collected works, at once making a claim for its originality (in its heavy reliance on male authorities to make the case for women) and effectively inviting its placement within the *querelle des femmes.*[1]

Gournay has already been situated generally in relation to that debate (see above, 13–16); our annotations to the *Equality* will document particular indebtedness to the contributions of Boccaccio, Agrippa, and Taillemont. Many (though not all) of her instances of notable women are to be found in the two former authors; the last is chiefly reflected in her celebration of learning and virtue, currently denied to women by male tyranny, as the means whereby they may accede to their appointed place in the divine creation. For Gournay, that place is emphatically an equal, not a superior, one, in contrast with the common tendency among advocates of women to "redirect the preference" to that sex, as Gournay puts it (below, 75). Even the generally egalitarian Taillemont, at once for argument's sake and under the spell of the courtly love tradition, tends to counter traditional misogynist arguments by standing them on their head, as when he maintains that woman's creation from human matter (the rib of Adam) proves not remoteness from God, as was frequently argued, but remoteness from the base clay of which the first man had been composed.[2]

The originality of Gournay's arguments in the *Equality* has sometimes been overblown—a tribute, perhaps, to her rhetorically effective presentation of them, which gains force from a passionately yet dexterously managed irony. There is, however, at least one vital aspect of her case for "mere" equality that goes to the heart of her distinctiveness as a thinker and writer in early modern France. For that case, as she makes it, is inextricable from her ideal of an intellectual community transcending gender and from her aspiration to join that community by dint of scholarly merit. It is originality of this kind to which she effectively lays claim when she draws the attention of the reader of her collected works to her extensive enlistment of male authorities

1. See Ilsley, *A Daughter of the Renaissance,* 205.
2. Taillemont, *Discours,* 113.

on behalf of women. At the same time, that claim does not obviate her palpable imaginative identification, throughout the *Equality,* with paragons of female strength, including physical strength, whom she draws from both the secular and religious spheres—or from both at once, in the case of Jeanne d'Arc.

Jeanne happens to be a conservative point of reference—a figure already serving to rally patriotic and religious sentiment. Nevertheless, another striking feature of Gournay's method is her generally free handling of religious issues: to adduce divine authority and instances in confirmation of human proofs was standard argumentative procedure in the period, but Gournay shows greater daring in this domain than do, say, Agrippa and Taillemont. This is especially clear when she insinuates a discrepancy between God's will and current teachings of the Church. Thus, with reference to the limited role allowed women in the religious life, she affirms the precedent of Mary Magdalene as a public preacher and maintains—even citing pagan in addition to early Christian practice—that women have an inherent right to administer the sacraments. The opposite side of this coin, undoubtedly the enabling condition of her iconoclasm, is a profound religious seriousness: these are evidently not arguments for argument's sake; for Gournay, they touch on the highest order of truth. She is also able, thanks to wide reading in theological texts, especially the Church Fathers, to bolster her opinions with reference to unimpeachable authorities, who are, of course, men. Nowhere, it may be added, is her propensity for choosing and using evidence selectively more apparent.

Comparison of the final published version of the *Equality* (1641) with the first (1622), of which translations are also available, serves to demonstrate not only Gournay's general habit of revision but also the particularly careful attention she bestowed on this essay over the last twenty years of her career. The text translated here is longer by roughly one-third, mainly as a result of "fleshing-out" the case with further illustrations—a procedure for which she had the notable precedent of Montaigne's successive versions of his *Essays.* In some cases (such as the naming of Hypatia [see below, 77 and n. 9]), Gournay is clarifying points previously made; more often, she is adding evidence, some of it gleaned from more recent reading. In a strict view, this elaboration may entail some cost to the focus and cohesiveness of the argument, but in practice the sheer intellectual exuberance of her additions, which tend to take on a life of their own, obscures any such detriment. In them the scholar's life-long curiosity joins compellingly with the female scholar's unabated commitment to justice for her sex. The consequent impulse to "get it all in" must have become increasingly acute as Gournay anticipated a decisively final publication.

To the Queen,[1] *on presenting her with*
The Equality of Men and Women

Madam:

Those who determined to assign a sun as a device for the late King your
father, with this motto, "There is no West for me," did better than they supposed, because in representing his greatness, which almost always, without
interruption, saw that Prince of Stars upon one of his territories, they rendered the device hereditary to your Majesty, presaging your virtues, the light
and felicity of peoples. It is, I say, Madam, in your Majesty that the Light of
Virtues shall have no West, when time has converted their flower into fruit;
and consequently the felicity of the French, which they illuminate, shall also
have no West. Now, while you are in the East of your age, as of your virtues,
deign, Madam, to resolve to arrive at their noon at the same time that you arrive at that of your years. I mean at the noon of your Virtues, which, in order
to mature, must benefit from leisure and culture. For there are several of the
most commendable—among others, religion, charity to the poor, chastity,
and marital love—that the noble instinct of Nature and fortunate birth may
inspire of themselves; of these you attained the noontide even in your morning. But truly, for that effort, one must have the requisite courage, courage as
great and potent as your Royalty (as great and potent as that is), Kings being
afflicted by this unhappiness—that the infernal plague of flatterers[2] who slip

1. Anne of Austria (1601–66), daughter of Philip III of Spain, who had married the French King
Louis XIII in 1615.

2. "La peste infernale des flatteurs"; the metaphor was firmly entrenched as a commonplace—
cf. Pierre de Ronsard, *La Franciade* 4.1515–17: "flateurs / Peste des Rois, courtizans et menteurs, /
Qui des plus grans assiegeant les oreilles . . ." [flatterers, the plague of kings, courtiers and liars,

into palaces renders Virtue, and her guide Clear-sightedness, of infinitely more difficult access for them than for their inferiors.

I know but one means by which you may hope to attain these two zeniths of age and the virtues at the same moment: that is, may it please your Majesty, by wholeheartedly plunging into sound writings concerning prudence and morality. For as soon as a Prince has heightened his mind by that exercise, the flatterers, finding themselves less subtle than he, no longer dare to trifle with him. And commonly potentates and kings cannot receive appropriate instruction except from the dead, because those who surround the great, being divided into two groups, the fools and the wicked (that is, those flatterers), neither know how nor wish to speak well in their hearing. The wise and well disposed can and wish to do so, but they do not dare. It is in Virtue, Madam, that persons of your rank must seek true loftiness and the Crown of Crowns, inasmuch as they have the power—but not the right—to offend against laws and justice, and they meet with as much danger and more shame than others do when they commit such excesses. Thus does a great king himself teach us—that all the glory of the daughter of the king is inward.

But what a country bumpkin am I! All others approach their princes and their kings by adoring and praising them; I dare to approach my Queen by preaching! But pardon my zeal, Madam, for I burn with desire to hear France cry, with applause, this acclamation, "The Light has no West for me," wherever your Majesty shall go, the new Sun of the Virtues; and I wish further to draw from you—so I hope from your worthy beginnings—one of the strongest proofs of the treatise that I offer at your feet to uphold the equality of men and women. And, not solely because of the unique greatness that is yours by birth and by marriage, you will serve as a mirror for your sex, and as an object of emulation for men, to the farthest extent of the universe, if you deign to raise yourself to the degree of merit and perfection that I propose to you by the aid of those great books. But as soon, Madam, as you have resolutely determined to shine forth with that precious brilliance, the sex as a whole will seem to be illuminated in the splendor of your rays. I am, Madam,

Your Majesty's most humble and obedient
subject and servant,
GOURNAY
1624

---

who, assailing the ears of the greatest . . .] (in *Oeuvres complètes*, ed. Jean Céard, Daniel Ménager, and Michel Simonin, 2 vols., Bibliothèque de la Pléiade [Paris, 1993], vol. 1).

THE EQUALITY OF MEN AND WOMEN

Most of those who take up the cause of women, opposing the arrogant preference for themselves that is asserted by men, give them full value for money, for they redirect the preference to them.[3] For my part, I fly all extremes; I am content to make them equal to men, given that nature, too, is as greatly opposed, in this respect, to superiority as to inferiority. But what am I saying? It is not enough for certain persons to prefer the masculine to the feminine sex; they must also confine women, by an absolute and obligatory rule, to the distaff—yea, to the distaff alone.[4] Still, what may console them for this contempt is that it comes only from those men whom they would wish least to resemble—persons who would lend plausibility to the reproaches that might be spewed upon the female sex, if they were of it, and who feel in their hearts that they have nothing to recommend them but the credit of being masculine. Because they have heard it cried in the streets that women lack value, as well as intellectual ability[5]—indeed, the constitution and physical make-up to arrive at the latter—their eloquence exults in preaching these maxims, and all the more richly for the fact that value, sufficiency, physical make-up, and constitution are imposing terms. They have not learned, on the other hand,

3. This includes Agrippa, who sets out to demonstrate women's "preeminence," but not Taillemont. On the context of the *querelle des femmes*, see Margaret L. King and Albert Rabil, Jr., "The Other Voice in Early Modern Europe: Introduction to the Series," in this volume, xviii; and Richard Hillman, "Introduction to Marie le Jars de Gournay (1565–1645)," also in this volume, 13–16.

4. Constant Venesoen, in his edition of *Égalité* in *Égalité des hommes et des femmes, Grief des dames, Le Proumenoir de Monsieur de Montaigne*, by Marie le Jars de Gournay (Geneva, 1993), n. 9, cites a proverb to this effect.

5. In this text, "intellectual ability" (which for humanists extended to moral development) often seems the most appropriate rendering of *suffisance*. Compare above, *Promenade*, n. 3.

that the chief quality of a dolt is to espouse causes on the basis of popular belief and hearsay.

Amid the chirping of their lofty conversation, hark how such intellects
compare the two sexes: in their opinion, the supreme excellence women may
achieve is to resemble ordinary men. They are as far from imagining that a
great woman might style herself a great man, if her sex were simply changed,
as from allowing that a man may raise himself to the level of a god. Men
braver than Hercules, truly, who merely took on a dozen monsters in a dozen
combats, while, with a mere single word, they vanquish half the world. But
isn't it beyond belief that those who seek to exalt and strengthen themselves
through the weakness of others feel compelled to insist that they can exalt or
fortify themselves by means of their own strength? And the best of it is that
they think themselves exonerated for their effrontery in vilifying the female
sex when they employ equal effrontery to praise, or rather to gild, themselves—sometimes (I say) in particular, sometimes in general, and, moreover,
in whatever wrong and false measure may be, as if the validity of their boasting gained weight and worth from their impudence. And God knows I am acquainted with some of those merry braggarts, among the most fervent in
their contempt for women, whose brags have even become proverbial. But
truly, if they lay claim to being men of refinement and sufficiency, since they
proclaim themselves to be so by edict, why would they not, by a contrary
edict, proclaim women to be stupid? It is only reasonable that their ball
should roll right to the end of its course. My God, doesn't the desire ever
come upon these embodiments of sufficiency to furnish a smidgeon of a just
and precise example and a fitting rule for perfection to that poor sex? And if
I judge well, either of the worthiness or of the capacity of women, I do not
propose at present to prove it with reasons, since the opinionated might dis-
pute them, nor with examples, since they are too common, but indeed only
by the authority of God himself, of the Fathers—the buttresses of His
Church—and of those great philosophers who have served as a light to the
universe. Let us rank those glorious witnesses in front and reserve God, then
the holy Fathers of his Church, for the innermost, as the treasure.

Plato, whose title of divine no one has disputed,[6] and consequently
Socrates, his interpreter and guarantor in his writings—if Plato is not rather in
them that of Socrates, his most divine preceptor, since they never had but a
single sense and a single mouth—attribute to women the same rights, faculties,

6. See Montaigne, *Essais*, 1.51.307A: "Platon a emporté ce surnom de divin par un consentement
universel, que aucun n'a essayé luy envier" [Plato has gained the sobriquet of "divine," which nobody begrudges him, by universal consensus].

and functions in their Republics, and everywhere else.[7] What is more, they maintain that women have often surpassed all the men of their nations, for indeed they have invented a number of the finest of the fine arts, even the Latin alphabet;[8] they have excelled, they have instructed magisterially and with sovereign authority over men, in all sorts of disciplines and virtues, in the most famous cities of antiquity, including Alexandria, the premier city of the Empire after Rome. Hypatia held such an exalted position in that much-celebrated place.[9] But did Themistoclea in Samothrace, the sister of Pythagoras, do any the less, not to mention the wise Theano, his wife?[10] For we are informed that the latter taught philosophy as he did, having had as a disciple even her brother, who had difficulty in finding in all of Greece disciples worthy of him. What, too, was Damo his daughter, in whose hands, as he died, he placed his Commentaries and the task of propagating his doctrine, with those mysteries and high seriousness that he practiced all his life?[11] We read even in Cicero, the Prince of Orators, what luster and vogue were enjoyed, at Rome and nearby,

7. Republics: plural, conceivably, because Gournay has both Plato and Socrates in mind as authors of *The Republic*, or because she is thinking less of that work's title than of the model it provides for forming future states. The section referred to is in bk. 5 (Plato, *The Republic* 5.3.451C–5.6.457B). The sweeping expression, "and everywhere else," reveals, as much as it conceals, Gournay's tendency to read selectively.

8. This legend is developed by Boccaccio, in particular—see his account of "Nicostrata, Who Was Called Carmenta," in *Concerning Famous Women*, 53–54 (chap. 25), to whom he also attributes grammar. Here Gournay conspicuously moderates the "extremism" of Henricus Cornelius Agrippa, who claims that women "have invented all the liberal arts" (*Declamation*, 76).

9. Born around 370 C.E., Hypatia, the daughter of Theon, was a philosopher and mathematician renowned for her knowledge and eloquence. In 415, when she was head of the school of Platonic philosophy in Alexandria, she was seized by a gang of men, who stripped her and cut her to pieces, evidently at the instigation of Christian monks. There is an account of her in *Suidas* (see below, 85, and n. 40), and Gournay may also have read about her in a compilation known as the *Historiae Ecclesiasticae Scriptores Graeci* (Greek writers on the history of the church), which was produced in several editions during the period; see that of N. Chesnau (Paris, 1571), 569–70 (570 misnumbered as 569). Hypatia received an ample notice in the late seventeenth-century survey of Ménage, *The History of Women Philosophers*, 25–29, and her significance is increasingly recognized today. See Mary Ellen Waithe, "Hypatia of Alexandria," in *A History of Women Philosophers*, 1:169–95, and "Finding Bits and Pieces of Hypatia," in *Hypatia's Daughters: Fifteen Hundred Years of Women Philosophers*, ed. Linda Lopez McAlister (Bloomington, Ind., 1996), 4–15.

   Hypatia was clearly in Gournay's mind even in her first version of the *Equality*, where she similarly refers to Alexandria. This sentence initiates, however, a series of embellishments of the original text.

10. Modern texts of Diogenes Laertius (8.21) identify Themistoclea as the Delphic priestess, rather than the sister, from whom (according to Aristoxenus) the philosopher Pythagoras (ca. 582–500 B.C.E.) was supposed to have derived his doctrines. Compare Ménage, *History of Women Philosophers*, 47–48. On Theano, see above, *Promenade*, n. 48.

11. Damo (as "Dama") is said by Agrippa (who has likewise just mentioned Theano) to have been "renowned in explaining her father's veiled opinions" (*Declamation*, 81). Another tradition

by the eloquence of Cornelia, the mother of the Gracchi, and, further, by that of Laelia, the daughter of Caius Laelius, who in my opinion was Sylla.[12] Neither did the daughter of Laelius, any more than that of Hortensius, fail to receive a famous encomium in Quintilian on the subject of that exquisite virtue.[13] But then if Tycho Brahe, the famous astronomer and Danish baron,[14] had lived in our day, would he not have celebrated that new star recently discovered in his region—let us call her thus—Mademoiselle van Schurman,[15] the rival of those illustrious ladies in eloquence, and of their lyric poets too, even in their own Latin language, and who, besides that language, possesses all the others, ancient and modern, and all the liberal and noble arts? But would Athens, august queen of Greece and learning, be alone among the foremost cities in not having seen women triumph in the highest rank of the preceptors of humankind, as much through their illustrious and prolific writings as by the spoken word? Arete, the

---

holds that Pythagoras, in entrusting his writings to her, forbade her to publish them and that she loyally obeyed (Diogenes Laertius, 8.42). Compare Ménage, *History of Women Philosophers*, 53–54.

12. Cornelia (ca. 189–110 B.C.E.) educated her two sons, Caius Sempronius Gracchus and Titus Sempronius Gracchus, in oratory in the Greek tradition and to a life of public service on behalf of plebeian interests; after they were successively murdered, she devoted herself to letters. Laelia (185–115 B.C.E.) was the daughter of Caius Laelius Sapiens. It is not clear to us why Gournay identifies the latter with Lucius Cornelius Sylla (or Sulla), ca. 138–78 B.C., the notoriously ruthless Roman general and politician who, through civil war, made himself de facto monarch of the republic and was eventually forced to abdicate. Cicero, in *Brutus*, offers qualified praise of the eloquence of the Gracchi (27.103–4; 97.333)—whose political ideas he detested—and gives full credit for it to their mother (27.104; 58.211). In the latter instance, Cicero's point is the importance of a parent's influence on rhetorical style, and he goes on to support it with praise of Laelia, who was his wife's mother and whom he elsewhere cites for her natural and unaffected speech (*De Oratore* 3.12.45). Agrippa (*Declamation*, 83) similarly uses the training in eloquence given by Cornelia to her sons as an instance of the formative role of nurses and mothers; see also Albert Rabil, Jr., in Agrippa's *Declamation*, 73 n. 143.

13. The daughter of Hortensius was Hortensia, known for having delivered an effective public oration on behalf of women; the passage in Quintilian mirrors Cicero's emphasis on parental education and cites Cornelia and Laelia before mentioning Hortensia, whose declamation "is still read and not merely as a compliment to her sex" (*Institutia Oratoria*, trans. and ed. H. E. Butler, 4 vols., Loeb Classical Library [London and Cambridge, Mass., 1920], 1:22–23 [1.1.6]). Hortensia's story is told by Boccaccio, *Concerning Famous Women*, 185 (chap. 82), who instead relied (Guarino, in *Concerning Famous Women*, 256) on Valerius Maximus 8.3.3. She is also cited by Agrippa, *Declamation*, 82. It may be relevant that Hortensius was connected with Sulla by way of his sister, who enticed the dictator to marry her (Rabil in Agrippa's *Declamation*, 82 n. 175); Plutarch allows her to have been of excellent character, but the enticement was due to her beauty (*Lives* 35.4–5). In 62 B.C.E., Hortensius, together with Cicero, also successfully defended Sulla's kinsman, Publius Cornelius Sulla, against the charge of complicity in subversion fomented by Catiline.

14. Tycho Brahe (1546–1601), born in what is now Sweden, observed the stars and planets with great accuracy.

15. This reference first appears in the edition of 1634. On Anna Maria van Schurman, see in this series, *Whether a Christian Woman Should Be Educated and Other Writings from Her Intellectual Circle*, ed. and trans. Joyce Irwin (Chicago, 1998).

daughter of Aristippus, acquired in that glorious city a hundred and ten
philosophers as disciples, publicly occupying the chair that her father had left
vacant by his death; and because, apart from that, she had composed excellent
writings, the Greeks honored her with this praise: that she had had the pen of
her father, the soul of Socrates, the tongue of Homer.[16]

I single out here only those women who have taught publicly in the most
celebrated places, and with a brilliant luster. For it would be a tedious business, because an infinite one, to enumerate the other great and learned minds
of women. Why indeed would the peerless Queen of Sheba have adored the
wisdom of Solomon, even across as many seas and territories as separated
them, if not because she knew it better than all her age?[17] Or why would she
have known it better, except by a corresponding wisdom, equal or closer to
it than all those of the other minds of that time? It is in thus sustaining the esteem and deference that women have deserved that that double miracle of
Nature—preceptor and disciple—named at the opening of this section believed that he gave more weight to certain speeches of great importance if he
pronounced them in his books through the mouths of Diotima and Aspasia:[18]
Diotima, whom he did not at all shrink from terming his mistress and pre-
ceptress in several of the most exalted branches of learning—he, the preceptor and master of all the nations under the sun.

From the subject Theodoret so readily broaches in the *Oration Concerning
Faith*, it seems to me quite evident that he found a favorable opinion of the

16. On Arete (whose name means "virtue"), see Diogenes Laertius, 2.72, 86), although Gournay
appears to have taken her information chiefly from Boccaccio, *Concerning Famous Women*, to judge
from H. J. Mozans, *Women in Science* (New York, 1913), 197–99 and 198 n. 1. Compare Mary Ellen
Waithe, "Arete, Asclepigenia, Axiothea, Cleobulina, Hipparchia, and Lasthenia," in *A History of
Women Philosophers*, 1:197–201. Gournay had a special interest in Arete's father, the philosopher
Aristippus of Cyrene (ca. 435–350 B.C.E.), thanks, presumably, to the account of Diogenes Laertius, 2.65–104, and the numerous references to him by Montaigne. See *Preface*, 39 n. 26.

17. See 1 Kings 10:1–13 and 2 Chron. 9:1–12. As "Nicaula, Queen of Ethiopia," she is the subject of chap. 41 of Boccaccio's *Concerning Famous Women*, ed. Guarino (93–94), which, as Guarino notes (in *Concerning Famous Women*, 255), draws on Flavius Josephus (see the latter's *Jewish
Antiquities* 8.165–75). The story also figures in Agrippa (*Declamation*, 85), who identifies her,
with Boccaccio, as Nicaula and further cites the New Testament prophecy (Matt. 12:42 and
Luke 11:31) that she "is going to judge the men of Jerusalem" (96; Rabil in Agrippa's *Declamation*, 96 n. 233).

18. Diotima of Mantinea: a legendary priestess for whose wisdom Socrates, in Plato's *Symposium*
(201D–212B), expresses his admiration and to whom he attributes his ideas on love.

Aspasia: for many years the companion of Pericles, ruler of Athens; she is supposed to have
been skilled in rhetoric and to have taken part in intellectual discussions with men, including
Socrates. On Aspasia and Diotima, see also *A History of Women Philosophers*, ed. Waithe, 1:75–116.
Gournay's references here are further evidence, it seems, of her debt to Agrippa's defense of
women (*Declamation*, 81, and Rabil in *Declamation*, 81 n. 173), although Aspasia is also singled out
by Jerome (see below, n. 81).

sex highly plausible.[19] Then look at that long and magnificent comparison
that the famous philosopher Maximus of Tyre makes between the mode of
loving of Socrates himself and that of the great Sappho.[20] To what extent,
too, does that king of sages delight himself with the hope of conversing in
the other world with the sufficiency of the great men and the great women
whom the ages have fostered; and what pleasures does he promise himself
from that exercise in the divine *Apology* where his great disciple reports his
last words?[21] After all these testimonies from Socrates on the subject of
women, it is easy to see that if, in the *Symposium*, he lets slip some remark of
Xenophon disparaging their prudence, in comparison with that of men,[22] he
is considering them according to the ignorance and inexperience in which
they are nurtured, or rather, at the worst, in general, intending to leave ample room for frequent exceptions—something that the blatherers[23] we are
discussing are far from comprehending. With regard to Plato, we are also told
that he did not wish to begin teaching unless Lastemia (I have read the name
in this form) and Axiothea had arrived among his auditors, saying that the

19. Theodoret (ca. 393–466), Bishop of Cyrrhus (in Syria), one of the Church Fathers. Gournay seems likely to be referring to his commentary on the Apostles' Creed, where he is indeed
concerned with faith and where, typically for Theodoret, he emphasizes the dogma that Christ
derived human nature from the Virgin Mary. Also to the point, perhaps, is Theodoret's work
commonly known as the *Philoteus* or *Religious History*, which introduces several accounts of holy
women in the following (by no means unequivocal) terms: "Having written the lives of these
heroic men, I believe that it will be useful also to mention women who have struggled in no lesser
way, if not with even greater strength. They deserve, indeed, still greater praises, these women
who, though having a weaker nature, have given proof of the same courage as the men and have
delivered their sex from its hereditary shame" (Théodoret de Cyr, "Histoire Philothée," in *Histoire des moines de Syrie*, Sources Chrétiennes 257 [Paris, 1979], 2:29.1; our translation).

20. Maximus of Tyre: Greek sophistic philosopher of ca. 125–85 C.E., whose work would have
been available to Gournay in Latin and French translation, as well as in the original. The passage
mentioned may be found in *The Dissertations of Maximus of Tyre*, trans. Thomas Taylor, 2 vols. (London, 1804), 1:90–94 (dissertation 8); the discussion is conducted very much in the shadow of
Plato, with this dissertation on the "Amatory Art of Socrates" including references to Aspasia
and, especially, Diotima. Gournay would have found further references to Sappho, one of the
most celebrated ancient Greek poets (b. ca. 612 B.C.E.), in many classical authors. She is also
praised in chap. 45 of Boccaccio, *Concerning Famous Women*, 99–100.

21. See Plato, *Apology* (in *Euthyphro, Apology, etc.*, trans. and ed. Harold North Fowler, Loeb Classical Library [London and Cambridge, Mass., 1914], 142–43 [41C]), where Socrates indeed
specifies "both men and women."

22. Socrates' remark comes in response to a display of skill by a dancer: "This girl's feat, gentlemen, is only one of many proofs that woman's nature is really not a whit inferior to man's, except in its lack of judgment and physical strength" (Xenophon, *Symposium*, trans. and ed. O. J.
Todd, in *Anabasis, Books IV–VII, Symposium and Apology*, Loeb Classical Library [London and
New York, 1922], 392–93 [2.9]).

23. *Deviseurs*—corrected from *diverseurs*, following the 1641 list of errata.

former was intelligence, the latter memory, and that they could understand and retain what he had to say.[24]

If, therefore, women attain less often than men to the heights of excellence, it is a marvel that the lack of good education—indeed, the abundance of outright and blatantly bad education—does not do worse and prevent them from doing so entirely. If proof is needed, is there more difference between them and men than among themselves—according to the training they receive, according to whether they are brought up in a city or a village, or according to nationality? Therefore, why should not their training in public matters and in letters, of a kind equal to men's, fill up the gap that commonly appears between their minds and those of men, when we see, likewise, that such training is of such importance that, because just one of its branches—namely, dealing with the world—is common among French and English women and lacking among the Italian, the latter are in general so far exceeded by the former?[25] I say in general because in particular the ladies of Italy sometimes excel; and we have drawn from them queens and princesses who did not lack intellectual ability.[26] Why indeed might not the right sort of upbringing succeed in filling the gap between the understandings of men and theirs, given that in the example I just cited, those of inferior birth surmount their betters purely and simply by dint of this dealing and engagement with the world? For the air breathed by the women of Italy is more subtle and fit for rendering the mind so than that of England or France, as appears by the

24. Following Diogenes Laertius, 3.46 and 4.2, Lastheneia of Mantinea and Axiothea of Phlius are mentioned by Agrippa as disciples of Plato (*Declamation*, 81; and Rabil in *Declamation*, 81 n. 173). We have been unable, however, to trace the detail supplied by Gournay, which appears in neither these nor two other more remote but conceivable sources: Themistius, *Orationes* 23.295C; and Clement of Alexandria, *The Miscellanies* (*Stromata*). It is nonetheless striking that Clement, a Greek Church Father of the second century, praises both Lastheneia and Axiothea in a chapter devoted to women's potential for virtuous excellence (*The Miscellanies* [*Stromata*], bks. 2–8 in *The Writings of Clement of Alexandria*, trans. William Wilson, 2 vols., Ante-Nicene Christian Library, vol. 12 [Edinburgh, 1869], 2:193–96 [4.19]) and in the company of the following exempla also cited by Gournay: Judith, Theano, Arete, Aspasia, Corinna, and Sappho. In another chapter, while granting the generally superior abilities of males, he praises women's capacity to endure the torments of martyrdom, insists that virtue is the same for both sexes, and opines that women should engage in philosophy (165–70 [4.8]). Clement's work would have been available to Gournay in Latin translation, as well as in the Greek original.

25. As Venesoen points out (in Gournay's *Égalité des hommes et des femmes*, 44 n. 19), the restrictions placed on Italian women with regard to normal social contact had been deplored by Montaigne (*Essais*, 3.5.883B).

26. The first edition (1622) specified "deux Reynes à la prudence desquelles la France a trop d'obligation" [two queens to whose prudence France is only too obliged] (*Égalité des hommes et des femmes*, ed. Venesoen, 44)—obviously Marie de' Medici and Catherine de' Medici.

ability of the men of the Italian climate when compared ordinarily with that of Frenchmen and Englishmen; but I have touched on this idea elsewhere.

Plutarch, in his little work on the virtuous deeds of women, maintains that the virtue of the man and that of the woman are the same thing.[27] Seneca, by the same token, affirms in the *Consolations* that one cannot suppose Nature to have treated women harshly or restricted and curtailed their virtues and their intellects more than the virtues and intellects of men; but, on the contrary, she has endowed them with equal vigor and with resources sufficient for everything honorable and praiseworthy.[28] Let us look, after these two, at what judgment the third chief of the Triumvirate of Wisdom human and moral makes of them in his *Essays*.[29] It seems to him, he says—hence, he does not know why—that one rarely finds women worthy of commanding men.[30] Is this not to place them, individually, in equal counterpoise to men and to confess that, if he does not so place them in general, he is afraid of being wrong, though he can excuse his restriction by the poor and unseemly manner in which that sex is nurtured? Nor does he neglect, moreover, to cite favorably in another place in the same book that authority which Plato grants to them in his Republic and the fact that Antisthenes denies all difference in ability and in virtue between the two sexes.[31] As for the philosopher Aristotle, in the course of enquiring into heaven and earth, he has by no means contradicted the opinion that favors women, unless he has done so in general terms because of their poor upbringing, and without ruling out exceptions; thus he has confirmed that opinion, relying, apparently, on the sayings of his spiritual father and grandfather, Socrates and Plato, as on something constant and determined by the authority of such sages, through whose mouths (it must be admitted) the entire human race, and reason itself, have pronounced their decree.[32]

27. Plutarch, *Moralia, Bravery of Women* 243A; this translation of the title accurately reflects the sort of "virtue" primarily illustrated by Plutarch's collection of stories.

28. See Seneca, *Moral Essays, Ad Marciam de Consolatione* 16.1.

29. The reference, of course, is to Montaigne, who is similarly characterized in *Promenade*—see above, 35.

30. Gournay refers to Montaigne's *Essais,* 2.8.398A, but her reading is hard to square with what Montaigne goes on to say about the untrustworthiness of women's judgments.

31. Montaigne, *Essais,* 3.5.897C. "Virtue is the same for women as for men" was a saying of the Athenian philosopher Antisthenes (ca. 445–360 B.C.E.), founder of the Cynic school (Diogenes Laertius, 6.12). Gournay chooses at this point to ignore Xenophon's *Symposium* (392–93 [2.10]), where, following the remark of Socrates cited above, 80 and n. 22, Antisthenes teases him about his inability to "educate" his notoriously shrewish wife, Xanthippe.

32. There is no point in adducing here the dozens of key passages, ranging over a number of works in his vast oeuvre, where Aristotle sets forth his views on women, both biological and social. Those essentially negative views, which had been enormously influential for hundreds of

Must I adduce a vast number of other intellects, ancient and modern, of illustrious name? Or, among the latter, Erasmus, Politian, Boccaccio, Tasso in his works, Agrippa, the honorable and judicious preceptor of courtiers, and so many famous poets, all of them together so thoroughly opposed to the disdainers of the female sex and such partisans of its advantages, aptitude, and readiness for all praiseworthy functions and practices and for great undertakings?[33] In truth, ladies console themselves with the fact that the decriers of their merit cannot prove that they themselves are capable people if all these authors, old and new, are so, and that such a man will not say—even if he believes it—that the merit and the advantages of the female sex fall short, next to those of the masculine, until he has passed off all these writers as dreamers, so as to impugn their testimony so contrary to such a statement, should he undertake to pronounce it. And he would still have to proclaim as dreamers entire peoples, even some of the most astute, including those of Smyrna, according to Tacitus, who at one time, in order to establish, among the Romans, their precedence in nobility over their neighbors, claimed to have descended, either from Tantalus, the son of Jupiter, or from Theseus, the grandson of Neptune, or from an Amazon, whom, consequently, they set equal to those gods in dignity.[34] The inhabitants of Lesbos sought no less glory in the birth of Sappho, since it is found everywhere today, even in Holland, that their money carried as its only mark the figure of a young woman holding the lyre with this word, Lesbos. Was this not to recognize that the greatest honor they and their island had ever had was to nurture the child-

---

years before Gournay's era, were already beginning to be challenged by advocates of women, and her uphill struggle to reconcile traditional intellectual authority with progressive thinking is reflected in the mixture of equivocation and rhetorical overkill here. Both for documentation and for a good sense of the issues from a feminist perspective, see Maryanne Cline Horowitz, "Aristotle and Women," *Journal of the History of Biology* 9 (1974): 183–213. For Aristotle on women in the Renaissance context, see Ian Maclean, *The Renaissance Notion of Women* (Cambridge, 1980).

33. As previously mentioned (see above, 14), Gournay is indebted to the explicit encomiums of women written by Boccaccio and, especially, by Agrippa. In general, however, her tendency to identify authors she admired as advocates of women—a tendency most notable in the case of Montaigne—involves some selective reading and wishful thinking. This is true for Desiderius Erasmus, the Dutch humanist (ca. 1466–1536), as well as for the two Italian poets, Torquato Tasso (1544–95) and Politian, i.e., Angelo Poliziano (1454–94). All three figures, however, did contribute to the burgeoning literature on women by way of such topics as love and marriage; see their listings in Kelso's exhaustive bibliography (*Doctrine for the Lady of the Renaissance*, 326–424). The "preceptor of couriers" is Baldassare Castiglione (1478–1529), who wrote the enormously influential (and heavily Neoplatonic) *Il Cortegiano* (The courtier). Again, see Kelso, 210–22, for a summary of Castiglione's prescriptions for women as courtiers, esp. in relation to the ideal of courtly love.

34. Tacitus, *Annals* 4.56, records this argument in the context of a competition among Asian cities for the privilege of building a temple dedicated to the Roman imperial family and the senate.

hood of that heroine? And since we have happened upon the subject of women poets, we learn that Corinna publicly took the prize over Pindar in their art and that at the age of nineteen, the last year of her life, Erinna had made a poem of three hundred verses achieving such a height of excellence that it paralleled in majesty those of Homer and plunged Alexander into doubt as to whether he must think more highly of the good fortune of Achilles for having met with that great poet to be his herald, or that of the poet himself for having had as his rival such a heroine.[35] Have ladies possessed the knowledge to choose, between those two poets, to whom to accord gloriously the victory, or at least equal standing?

On the question of the Salic law, which deprives women of the crown, it applies only in France. And it was invented in the time of Pharamond,[36] solely because of the wars against the Empire, whose yoke our forefathers were throwing off, the female sex seemingly being physically less fit for bearing arms because of the necessity of bearing and nourishing children. It must still be noted, however, that, the peers of France having originally been created to serve as virtual associates of royalty, as their name makes clear, the lady peeresses in their own right had a seat, privilege, and voice in deliberations wherever the peers did, and of the same extent.[37] One can consult Hotman for the etymology of peers, and Du Tillet and Matthieu in the *Histoire du Roy* for the peeresses.[38] So, too, it is worth considering that the Lacedaemonians, that brave and generous people, consulted with their wives on all busi-

35. Corinna of Tanagra: see Pausanias, *Description of Greece* 9.22.3, who explains her victory over Pindar with reference to her dialect and her beauty. Erinna: see, again, Agrippa, *Declamation*, who includes in his list of female orators and poets "Erinna of Telos or of Lesbos, who was surnamed the epigrammatist" (82). The reference to Lesbos may be due to an erroneous association with Sappho, with whom she was probably not contemporary. She was especially well known for a poem in memory of a girlhood friend. For further references to both women, see Rabil, in Agrippa's *Declamation*, 82–83 n. 176. We have not traced Gournay's story about Alexander, which looks to be grafted onto Plutarch's report, in his life of Alexander, that at the tomb of Achilles that monarch declared "the hero happy in having, while he lived, a faithful friend, and after death, a great herald of his fame" (Plutarch, *Lives*, 7:263 [Alexander, 15.4]).

36. Pharamond: a figure from Arthurian romance whom legend credits with founding the line of Merovingian kings in the fifth century C.E.

37. As Venesoen notes (in Gournay's *Égalité des hommes et des femmes*, 47 n. 35), this fact comes by way of Montaigne, *Essais*, 1.41.256C.

38. See François Hotman, *Francogallia*, ed. Ralph E. Giesey and J. H. M. Salmon, trans. J. H. M. Salmon, Cambridge Studies in the History and Theory of Politics (Cambridge, 1972), 386–89. No cataloged title of either Du Tillet or Matthieu corresponds precisely to that cited by Gournay. Jean Du Tillet (d. 1570), a churchman, wrote *La Chronique des roys de France* (Chronicle of French kings), first published in Latin in 1539, then translated and several times updated until the reign of Henri III. Pierre Matthieu, 1563–1621, produced biblical and legal commentary, poetry, and drama (including vitriolic texts on behalf of the ultra-Catholic Holy League), before

ness, public and private, by the account of Plutarch;[39] and Pausanias, Suidas, Fulgose, and Laertius[40] will answer for most of the other authorities or testimonies that I gathered above—to which I will add that the *Theater of Human Life*, with the *Dial of Princes*,[41] which I can call to witness in such a case, recount much new information on this subject, for which they cite their authorities. Nevertheless it has served the French well to develop the device of female regents[42] as the equivalent of kings during royal minorities. For without this, how many would have had their states overthrown? According to Tacitus, the Germans—those bellicose tribes—who after more than two hundred years of war, were proclaimed in triumph more often than vanquished,[43]

---

becoming, in effect, official historian under Henri IV; there had been multiple editions of his historical works, which concentrate on late sixteenth-century France.

39. Plutarch, *Lives*, Lycurgus, 14.1–3, and comparison of Lycurgus and Numa, 3.5.

40. Pausanias, whose *Description of Greece* has previously been cited, was active around 150 C.E. *Suidas* (also *Suda*), is now commonly considered to designate the title, rather than the author, of this compilation of information on classical literature and history, which probably dates from the latter part of the tenth century C.E.

Gournay's "Fulgose," in our opinion, must be Battista Fregoso, regularly identified as Baptista Fulgosius in the early editions of his work; Doge of Venice from 1453 to 1504, he produced a compendium of memorable sayings and deeds, which, in Latin translation (*Bap. Fulgosii factorum dictorum que memorabilium libri IX*), went through at least eight editions between 1509 and 1604. Arnould (letter to Richard Hillman, 16 December 1999) has supported this identification and pointed out that bk. 8, chap. 3, of Fregoso's work, entitled "De fœminis qui doctrine excelluerunt" (Of women who have excelled in learning) was, in turn, included in *De Memorabilibus et Claris Mulieribus* (Of memorable and famous women) by Joannes Ravisius Textor (Paris, 1521).

As for Diogenes Laertius, a number of our notes reflect Gournay's considerable debt to his collection of philosophers' lives; nothing is known about the author, but he is usually assigned to the earlier part of the third century C.E.

41. *The Diall of Princes* is the title of Thomas North's translation (1568) of the enormously popular Spanish work of moral counsel, *Relox de principes o Libro aureo des Emperador Marco Aurelio*, by Antonio de Guevara (1529). Compare above, *Promenade*, n. 57. The translation into French (by René Berthault de la Grise, as *L'Horloge des princes*) was first published in 1531; there were numerous subsequent editions, including one in 1608.

Theater of Human Life ("Theatre de la vie humaine") alludes, according to Arnould (letter to Hillman, December 1999), to the *Theatrum vitae humanae* produced in the second half of the sixteenth century by Theodor Zwinger, who adapted the work of Conrad Lycosthenes (or Lykosthenes). The scope of this vast compilation of instances, which was owned by Montaigne, may be judged from part of the title of the 1565 Basel edition: *omnium fere eorum quae in hominem cadere possunt bonorum atque malorum exempla historica* (historical examples of almost all the good and bad things that can happen to mankind).

42. Venesoen, in Gournay's *Égalité des hommes et des femmes*, 47 n. 37, traces the practice back to Blanche of Castille, 1188–1252.

43. See Tacitus, *Germania*, trans. and ed. Maurice Hutton, rev. E. H. Warminton (in *Agricola, Diologus*, vol. 1 of *Tacitus in Five Volumes*, rev. ed., Loeb Classical Library [London and Cambridge, Mass., 1970]), chap. 37.

brought a dowry to their wives, not the other way round;[44] and likewise, what is more, they had some nations among them who were never ruled except by that sex.[45] And when Aeneas presents to Dido the crown and scepter of Ilium,[46] the scholiasts say that this comes from the fact that ladies who were elder daughters, such as that princess, formerly reigned in royal houses. Could one wish for two more forceful refutations of the Salic law (if it can endure two refutations)? Thus it is that our ancient Gauls did not disdain women, nor the Carthaginians with them, when, being united in the army of Hannibal to pass through the Alps, they established the women of Gaul to serve as arbiters of their quarrels.[47] And if men in many places rob the sex of its portion of the greatest advantages, they are wrong to make a right of their usurpation and tyranny; for inequality in physical force, more than in spiritual strength or other branches of merit, is far and away the cause of that thievery and of the tolerance of it: physical force, which ranks, moreover, so low among the virtues that beasts exceed men in it by more than men exceed women.[48] And if that same historian Tacitus teaches us that where force prevails, fairness, integrity, even modesty are attributed to the conqueror,[49] it is scarcely astonishing that prudence, wisdom, and every sort of good quality in general are the prerogatives of these men of ours, to the exclusion of women, excluded as they are, too, from all worldly advantages.[50]

Further, the human animal, taken rightly, is neither man nor woman, the sexes having been made double, not so as to constitute a difference in species, but for the sake of propagation alone.[51] The unique form and distinction of that

---

44. Ibid., chap. 18.

45. Ibid., chap. 45. Gournay does not take up Tacitus's comment that such tribes have thereby "fallen lower . . . even than slaves" (211 [chap. 45]).

46. That is, Troy. The reference is to *Aeneid* 1.653–55. Dido also serves both Boccaccio (*Concerning Famous Women*, 86–92 [chap. 40]) and Agrippa (*Declamation*, 74, 86) as an exemplum of a virtuous and powerful woman.

47. Gournay seems to have adapted the point from Agrippa (*Declamation*, 94), who virtually translates his own source (Plutarch, *Bravery of Women*, 246C).

48. Taillemont, *Discours*, 116, makes a similar point about physical strength and women's relative lack of it.

49. Gournay is again drawing on the *Germania*; her terms here ("l'équité, l'integrité, la modestie mesme") faithfully paraphrase the Latin text ("modestia ac probitas"), while her mention of "wisdom" (*sagesse*) immediately following picks up *sapientiam* in the next sentence of Tacitus (186–87 [chap. 36]).

50. On male conquest and tyranny with respect to women, cf. Agrippa, *Declamation*, 94–96; and Taillemont, *Discours*, esp. 119–20.

51. With Gournay's argument in this section, cf. Agrippa, *Declamation*, 43. See also Plato, *The Republic*: "If it appears that [the sexes] differ only in just this respect that the female bears and the male begets, we shall say that no proof has yet been produced that the woman differs from the man for our purposes" (trans. and ed. Paul Shorey, rev. ed., 2 vols., Loeb Classical Library [London and Cambridge, Mass., 1937], 1:444–45 [5.5.454D–E]).

animal consists only in its rational soul. And if it is permitted to laugh in the course of our journey, the jest would not be out of season that teaches us that there is nothing more like a cat on a windowsill than a female cat. Man and woman are so thoroughly one that if man is more than woman, woman is more than man. Man was created man and female—so says scripture, not reckoning the two except as one;[52] and Jesus Christ is called Son of Man, although he is that only of woman—the whole and consummate perfection of the proof of this unity of the two sexes.[53] I speak thus according to the great Saint Basil in his first homily on the Hexameron:[54] the virtue of man and of woman are the same thing, since God bestowed on them the same creation and the same honor: *masculum et feminam fecit eos.*[55] Now in those whose nature is one and the same, it must be concluded that their actions are so as well, and that the esteem and recompense belonging to these are equal, where the works are equal. There, then, is the declaration of that powerful champion and venerable witness of the Church.

It is not amiss to recall on this point that certain ancient hair-splitters carried their arrogance to the inane extreme of arguing against the image of God in the female sex, as opposed to man; on this basis, according to their reckoning, they had to make the beard characteristic of that image. It was consequently necessary, moreover, to refuse to women the image of man, since they could not resemble him without resembling the other whose image he bore. God himself has distributed the gifts of prophecy impartially to women along with men and has also established them as judges, instructors, and leaders of his faithful people in peace and war, in the persons of Huldah and Deborah;[56] further, He caused them to enjoy, with that people, the triumphs of great

52. Gournay's biblical readings tend to confirm the influence of Agrippa on the French feminist tradition—see Rabil's introdroduction to Agrippa's *Declamation,* 28 n. 53.

53. Compare Agrippa, *Declamation,* 64.

54. Basil of Caesaria, ca. 320–379, one of the Church Fathers. The passage referred to is found not in the first of the Nine Homilies on the Hexameron but, rather, in the first (usually known as Homily 10) of two later additions on the creation of mankind. This text is available in French translation in Basile de Césarée, *Sur l'origine de l'homme (Hom. X et XI de l'Hexaéméron),* ed. and trans. Alexis Smets and Michel Van Esbroeck, Sources Chrétiennes 160 (Paris, 1970); see 232–33 (1.29.1) It is noteworthy that Gournay drops the negative element: "Equally honorable are the natures of each, equal their virtues, equal their reward, and identical their condemnation" (our translation).

55. Genesis 1:27: "So God created man in his own image, in the image of God created he him; male and female created he them"; this is the textual cornerstone of Agrippa's argument (*Declamation,* 43), as well as of that of Taillemont (*Discours,* 112–13), whose concern for the fate of women's souls more closely matches Gournay's.

56. Huldah ("Olda" in Gournay's text), and Deborah were Old Testament prophetesses (2 Kings 22:14–20; Judg. 4:4–5:15). Again, there are precedents in Agrippa (*Declamation,* 76, 80, 85). See also below, n. 81.

victories, in witness whereof their hymns of praise have the honor of finding
a place in the Holy Bible, and likewise those of Marie, the sister of Moses, and
Anna, the daughter of Phanuel.[57] What is more, they have many times prevailed and triumphed in various regions of the world—and over whom? Cyrus
and Theseus;[58] to these two one may add Hercules, whom they have, if not
vanquished, at least well thrashed.[59] Likewise, the fall of Penthesilia gave the
crowning touch to the glory of Achilles—you have only to hear Seneca and
Ronsard speak of him:

> The amazon he vanquished, final terror of the Greeks.
> Penthesilia he cast into the dust.[60]

Nor could Virgil consent to the death of Camilla in the midst of a furious
army, which seemed to fear nothing but her, except by means of ambush and
the surprise of a shot from far off.[61] Epicharis, Leaena, Porcia, the mother in
Maccabees—will they serve us as proof of how capable women are of that
other triumph, the magnanimous strength that consists in constancy and endurance of the most rigorous sufferings?[62] Have they, moreover, excelled

57. Agrippa (*Declamation*, 76–77, 80) likewise cites the sister of Moses (see Exod. 15:20–21;
Num. 26:59)—whose name was Miriam, however, not Marie—as well as Anna. Not surprisingly, neither writer mentions God's disgrace and punishment of the former (Num. 12:1–15). According to Luke 2:36–38, Anna was a prophetess who received the child Jesus in the temple. She
served as a type of the virtuous woman for Saint Jerome—see *Letters*, in *The Principal Works*, 127.

58. Cyrus died in battle against Thamyris (or Tomyris), the queen of Scythia, whose story figures in Boccaccio, *Concerning Famous Women*, 104–6 (chap. 47), and Agrippa, *Declamation*, 86. Notable classical sources are Herodotus, 1.214; and Valerius Maximus, 8.10, Ext. 1. Plutarch, *Lives*,
Theseus, 26–27, recounts the wars of Theseus against the Amazons. Boccaccio, 40 (chap. 18),
portrays their furious retaliation for that hero's abduction of Hippolyta.

59. The allusion is to the great resistance offered by the Amazons to Hercules' achievement of
the girdle of Hippolyta, his Ninth Labor. Compare Boccaccio, *Concerning Famous Women*, 40
(chap. 18), where, however, the queen is Antiope.

60. Penthesilia was a legendary queen of the Amazons—see *Aeneid* 1.490–93 and 11.661–63;
cf. Boccaccio, *Concerning Famous Women*, 65–66 (chap. 30). The first of Gournay's lines translates
Seneca, *Troades* 243; Ronsard makes passing mention of Penthesilia, likewise as the ultimate conquest of Achilles, in "Institution pour l'adolescence du Roy Très-Chrestien Charles IXᵉ de ce
nom" (in *Oeuvres complètes*, ed. Jean Céard et al., 2:1007, line 45). The context in Seneca renders
Gournay's allusion intriguingly double-edged, since Pyrrhus, the son of Achilles, is detailing his
father's achievements in order to justify sacrificing Polyxena to Achilles's vengeful spirit—an
emblem of female martyrdom appropriated by Gournay for herself in the *Apology* (see below, 148
and n. 71 in the same work).

61. Camilla was the queen of the Volscians, allied with Turnus against the forces of Aeneas and
finally slain with a spear thrown by Arruns. See *Aeneid* 11.432–33, 498 ff., 532 ff., and esp. 648–
835. She, too, figures in Boccaccio, *Concerning Famous Women*, 79–80 (chap. 37), and is mentioned
by Agrippa, *Declamation*, 74, 86.

62. Epicharis, Leaena, and Porcia are all included in Boccaccio, *Concerning Famous Women*.
Epicharis, though of base birth and shameful morals, heroically resisted torture and committed

less in keeping faith, which comprises all the chief virtues, than in strength, considered in all its aspects? Paterculus informs us that during the Roman proscriptions, the fidelity of children was nonexistent, that of freedmen slight, that of women preeminent.[63]

And if Saint Paul, to follow my trail of testimonies from the saints, forbids them the ministry and commands them to keep silence in church?[64] It is plain that this is not at all out of contempt but rather, indeed, only for fear lest they should arouse temptations by that display, so plain and public, that must be made in the course of ministering and preaching, since they are of greater grace and beauty than men. It is clear as day, I affirm, that contempt has nothing to do with it, since that Apostle speaks of Thesbé as his cohelper in the work of our Lord[65]—apart from the fact that Saint Thecla and Apphia have a place among his dearest children and dis-

---

suicide rather than reveal information about a conspiracy against the Roman emperor Nero (209–11 [chap. 91]). Her story was further accessible in Tacitus's *Annals* 15.51 and 15.57, which was Boccaccio's own source (Guarino in *Concerning Famous Women*, 256).

According to Boccaccio, 107–9 (chap. 48), the prostitute Leaena similarly endured torments and finally bit off and spat out her tongue to avoid betraying the conspirators against an Athenian tyrant. Although she is briefly mentioned by Pausanias, *Description of Greece* 1.23.2, the main classical source for her story, as Guarino indicates (255), is Pliny, *Natural History* 7.23, where her endurance is termed "most famous." There, however, it is Anaxarchus who is credited, later in the same passage, with biting off his tongue. Boccaccio evidently followed the later account of Tertullian (one of the Church Fathers), who, it seems, may have read Pliny carelessly. Compare Ménage, *History of Women Philosophers*, 56. Gournay's text actually reads "Læena," and Arnould has suggested (letter to Hillman, 16 December 1999) that she may have had in mind Lerna, to whom the Athenians raised a bronze statue of a tongueless lioness in token of her constancy and love of country. This reference might have been found in *Le Bouclier des Dames, contenant toutes leurs belles perfections* (The ladies' shield, containing all their great perfections), by Louis de Bermen, seigneur de la Martinière, a rare volume published in Rouen in 1621.

The fame of Porcia (or Portia) is more widespread, although Agrippa (*Declamation*, 73) makes her the wife of Marcus Cato rather than his daughter; she was, instead, the wife of Marcus Brutus, the prominent conspirator against Julius Caesar. As Guarino observes (256), Boccaccio incorporates the two mentions of her by Valerius Maximus, 3.2.15 and 4.6.5, by having her first test her capacity to endure pain, then, after her husband's death, commit suicide by swallowing live coals. Plutarch also gives these details in his biography of Marcus Brutus, 13.3–11 and 53.5. The mother referred to in the Apocryphal books of the Bible known as 1 and 4 Maccabees was willing to see her seven sons killed, then to sacrifice herself, for their faith—see 2 Macc. 7 and the amplification of the story, including extended praise of the mother, in 4 Macc. 8–18.

63. That is, their loyalty to the proscribed men—see Velleius Paterculus (ca. 19 B.C.E.–after 30 C.E.), *Compendium of Roman History* 2.67.2. The historian's point is that the sons were corrupted by self-interest.

64. See 1 Tim. 2:12 and 1 Cor. 14:34–35. Agrippa, *Declamation*, 96, also needs to explain away this injunction, though he uses a different argument.

65. The name Thesbé is not found in the Bible; Venesoen, in Gournay's *Égalité des hommes et des femmes*, 51 n. 56, plausibly suggests an error for Phoebe (Rom. 16:1–2), who is praised by Paul immediately prior to his commendation, in terms resembling Gournay's, of two other women, Priscilla and Aquila (Rom. 16:3).

ciples.[66] Not to mention the great credit of Saint Petronilla[67] with respect to Saint Peter—or to add that Mary Magdalene is named in the Church as equal to the Apostles ("Par Apostolis"), among other places in the calendar of the Greeks published by Génébrard.[68] Indeed, the Church and those very Apostles allowed an exception to that rule of silence for her, who preached for thirty years in the Baume of Marseilles, as all of Provence reports.[69] And if someone impugns this testimony of the preaching of the Magdalene, let them be asked what else the Sibyls were doing but preaching about God's universe by divine inspiration, in anticipation of the future coming of Jesus Christ?[70] And he would then have to tell us whether he can deny the preaching of Saint Catherine of Siena, which the good and holy Bishop of Geneva has just taught me about.[71] Moreover, all nations grant

66. According to the second-century *Acts of Paul and Thecla* (in *Apocryphal Books of the New Testament, The Twelve Patriarchs, etc., The Ante-Nicene Fathers,* ed. Alexander Roberts and James Donaldson, rev. ed. A. Cleveland Coxe [Buffalo, N.Y., 1886], 8:487–92), Thecla dedicated herself to virginity and followed Paul (at one point traveling to meet him in boy's clothing); she preached the gospel in Iconium, and a chapel dedicated to her honor in St. Peter's, Rome, became the chapel of the kings of France. Paul sends greetings to Apphia, among his fellow laborers, in Philemon 1:1.

67. Petronilla (or Petronille): according to legend, the daughter of Saint Peter, probably in a spiritual sense. Saint Francis of Sales speaks of Peter's "particular love" for her—and, in the same breath, of Paul's for Thecla (*Introduction to the Devout Life*, 141); she was supposedly martyred after refusing to wed.

68. Gilbert Génébrard (1537–97), Benedictine monk; active in the Catholic League during the wars of religion, he was named Archbishop of Aix by the duke of Mayenne. His most highly regarded work is a Latin commentary on the Psalms of David (1577).

69. The so-called Sainte Baume (sacred grotto), northeast of Marseilles, had been a center of pilgrimage for centuries because of its association with Mary Magdalene, supposed to have spent thirty-three years there; in the pre-Christian era, it was associated with a fertility cult.

70. Sibyls: women who, in classical times, were thought to possess the power of prophecy—a point endorsed by Agrippa (*Declamation,* 76, 80). Especially renowned was the Sibyl of Cumae. Christian tradition often extended their foresight to the coming of Christ—see, e.g., Boccaccio, *Concerning Famous Women,* 41–42 (chap. 19) and 50–51 (chap. 24). Saint Augustine, *The City of God against the Pagans* 10.27, so expounds the reference to the Sibyl of Cumae in Virgil's famous fourth *Eclogue.*

71. Saint Catherine of Siena (1347–80): influential visionary and theologian, author of letters and a much read work of meditations and revelations called the *Dialogue* or *Treatise on Divine Providence.* The Bishop of Geneva referred to is Saint Francis de Sales (1567–1622), who held that post from 1602 until his death. Both his *Introduction à la vie dévote* (Introduction to the devout life), first published in 1609, then revised and expanded in 1619, and his *Traité de l'amour de Dieu* (Treatise on the love of God), which appeared in 1616, make reference to Catherine of Siena, although the 1622 edition of the *Equality* does not. Curiously, while Catherine's charitable works come in for due praise from Francis, her preaching is not stressed but, rather, her intense, quasi-erotic, mysticism, as when she "shared the burning pain of our Saviour's wounds" and "gratifying love set a keen edge on aching pity" (*The Love of God,* trans. Vincent Kerns [London, 1962], 194). Moreover, Francis advises that in her "there is more to admire than to imitate" (*Introduction to the Devout Life,* 76). See also above, "Introduction to Marie le Jars de Gournay," 15.

the priesthood to women impartially with men, and Christians must at least agree that they are capable of administering the sacrament of baptism. Then, if the right to administer that one has been justly accorded, how can they be justly denied the capacity to administer the others?[72]

As for the claim that necessity, because of the death of little children, compelled the ancient Fathers to establish this practice against their will, surely they would never have believed that this necessity could excuse such prevarication as to bestow permission to violate and profane the administering of a sacrament. In the end, one sees plainly that in granting this power to women they esteemed them worthy of it and that they have not forbidden them to administer the other sacraments except in order always to preserve more complete the authority of men, whether because they themselves were of the male sex or, rightly or wrongly, so that peace between the two sexes might be better assured by the weakness and repression of one of them. Truly, Saint Jerome wrote wisely in his Letters that with regard to serving God, the spirit and the doctrine must be considered—not a person's sex.[73] This pronouncement should be applied generally so as to allow to women, on still stronger grounds, all other branches of knowledge and all the most excellent and soundest actions, to put it in a word, of the most exalted kind.

And this too would be to follow the intentions of the same Saint, who in all his writings highly honors and grants authority to that sex, hence dedicating to the maiden Eustochium his commentaries on Ezekiel, although it was forbidden even to priests to study that prophet before the age of thirty.[74] Whoever will read what Saint Gregory, too, writes on the subject of his sister[75] will

72. Venesoen, in Gournay's *Égalité des hommes et des femmes*, 53 n. 61, documents Gournay's simplification of this question.

73. Gournay perhaps has in mind Jerome's statement in *Letters*, 127.5, justifying his great esteem for the holy Marcella (the friend of Paula and preceptor of Eustochium): "For we judge of people's virtue not by their sex but by their character" (p. 255). This belongs to the same discussion of women's apostolic role on which she will shortly be drawing. Gournay is at least making a reasonable inference from a number of Jerome's letters to and about his female associates— see, e.g., *Letters* 22, 24, 59, 108, and 130—as well as from the prologue to his commentary on Zephaniah (see below, n. 81).

74. Eustochium (ca. 368–420) was an important follower of Jerome, a founder of monasteries and an accomplished biblical scholar. Besides dedicating to her his commentaries on Isaiah, Ezekiel, and Zephaniah, he addressed several letters to her. Gournay borrows a number of her examples of outstanding women from Jerome, although her generalization about his favoring of the sex presumes, of course, his insistence on chastity and praise of asceticism and virginity— see, notably, *Against Jovinianus* (in *The Principal Works*), 346–416, on which Chaucer's Wife of Bath draws in idiosyncratic fashion.

75. The sister of Saint Gregory of Nyssa was the religious Macrina, whose holy asceticism is admiringly chronicled by her brother in *The Life of St. Macrina*—see Saint Gregory of Nyssa,

find him no less favorable to women than is Saint Jerome. I was reading the other day a blatherer who declaimed against the prerogative that the Protestants commonly accord to the supposed insufficiency of women to explore freely in scripture. In this, I found he was as right as right could be, if he had made a similar objection to the insufficiency of men in the case of such a general permission—insufficiency, however, that he is unable to see because they, like him, have the honor of wearing a beard. Further, Saint John, the Eagle[76] and the most cherished of the Evangelists, did not disdain women, any more than Saint Peter and Saint Paul, and those three Fathers (I mean Saint Basil, Saint Jerome, and Saint Gregory), since he addresses his Letters to them in particular—to say nothing of innumerable other saints, or Fathers of the Church, who take the same position in their writings.

As for the accomplishment of Judith,[77] I would not deign to mention it, so particular was it—that is, dependent on the initiative and the will of its author. No more will I speak of the others of that caliber, though they are immense in quantity, as they are equally heroic in qualities of every kind as those that are the crowning glory of the most illustrious men. I do not record private deeds, for fear that they might seem to be mere ebullient manifestations of personal energy rather than of the advantages and endowments of the female sex. But that of Judith deserves a place here, since it is true that her plan, coming into the heart of a young woman among so many feeble-hearted men, in such need, in such a difficult enterprise, and for such a benefit as the salvation of a people and of a city faithful to God, seems to be rather an inspired favor and a gift of divine and special grace toward women than a purely human and voluntary action. So, too, appears that of the Maid of Orléans, accompanied by much the same circumstances but of more extensive value, inasmuch as it extended even to the salvation of a great kingdom and its prince.

> That illustrious Amazon, whom Mars took pains to teach,
> Mows down squadrons, and braves hazards,
> Wearing the hard breastplate upon her round breast
> Whose rosy nipple sparkles with graces:

Ascetical Works, trans. Virginia Woods Callahan (Washington, D.C., 1967), 163–91; she also figures as the "teacher" in Gregory's dialogue *On the Soul and the Resurrection* (in *Ascetical Works,* 198–272).

76. Saint John was known as the Eagle of Patmos, where he was supposed to have composed *Revelation,* and the eagle was his traditional iconographic symbol in art and architecture.

77. The Book of Judith recounts this widow's courageous redemption of the besieged Jewish city of Bethalia; having used her beauty to captivate the besieging general, Holofernes, she then cut off his head. Jerome also praises her in several places, using at one point terms taken up by Agrippa (*Declamation,* 87–88; and Rabil in *Declamation,* n. 194).

To crown her head with glory and laurels,
She, a mere virgin, dares to confront the most famous warriors.[78]

Let us add that the Magdalene is the only living being to whom the Redeemer ever spoke these words and promised this august grace: Wherever the gospel is preached, you shall be spoken of.[79] What is more, Jesus Christ declared the supreme joy and glory of his resurrection to women first of all,[80] so as to render them, according to the famous expression of Saint Jerome in his prologue to the prophet Zephaniah, female apostles to the Apostles themselves[81]—and, as we know, with an express mission: Go, he said to that

---

78. Ceste illustre Amazone instruicte aux soins de Mars,
    Fauche les escadrons, & brave les hazars:
    Vestant le dur plastron sur sa ronde mammelle,
    Dont le bouton pourpré de graces estincelle
    Pour couronner son chef de gloire & de lauriers,
    Vierge elle ose affronter les plus fameux gueriers.

The French is Gournay's own translation of the *Aeneid:*

    ducit Amazonidum lunatis agmina peltis
    Penthesilia furens mediisque in milibus ardet,
    aurea subnectens exsertae cingula mammae
    bellatrix, audetque viris concurrere virgo.

    (1.490–93)

The combination of sexual modesty with intimations of divine blessing in Gournay's flamboyant rendering brings the queen of the Amazons close to the popular images of Jeanne d'Arc, who qualified for Estienne Pasquier, e.g., writing in 1612, as "nostre Amazone" (*Lettres familières*, ed. D. Thickett [Paris, 1974], 374). Agrippa also compares Jeanne to an Amazon (*Declamation*, 88), and she had figured in the tradition of the praise of women since Christine de Pizan (a contemporary) and Martin Le Franc (*Le Champion des dames*) toward the mid-fifteenth century—see Rabil, introduction to Agrippa's *Declamation*, 22 and 88–89 n. 200. Gournay herself composed several poems in Jeanne's honor—see Ilsley, *A Daughter of the Renaissance*, 292–93.

79. Matthew 26:13, though the association of the woman mentioned there with Mary Magdalene is merely traditional.

80. Matthew 28:1–10; Mark 16:1–8; Luke 24:1–12; John 20:1–18. The same point is made by Agrippa, *Declamation*, 64; see also Rabil in *Declamation*, 64 n. 104.

81. The prologue to Jerome's commentary on Zephaniah (or Sophonias) was addressed to Paula and Eustochium. Obviously a key text for Gournay—after all, its authority was impeccable—this very brief piece (barely a page in modern type) not only contains the biblical reference and the phrase in question but also supplies a list of exceptional women from religious and secular history that overlaps considerably with her exempla: the biblical instances include Huldah (as "Olda"), Deborah, Judith, Anna, and Elizabeth; among the secular women praised are Aspasia (by way of Plato), Sappho, Porcia (for rivaling in constancy both her father, Cato, and her husband, Brutus), and Cornelia, the mother of the Gracchi. The last is even paired with Carneades (cf. below, *Complaint*, n. 3), "eloquentissimus philosophorum, acutissimus rhetorum" [the most eloquent of philosophers, the most sharp-minded of orators] (*In Sophoniam Prophetam, S. Hieronymi Presbyteri Opera*, pt. 1.6 [*Commentarii in Prophetas Minores*], ed. M. Adriaen, Corpus Christianorum Series Latina, vol. 76A [Turnhout, 1970], 655), who, although accustomed to the plaudits of

very woman, and relate what you have seen to the Apostles and Peter.[82] On this point, it must be noted that he revealed his new birth in the same instance and in the same way to women as to men, in the person of Anna, the daughter of Phanuel, mentioned above, who recognized him by prophetic spirit along with the good old man Saint Simeon at the time when he was circumcised, and before them Saint Elizabeth, from the time when he was still enfolded within the hidden places of the womb of the Virgin.[83] That birth, moreover, was predicted by the Sibyls, whom I recently mentioned, alone among the Gentiles: a transcendent privilege for the female sex. What honor accorded to women was, as well, the dream that occurred in Pilate's house, directed to one of them to the exclusion of men, and on such and so exalted an occasion?[84] And if men boast that Jesus Christ was born of their sex, we answer that it had to be thus for necessary reasons of decency, since he would have been unable without scandal to mingle as a young person and at all hours of the day and night among the crowds in order to convert, succor, and save the human race, if he had been of the female sex, especially in the face of the malice of the Jews.

But further, if anyone is so dull as to imagine masculine or feminine in God—for although His name may seem to have a masculine sound to it, it does not follow that one sex needs to be chosen above the other to honor or exalt the incarnation of His Son—such a person shows in a plain light that he is just as bad a philosopher as he is a theologian. On the other hand, the advantage that men possess by virtue of His incarnation in their sex (if they can draw an advantage from it, given the necessity noted earlier) is counterbalanced by His priceless conception in the body of a woman, by the entire perfection of that women—the only one to carry that title of perfect among all purely human creatures since the fall of our first parents—and by her Assumption, also unique in a human being. What is more, it may perhaps be said of her humanity that she exceeds that of Jesus Christ in this prerogative—that sex was by no means necessary in him for the Passion and for the Resurrection and the redemption of human beings,

---

public men and scholars, felt no shame at philosophizing with her in her home. See also Jerome, *Letters*, 127.5.

82. Mark 16:7. The privilege accorded Mary Magdalene in particular, which also figures in Jerome's *Letters*, 127.5, was sometimes cited in the Middle Ages on behalf of women—see Rabil, introduction to Agrippa's *Declamation*, 15 and 15 n. 32.

83. For Simeon (or Simon) and Anna, see Luke 2:25–38; for Elizabeth, see Luke 1:41–42. It sheds some light on Gournay's train of references to note that the biblical Anna is compared by Jerome to the virtuous woman Marcella (to the latter's advantage) in *Letters*, 127.

84. See Matt. 27:19. The reference is to Procula, the wife of Pilate.

his very functions, while it was so in her for motherhood, which was likewise her function.

Finally, if Scripture has declared the husband the head of the wife,[85] the greatest folly that men can commit is to take that as a license conferred by their worthiness. For in view of the instances, authorities, and reasons noted in this discourse, by which is proved the equality—let us even say the unity—of graces and favors on the part of God toward the two sexes, and in view of the fact that God declares, "The two shall be but one," and then declares, "The man shall leave mother and father and give himself to his wife,"[86] it appears that this declaration of the gospel is made solely for the express need of fostering peace in marriage. This need would require, undoubtedly, that one of the conjugal partners should yield to the other; for the usual weakness of intellects made it impossible for concord to be born of reason, as should have been the case in a just balance of mutual authority; nor, because of the imposing presence of the male, could the submission come from his side. And however true it may be, as some maintain, that such submission was imposed on woman in punishment for the sin of eating the apple,[87] that still hardly constitutes a decisive pronouncement in favor of the supposed superior worth of man. If one supposed that scripture commanded her to submit to man, as being unworthy of opposing him, consider the absurdity that would follow: woman would find herself worthy of having been made in the image of the Creator, worthy of the holy Eucharist, of the mysteries of the redemption, of paradise, and of the sight—indeed the possession—of God, yet not of the advantages and privileges of man. Would this not declare man to be more precious and more exalted than all these things, and hence commit the gravest of blasphemies?

85. 1 Cor. 11:3; the most commonly cited biblical authority for man's dominion over women was Gen. 3:16.

86. See Gen. 2:23–24; Matt. 19:4–5; Mark 10:6–8; Eph. 5:21–33.

87. This was standard misogynist theology from the earliest days of the Church but had been notably rebutted by Agrippa (*Declamation*, 62–63).

THE LADIES' COMPLAINT
(1 6 4 1)

INTRODUCTION

The general caveat against considering Gournay's two explicitly feminist essays in isolation gains particular point when the affiliations of the later one (first published 1626) are considered. Ilsley terms the much shorter *Complaint* "an outburst of temper based on [the author's] own bitter experience," by contrast with the more deliberative and abstract *Equality*.[1] This is certainly true to first impressions, and there is no questioning the personal bitterness behind Gournay's treatment of male misogyny—in either essay, for that matter. Still, it is hardly slighting her as an author to recognize the impression of "outburst" as itself a skillfully contrived literary effect, and such a perspective imposes itself through a comparison with other texts. The *Complaint* thereby emerges as a rhetorical "set piece," complementing the forceful but abstract ironies of the *Equality* with a satirical scorn appropriate to the actual behavior of men in contemporary society—especially of those pretenders to intellectual sophistication who concealed their personal inadequacy behind the mask of male superiority. Indeed, in its conclusion, the *Complaint* makes explicit reference to the *Equality* as a virtual companion piece (see below, 105) and evokes the progression of that text's argument from the wisdom of pagan philosophers to the unchallengeable tenets of Christian doctrine.

The bulk of the *Complaint*, however, recycles—"outburst" and all—material that was dropped from one of Gournay's earliest published works, the *Preface* to her first edition of Montaigne's *Essays*, which dates back some thirty years (to 1595). The *Complaint's* opening gambit, with its ironic deployment of biblical language, derives from Gournay's jumping-off place, in the precursor text, for an acerbic depiction of misogynist boorishness in conversation, as she had repeatedly experienced it. That account continues to serve as a framework, which she now fills in with rhetorical polish and adapts more

---

1. Ilsley, *A Daughter of the Renaissance*, 209.

insistently to the general condition of women, as may be seen from the following passages:

> Even had I the arguments of Carneades, there is no one so much a weakling that he will not rebuke me, to the grave approbation of the company present, with a smile, a nod, or some jest, which will have the effect of saying, "It's a woman speaking." (*Preface*, 35)

> If women possessed the arguments and the profound thoughts of Carneades, there is no man, however mediocre, who does not put them in their place with the approval of most of the company, when, with merely a smile or some slight shaking of his head, his mute eloquence pronounces, "It's a women speaking." (Below, 101)

Such reworking of earlier texts, enacting at once continuity and discontinuity, is a pervasive characteristic of Gournay's canon.

So, too, is an intriguing tendency to fence with the (overwhelmingly male) reading public in the promulgation of controversial opinions—a tendency that may be related, in turn, to a basic personal ambivalence. Gournay obviously (and admittedly) thirsted for esteem, indeed fame, as a writer; at the same time, she felt driven to articulate forcefully her most deeply held convictions, including her critical perception of male-female relations. Hence, some of the very passages that originally made the *Preface* too hot to handle, and so compelled its neophyte author to withdraw it, virtually burst into flame in her maturity, when she had less to lose. At the same time, the amplified bluntness and broader scope of her new text also reflect a change in context, and so highlight the fact that Gournay's most fundamental and sustained ambivalence, throughout her adult life, involved her position as Montaigne's "daughter."

The focus of the feminist elements in the *Preface* was originally blurred by that piece's larger project, which was not protest and self-affirmation (though these are everywhere apparent) but, rather, the passionate championship of the male author who supplied the volume, even the editor herself, with a raison d'être. On him, she announced, her very identity depended absolutely: "I cannot, Reader, use another name for him, for I am not myself except insofar as I am his daughter" (*Preface*, 29). The result was what Rigolot has aptly identified, in the introduction to his edition, as a conflicted "dédoublement intentionnel" [split orientation], whereby Gournay spoke at once on her own behalf and as Montaigne's "daughter."[2] By contrast, when

---

2. Rigolot, introduction to "Préface à l'édition des *Essais* de Montaigne," 17.

her antimisogynist attack surfaces again in the eminently focused form of the *Complaint*, and in her first collected works (entitled, we should bear in mind, *L'Ombre de la Damoiselle de Gournay* [The shadow of Miss de Gournay]), the discussion need no longer be conducted in Montaigne's shadow.

Still, that discussion remains dependent on Montaigne in a concrete and fundamental way. In addition to incidental allusions to the *Essays*, such as pervade Gournay's oeuvre, she concludes her assault on offensive (and inept) conversationalists as follows: "Let these few words suffice on the subject of conversation, with particular regard to the participation of women; for concerning the art of conversation in general, and its perfections and defects, the *Essays* deal with this to the point of excellence" (below, 103). The allusion acknowledges (at least indirectly) the fact that she has been adapting to feminist purposes the style of Montaigne's lively catalog of conversational abuses in "De l'Art de conferer" (On the art of conversing; see *Complaint*, n. 2), which thus acquires the status of a "fathering" text. No such acknowledgment appeared in the *Preface*, and it is as if Gournay now feels a need to compensate for casting a shadow of her own.

She may even be compensating for the new direction the *Complaint* proceeds to take: "Let us note in this discourse that not only the vulgar among the literati stumble in this error against the female sex, but among those, living and dead, who have acquired a certain name in letters in our age—sometimes, I declare, decked out in serious robes—some have been known who had absolute contempt for the works of women, without stooping to amuse themselves by reading them, so as to know what stuff they were made of" (below, 103). It suits Gournay's hard-won and controversial position as an established "woman of letters" that the orientation of her essay, by comparison with the precursor passages in the *Preface*, is less generally social, more specifically literary and intellectual. She may be using as a springboard the same supposed sophisticate who, "uttering thirty idiocies, will still take the prize by his beard" (below, 102), but her ultimate target is more serious: the magisterial "strokes of contempt" delivered by "doctors with moustaches" (103). She would hardly have included Montaigne in this group, yet her description nevertheless remains congruent, not only with attitudes evinced at several points in the *Essays*, but also with the silence she attributes to him in response to her purported gift of the *Promenade*. In the final analysis, the residual hints of ambivalence in the *Complaint* are supported by the fact that, while Gournay never ceased to revise and republish her early tribute and offering, which indeed helped to make her literary reputation, she never again wrote in the "typically" feminine form of romantic fiction.

If the *Complaint* of 1626 was largely a product of revision, once established as a text in its own right, it remained remarkably stable through its successive editions. The usual process of supplementation and expansion had already taken place, after all, and the impact of the piece as a scornful effusion depended on its sustained energy and conciseness. Indeed, the limited and local sculpting evident in Gournay's final version enhances this effect. Notably eliminated are a few sentences, anchored by a quotation from Horace, in which reflection momentarily prevails over diatribe.

THE LADIES' COMPLAINT

Blessed art thou,[1] Reader, if you are not of that sex to which one forbids every-thing of value, thereby depriving it of liberty; indeed, to which one also for-bids almost all the virtues, removing from it public duties, responsibilities, and functions—in a word, cutting it off from power, by the moderate exercise of which most of the virtues are formed—with the object of setting up as its only happiness, its crowning and exclusive virtues, ignorance, servitude, and a ca-pacity to play the fool if a woman likes that game. Blessed again are you, since you can be wise without offense, your masculinity allowing you—as much as one forbids these to women—every action of lofty purpose, every preemi-nent judgment, and every expression of subtle speculation.

But to hold my peace, for the moment, about the other grievances of this sex, in how unjust a manner is it commonly treated, I ask you, in conversa-tions, insofar as women engage in them?[2] And I am so little (or, more prop-erly, so greatly) vain that I do not fear to confess that I know it from my own experience. If women possessed the arguments and the profound thoughts of Carneades,[3] there is no man, however mediocre, who does not put them in their place with the approval of most of the company, when, with merely a smile or some slight shaking of his head, his mute eloquence pronounces, "It's

1. Our translation seeks to capture the effect of this allusion to the Beatitudes; cf. Gournay's *Preface*, n. 22.

2. With the passage that follows, cf. Montaigne, "De l'art de conferer" (On the art of convers-ing) in *Essais*, 3.8.926B, C.

3. That is, the Sceptic philosopher Carneades of Cyrene (ca. 214–129 B.C.E.). In *De Finibus Bono-rum et Malorum* (trans. and ed. H. Rackham, 2d ed., Loeb Classical Library [London and Cam-bridge, Mass., 1931], 395 [5.2.4]), Cicero, who encountered Carneades in Rome, terms him a "mighty intellect" and has Cato, in a dialogue, pay tribute to "his exceptional proficiency in logic and his consummate eloquence" (261 [3.12.41]).

a women speaking." One will rebuff as sour prickliness, or at least as obstinacy, any kind of resistance that women might make, however discreetly couched, against the decrees of his judgment, whether because he doesn't believe that they could strike his precious head by any other force than that of sourness and obstinacy, or because, in his heart of hearts sensing himself too dull for the combat, he needs to fabricate a trumped-up quarrel in order to flee the blows. And it is not too foolish a stratagem to grab hold of, so as to avoid an engagement with certain minds that he would perhaps have difficulty in vanquishing.

Another, stymied by his weakness in midcareer, under the color of not wishing to annoy a person of our stripe—or of our dress—will be termed at once victorious and courteous. Another still, although he may esteem a woman capable of sustaining a debate, will judge that decorum forbids him from engaging in a legitimate duel with that intellect, because he grounds his sense of decorum in the sound judgment of the vulgar, who disdain the sex in this regard. All things considered, to lead a vulgar person by the nose is a far cry from taking pride in having him lead us by the nose! But to go on. This fellow here, uttering thirty idiocies, will still take the prize by his beard, or by a self-satisfied conviction of his own supposed capacity, which the company and he himself measure according to its utility and modishness, without considering that his inane jibes very often occur to him because he is more ridiculous or more basely flattering than his companions, or as the result of some spineless submission or other vice—or thanks to the good grace and favor of some person who would not grant a place in his heart, nor intimacy, to anyone more able.

That fellow there will be struck, yet not have the intelligence to discern the blow delivered by a female hand. And some other will discern and feel it, only, for the sake of eluding it, to turn the discourse into mockery, or rather into a fusillade of incessant cackling; or he straightens it out and diverts it elsewhere, and commences to spew, like a pedant, a torrent of gems that nobody asked for; or out of silly ostentation, he mystifies it and confuses it with logical circus tricks, believing that he can dazzle his antagonist by the mere lightning bolts of his learning, thanks to the odd angles or perspectives from which he displays them. Such people know, in so behaving, how easy it is to exploit the ear of the onlooker, who cannot discover whether those pretty speeches amount to flight or victory, very rarely finding himself able to make a judgment about the order and conduct of a conversation and about the strength of those who stir it up, and also very rarely able to avoid being dazzled by the intensity of that empty knowledge which presumptuous vanity spits forth, as if it were a question of reciting his lessons. Thus, in order to carry off the prize, it is enough for these gentlemen to wriggle out of the combat, and they can harvest as much glory as they wish to spare pains. Let these few words suffice on the subject of conversation, with particular regard to the participation of women; for concerning the art of conversation in general, and its perfections and defects, the *Essays* deal with this to the point of excellence.[4]

Let us note in this discourse that not only the vulgar among the literati stumble in this error against the female sex, but among those, living and dead, who have acquired a certain name in letters in our age—sometimes, I declare, decked out in serious robes[5]—some have been known who had absolute contempt for the works of women, without stooping to amuse themselves by reading them, so as to know what stuff they were made of, or to accept opinions or advice that they might encounter in them, and without first wishing to be informed if they themselves could produce some that would merit reading by all sorts of women. That leads me to suspect that even in reading the writings of men, they are more perspicuous in anatomizing their beards than in anatomizing their arguments. These strokes of contempt from such doctors with moustaches are in truth highly serviceable, according to popular taste, in bringing out the luster of their wisdom, since, in order to render a man esteemed among the common people, that beast with many heads—especially at Court—it suffices that this man disdain that one and the other, and that he swear to be, in his own right, "foremost in the world,"[6] following the example of that poor mad woman who believed that she was making herself a model of beauty by going around crying out in our Parisian streets, her hands on her hips, "Come see how pretty I am!"

But I would wish, in charity, that these people had only added a further sophisticated touch to the one just mentioned. That is, to make us see that the worth of their intellects everywhere surpassed that of women head for head, or rather, as second best, that it equaled that of their neighbors—even neighbors, I declare, not quite top-notch. That means that, in the muster rolls of those among them who dare to write, we would not read wretched

---

4. That is, in "De l'art de conferer."

5. Venesoen, in his edition of *Grief des dames* in Gournay's *Égalité des hommes et des femmes, Grief des dames, Le Proumenoir de Monsieur de Montaigne*, 66 n. 18, makes a persuasive case that the reference is to the legal profession, one member of which was probably responsible for a satire of the *Equality* in a piece first published in 1622 (with further editions in the three succeeding years).

6. "Prime del mondo": Montaigne says (speaking of Epaminondas), "estre le premier de la Grece, c'est facilement estre le prime du monde" [to be the first man of Greece is easily to be the foremost man in the world] (*Essais*, 2.36.756A). It is not clear why Gournay interpolates the archaic (or Italian) form *del*.

translations, if they busy themselves with paraphrasing a good author; feeble and pedestrian conceptions, if they undertake to lecture; frequent contradictions, innumerable lapses, a judgment blind in choosing and to the
consequences of things; works whose only piquancy comes from a light stylistic make-up applied over missing substance, like beaten egg whites.

À propos, I happened the other day upon an introductory Epistle by a certain prominent person, one of those who make a display of never amusing
themselves by reading anything a woman has written:[7] for heaven's sake—
what gems, what glory, what an Orient, what splendor, what a Palestine,
fetched back from a hundred leagues beyond Mount Lebanon![8] For heaven's
sake, what chicken scrawl, passing for as many Phoenixes in their master's
opinion! And how far are they from good stylistic effects, those who seek
them out in linguistic excess or display, especially in prose? Those to whom
nature gives a skinny body, says a man of great merit, plump it out with stuffing, and those whose imagination conceives shrunken or dry matter make it
swell with their speech.[9] And what shame it is that France views the merit of
writers with such a bleary eye and blurred judgment that it has accorded a
reputation for writing excellently to an author who, like the begetter of that
Epistle, has never had any quality to recommend him except that cosmetic
artifice, backed up by a certain scholastic learning.[10] I am the more reluctant
to name him because he is dead.

Finally (to return to loving my neighbor), I would also like it if any of
that flock of intellectuals or writers who disdain this poor mistreated sex
would cease to employ the printers, so that they might at least leave us in
doubt whether or not they know how to compose a book. For they inform us
that they cannot by building up their own by the labor of others—building

---

7. Dezon-Jones, in her edition in *Fragments*, 132 n. 5, detects an allusion to Vincent Voiture
(1597–1648), who enjoyed a great reputation in the seventeenth century for his poetry, his letters, and his mastery of the art of conversation.

8. Venesoen, in Gournay's *Égalité des hommes et des femmes, Grief des dames, Le Proumenoir de Monsieur de
Montaigne*, 67 n. 21, explains the satirical dig here at Malherbe, the champion of innovation in
French poetry and of purity in the French language, who was an intellectual antagonist of Gour-
nay (cf. above, "Introduction to Marie le Jars de Gournay," 13).

9. The "man of great merit" is, not surprisingly, Montaigne. Gournay's French reproduces the
following sentence nearly verbatim, although Montaigne is, typically, more concise: "Ceux qui
ont le corps gresle, le grossissent d'embourrures: ceux qui ont la matiere exile, l'enflent de
paroles" [Those who have a skinny body plump it out with stuffing; those who have shrunken
matter make it swell with their speech] (*Essais*, 1.26.157C).

10. Venesoen, in Gournay's *Égalité des hommes et des femmes, Grief des dames, Le Proumenoir de Monsieur de
Montaigne*, 68 n. 24, proposes that her target here is Pierre Charron (1541–1603), the moralist,
philosopher, and theologian who had been an acquaintance of Montaigne.

them up in detail, I say, and sometimes wholesale, for fear lest that honest man whom the *Essays* ridiculed for the same vice in the time of their author should remain without company.[11] If I deigned to take the trouble to defend women against them, I would soon find my seconds in Socrates, Plato, Plutarch, Seneca, Antisthenes,[12] or, again, in Saint Basil, Saint Jerome, and intellects of that sort,[13] to whom these learned men so freely give the lie and a slap in the face when they make a distinction in merits and abilities, especially a universal distinction, between the two sexes. But they are sufficiently vanquished and punished by showing their stupidity when they condemn the particular by the general (if it were granted that in general the talent of women is inferior), and by showing it also through their audacity in disdaining the judgment of such great luminaries as those (not to mention some modern ones) and the eternal decree of God himself, who made the two sexes as a single creation and, moreover, honors women in his sacred history with all the gifts and benefits that he assigns to men, as I have more fully portrayed in *The Equality of Men and Women*.

Apart from all this, those cut from such cloth will suffer, if they please, from being put on notice: we do not know whether they are capable of defeating women by the sovereign law of their good pleasure, which condemns them and confines them to inadequacy, or whether there is glory for them in their efforts to dismiss them by contempt, from which they take pleasure in fashioning their thunderbolts. But we know of certain women who would never glory in so slight a thing as dismissing those men themselves, either in such a manner or by comparison. Further, they will know that the same sophistication they aim at in disdaining that sex without hearing it or reading its writings—that sex itself seeks it out, turning the tables on them, because it has heard them and has read the things that come from their hands. They will be able to treasure up, moreover, some dangerous words with an impeccable pedigree: that it is the part only of the most inept to live content with their ability, glancing at that of others over their shoulders—and that ignorance is the mother of presumption.

11. Gournay's use of the tag, *honneste-homme* (which here carries the requisite irony if translated literally), confirms her allusion to the dogmatically Aristotelian scholar in Pisa on whom Montaigne bestows the same epithet and whom he criticizes (*Essais*, 1.26.151B) for never thinking for himself.

12. On Antisthenes, see above, *Equality*, 82 and n. 31.

13. These secular and religious authorities are all invoked in the *Equality*, where Gournay (selectively) cites chapter and verse.

APOLOGY
FOR THE WOMAN WRITING
(1 6 4 1)

INTRODUCTION

We conclude our selection of Gournay's work with a relatively obscure text, not previously translated, which provocatively complements both the preceding feminist essays and the *Promenade*. The *Apology for the Woman Writing* is a late production and at the opposite extreme from romantic fiction—in its premise, at least, if not completely in its execution, as will be apparent. It is, in essence, a profuse autobiographical self-justification, with "apology" meaning "defense," on the model—invoked self-consciously and rather grandiosely—of Plato's *Apology of Socrates*. In defending herself, like the persecuted Greek philosopher, against slanders that menaced her reputation and, if not her life, her livelihood (by thwarting her prospects for patronage), Gournay composed what is undoubtedly the most revealing, on several levels, of her three major autobiographical pieces.[1]

The attacks to which Gournay responds in the *Apology* were motivated, in large measure, by contempt for her position as an independent unmarried woman with intellectual ambitions. They extended, however, to her supposed mismanagement of her household finances, as well as to her behavior in social relationships, which was sometimes perceived as alienating. What she relates of her life is skewed accordingly. There is no mention, for instance, of her mother's opposition to her scholarship, while she includes a minute account of her struggles to free the family from debt and of her expenses for alchemical experiments—details that, however dry in themselves, poignantly evoke the material hardship she endured for most of her nearly eighty years. In Gournay's typical manner, moreover, such information is energetically interspersed with learned and caustic commentary on ingratitude, poverty, and,

---

1. The other two are the *Copie de la vie de la Demoiselle de Gournay* (Representation of the life of Miss de Gournay) and the poem *Peincture de moeurs* (Character portrait). See above, 10.

especially, slander itself. She paints a particularly vivid picture of contemporary mores (indeed, of human nature) from her distinctive point of view—at
once sharp-sighted, embittered, and doggedly idealistic. The cumulative result is that, although it received, like the *Complaint*, its first publication in *L'Ombre* of 1626, the *Apology*, especially as subsequently elaborated for Gournay's
final collection, is sufficiently comprehensive and characteristic to stand as a
sort of terminal bookend to her career. More dramatically than anything else
she wrote, it demonstrates the particular interdependence of her "life and
works"—an interdependence so fascinating and, in literary terms, so fruitful
as to lead one critic, at least, to conclude that Gournay's "major contribution
to French literature may very well be the subtle art of self-portrait."[2]

Gournay dedicated the *Apology* to "a Prelate"—perhaps her cousin, as Ilsley proposes and as would suit the tone of respectful familiarity.[3] In any case,
the moral and spiritual authority of this unnamed churchman is clearly of
paramount importance, at least symbolically. The preamble addressing him
swells to more than twice the length of the second, and nominally more substantial, part of the piece. Regardless of Gournay's implicit reservations about
the Church in the *Equality*, this "father" serves, in effect, to anchor a long line
of male figures—once again both religious (Ezekiel) and secular (the Greek
philosophers)—whom she invokes as her moral sponsors and champions:
the *Apology* is replete, to the point of excess, with allusions to the classics, not
to mention the inevitable echoes of her intellectual "father," Montaigne.

At the same time, Gournay bolsters her self-justification by appealing
beyond her preferred *grands esprits* to some lesser ones more powerful in this
world: the dignitaries she had encountered on her 1597 visit to Belgium,
influential members of the French court, even King James of England. For
her objective, in proving herself worthy of admiration for her practical and
scholarly accomplishments, as well as for her upright character, is also to
prove herself worthy of the beneficent attention of her contemporaries.
More acutely than elsewhere, her theoretical, philosophical, and even satirical strains—here more than usually intertwined—tend toward practical
aims. Her idealistic contempt for riches goes hand in hand with a practical
horror of poverty.

The result is a text that—in contrast with the coherent argument of the
Equality or the focused anger of the *Complaint*—moves restlessly between the
poles of the abstract and the concrete, the disinterested and the intensely
personal, the hope for independence and the reality of dependence. Even her

---

2. Dezon-Jones, "Marie le Jars de Gournay (1565–1645)," 203.
3. Ilsley, *A Daughter of the Renaissance*, 127 n. 17.

interest in alchemy, the meeting-ground par excellence of extreme aspiration and expensive frustration, as her account makes clear, fits the pattern. Between these poles, Gournay's identity is tortuously, at times painfully, negotiated—and without resolution: her indefinite reference to herself in the title as "the woman writing" remains in tension with the down-to-earth account of her family history, not to mention the authorial status proclaimed for "la Demoiselle de Gournay" in the titles of her collections. And because identity is insistently the issue, exposed with special clarity is Gournay's conflicted attitude toward authority—authority that is inevitably masculine and that at once validates and negates her sense of self. In this respect, despite the large difference in genre, the *Apology* takes us back to her very origins as a writer in the *Promenade*, where her quasi-mystical ideal of communion among *grands esprits*—those of antiquity joining with Montaigne himself—was already at loggerheads with the imperatives of *histoire tragique*.

This comparison may be pursued to an ultimately disheartening conclusion. If the early narrative, under cover of its confident address to her "father," surreptitiously projects the author's anxieties about identity, as she fantasizes the tragic destruction of an idealistic young woman by the patriarchal forces enveloping her, the late autobiography evokes, despite itself, the image of a woman whose life is behind her. The very effort to revive a wounded public persona paradoxically takes on overtones of an act of self-immolation, in keeping with her poignant invocation of a classical sacrificial victim to masculine imperatives: "And what if, in the worst case, there is nothing left . . . but the fate of Polyxena—to fall honorably, since one must fall, and falling is in the course of human affairs?" (below, 148). The *Apology* thereby invites reading as a revisiting of Alinda's final speech and suicide—the romance heroine's last will and testament. There is, in the late work, an uncannily similar mixture of tones: despair, self-righteousness, self-pity, anger, vindictiveness. These come similarly attached to a reconsideration of her position vis-à-vis her family and of her betrayal by trusted friends. The preoccupation with slander harks back to the story of Paula and Melania (see above, 56). And here, too, the dedication to a spiritual "father" ultimately frames an angry revenge on the world that has betrayed her—a world, moreover, like that of the *Promenade*, in which women have not necessarily proved more trustworthy than men. On the model of the suicide of Alinda, at once active and passive, the *Apology* publicly performs self-vindication at the self's own cost. Socrates himself spoke so eloquently, after all, in anticipation of drinking hemlock.

Stanton has valuably opened the door to analyzing Gournay's *Apology* in terms of the female writing subject, trapped within "a tension between knowing and doing that subverts the efficacy of her discursive act in the very process of its accomplishment."[4] As it happens, the notion of urgent but thwarted communication is strikingly emblematized by another classical allusion. Among the *Apology*'s most evocative moments is Gournay's extraordinary comparison between the howl of protest to which the world's illtreatment has driven her—a virtual metonymy for the other voice—and the outcry that was compelled by nature in spite of nature from the mute son of Croesus, when death menaced his father (see below, 140). It is remarkable that this image equally resonates with the *Promenade;* indeed, it effectively implies a rapprochement between the two "daughters" within that work: the one who writes in the hope of pleasing her father—a father whom death had almost certainly already placed beyond her reach—and the other who consigns herself to the ultimate silence, in part because she has symbolically killed hers. Finally, then, our sample of texts, restricted though it is, abundantly illustrates a fundamental—and disquieting—continuity between the beginning and the end of Gournay's long, varied, and in many ways remarkably successful literary career.

4. Stanton, "Autogynography," 23.

APOLOGY FOR THE WOMAN WRITING—

To a Prelate[1]

The First Part of the Apology

When Nature provided man with a care for reputation, she undoubtedly gave him a useful counselor and a corrector of his wisdom,[2] his life, and his morals. But in proportion as she planted this care in his soul, with the same hand she opened him to the attacks of tongues, making him the slave, not only of his companion, but also of the most malicious, frivolous, and impudent part of that companion—the most indistinct, facile, and slippery in its effects, and just as often the least punished. This impunity proceeds as much from the incapacity of human beings to weigh good and bad actions in a just scale as from the pleasure that their ears take in becoming complicit, equally maliciously, with the calumnies and bad-mouthing of which the tongue is maliciously the author. And what if that prodigious worker of outrage and iniquity often goes so far as to insult, in fixed terms, the very virtues and merits of men, especially those of the best stamp? For the slanderer usually cannot perceive in his fellow man that which is excellent or outstanding, nor fail, in his stupidity, to decry that which he does not perceive; or if he has a certain subtlety along with his stupidity, he never spares, out of envy, to tarnish with insults the actions and qualities that he recognizes as praiseworthy in others but that he cannot lay claim to. So that, if one chooses to consider what good fortune or disaster,

---

1. The prelate in question may have been Charles de Hacqueville, Bishop of Soissons, who was Gournay's cousin (Ilsley, *A Daughter of the Renaissance*, 127 n. 17).

   Stanton, "Autogynography," 21–23, has observed the ambiguous referentiality of "the woman writing" ("celle qui escrit") and placed it in the context of the traditional "apology," or legal defense. It will be clear from Gournay's references that she was consciously writing in the shadow of the monumental model of the slandered Socrates.

2. The French term is *suffisance*, apparently used here in a general sense. Compare above, *Promenade*, n. 3, and *Equality*, n. 5.

joy or pain, has attended the life of a man worthy of particular esteem, it must almost always be that his very excellence tends toward disaster and misery as if having caused them, unless some external and fortuitous accident exempts him. At any rate, let us leave this point, about which, as it happens, I have said a few words elsewhere and will perhaps be constrained to say some others, or nearly the same thing, as this Apology unfolds.

Being bound by the course of nature to pass from this life before you, Monsieur, I console myself that an honorable prelate of distinguished birth and rare intelligence, such as you are, will arm his piety against those miserable blasts of babble that always follow ill fortune as persistently and pointedly as ill fortune follows me, so that you may bear witness after me that I deserved a better fate. Bear witness to it, I say, with all the more charity because the oblivion that exists beyond the tomb will leave me fewer defenders and because, on the other hand, the harsh and burning malignity I have aroused may cool off in the chill of my ashes, so as to allow favorable mouths to be believed—finally, when they will no longer be able to soothe me.

I confess my fault, if it is a fault, of tender sensitivity on the question of proper appearances; I like to have silence regarding what I do, if I cannot obtain praise, and I endure calumny with ill temper. But is it not valor and warlike strength, surpassing in vigor the strength of Socrates, not to worry any more about meeting in one's path a fool who might be offensive than about meeting a one-eyed man or a hunchback, not being obliged, he said, to be any more concerned with the imperfections of the intellect than with those of the body? And what judgment shall we make of the magnanimity of the philosopher Demetrius, who thirsted no more for the speeches of a fool or a shallow man than for his farts (which I am compelled to mention as he does), not perceiving any difference, as he said, whether such persons made noise from above or below?[3] On the other hand, we find in Philostratus an offering of insults to Hercules, as a means of amusing him worthy of his courage, inflicted on him one day by some angry villagers in memory of a similarly ample downpour of rain.[4]

It may well be, however, that no steadfastness of soul, except that of Socrates, ever arrived in a direct and constant manner at the point of dis-

3. Demetrius the Cynic philosopher, who lived in Rome during the first century C.E., was credited with this statement by his acquaintance Seneca (*Moral Epistles to Lucilius* 91.19). Gournay would also have found it in Montaigne, *Essais*, 2.16.624C.

4. There seem to have been four authors named Philostratus, from a single Lemnian family, and the attribution of various works to them remains uncertain. Gournay's reference here is to the

daining criticism of his faults and vices,[5] since well-regulated behavior and the virtues are ordinarily so dearly purchased by their possessors; and he who more persistently loves such ornaments, and acquires them, and deals in them at high price, finds greater difficulty in disdaining such criticism. Who can blame my hatred of calumny, if Solomon writes that it dries out the bones, troubles the wise man, and breaks the constancy of his spirit?[6] And if the Philosopher terms shame the greatest wrong among outward evils?[7] So natural is it, the horror of that monster extends even to the unreasoning animals, of which one could cite many examples; and certainly, among others, it may be supposed that the generous small animal, the ermine, which gives itself up to death rather than soil its virgin coat, would perhaps give itself up sooner yet, rather than endure that his fellows should merely believe that he

---

Imagines, probably written successively by two members of this family but usually ascribed to Flavius Philostratus, which describes and explains a cult of Hercules that involved ritual cursing. Arnould has pointed out (letter to Hillman, 16 December 1999) Gournay's probable use of the magnificently produced French translation by Blaise de Vigenère (*Les Images*), first published in 1578; see the facsimile reprint of this work, ed. Stephen Orgel, in *The Renaissance and the Gods*, vol. 22 (New York, 1976), 2.495–96 ("Thiodamus"). Gournay will subsequently be alluding to the life of Apollonius of Tyana (see below, 149) by a Flavius Philostratus (b. ca. 170 C.E.) also known as Philostratus the Elder or the Athenian.

5. An allusion especially to Plato's *Apology*.

6. An elusive reference, apparently mingling imagery from Prov. 15:30 ("a good report maketh the bones fat") and 17:22 ("a broken spirit drieth the bones"), attributed to Solomon, with the sustained attack on calumny in Ecclesiasticus. The latter reads, in part, "Curse the whisperer and doubletongued: for such have destroyed many that were at peace. A backbiting tongue hath disquieted many, and driven them from nation to nation: strong cities hath it pulled down, and overthrown the houses of great men. A backbiting tongue hath cast out virtuous women, and deprived them of their labors. Whoso hearkeneth unto it shall never find rest, and never dwell quietly. The stroke of the whip maketh marks in the flesh, but the stroke of the tongue breaketh the bones" (Ecclus. 28:13–17). In the Catholic Bible, this book, which is not part of the Jewish or Protestant canon, follows The Wisdom of Solomon as part of the "wisdom sequence" including Proverbs and The Song of Solomon.

7. "The Philosopher" is certainly Aristotle, commonly so designated in medieval and early modern texts, and cited elsewhere in the *Apology*. "Fear of just ill-repute" is one aspect of the virtue of "temperance" (*De Virtutibus et Vitiis* [Of the virtues and vices], trans. J. Solomon, in *The Works of Aristotle*, gen. ed. W. D. Ross, 11 vols. [Oxford, 1915], 1250b[4]). Gournay may further have in mind The "Art" of Rhetoric (trans. and ed. John Henry Freese, Loeb Classical Library [London and New York, 1926]), where there is the extended discussion of shame (1383–85a [2.6]). Also to the point would be the discussion of anger and hatred at 1382a–83b (2.4.30–2.5.22): slander is identified as a cause, evil as the intent, of hatred, and there is mention of "outraged virtue" (1382b [2.5.5]). Aristotle has already observed that those who have been slandered, or are readily susceptible to slander, attract wrongdoers (1372b [1.12.22]); he goes on to explain that one forensic means of removing prejudice "consists in attacking slander, showing how great an evil it is" (1416a [3.15.9]).

was soiled. Hence, Plato advises his citizens not to disdain reputation.[8] And the good old man Eleazar, that venerable sacrificial priest of the Jews, cared so much for it that, to avoid no less the imputation than the effect of having eaten pork, he suffered the most extreme torments, and then the ultimate agony, at the hands of the executioner of Antiochus Epiphanes.[9] Clearly, it was the imputation that mattered; for his friends wished him to substitute other flesh to eat under that name, in order to lend him the means to evade his sufferings and preserve his life without violating his religion, which the tyrant wished to make him abjure by means of that food.

It is nevertheless wholly impossible that persons of ill fortune should live in esteem, especially in this age and with our mores, or those of any other state that is old and sick. For if their affairs have always been or appeared unfortunate, nobody but the dregs of the common people, incapable of giving a just and pertinent opinion of their merit, will have taken the trouble to frequent them enough to testify as to what they are worth. If their affairs have been better or appeared to be so, as has been the case in my household (I know only too well how implausible these statements will seem to vulgar minds), those who did frequent them while this illusion lasted never fail to make themselves scarce when it has vanished, whether by quarreling or breaking with them. Having done so, they must still run down such persons however they can, as much to provide a color for the imputed wrong by which they justify this avoidance, as because they find themselves obliged generally to reduce to the status of fable and nonexistence whatever virtue may be found in him whose society they abandon, if they do not wish to be called fair-weather friends and the sort for whom the virtue of others dulls their own (or, more accurately, the reputation for virtue that they court). And in this derogation the way is smoothed for them by the abundance of false friends, their companions in the same moral bankruptcy, and no stranger, lacking acquaintance with the person they are sullying, can contradict them. I say, let their virtue be dulled! For in proportion as that of the friend whom ill fortune causes them to abandon is large—par-

8. Arnould has pointed out (letter to Hillman, 16 December 1999) that Gournay derives this statement from Montaigne, *Essais*, 2.16.629C (a passage that Villey [1297] traces to Ficino's translation of the *Laws*, 12). It may be more generally to the point that Socrates in the *Apology*, having devoted much attention to his undeserved reputations both for being wise and for corrupting the young, declares, then elaborates on, his refusal to appeal to the court's compassion "for the sake of my good name and yours and that of the whole state" (124–25 [23.34E]).

9. See 2 Macc. 6:18–31, esp. 21–28, and the more elaborate account in 4 Macc. 5–7, esp. 6:12–23. In both books, this story precedes that of the seven brothers and their mother, which Gournay cites in *Equality*—see above, 88.

ticularly a mild-mannered friend and one who does not harass anyone to obtain assistance in his difficulties—equally large is the corruption or failing
of the deserter. Let us use that word, which is most apt and carries the force
of three or four others.

What way of life is that of our age, if one is compelled to pass from the
particular to the general, and from the wrong done by false friends to that of
faulty morals? As little as a person is worth, he is honored with his possessions, and, as much as he is worth, he is disdained without them. Is this not
to honor the possessions, purely and simply? For his part, he who esteems
others solely according to the favors of Fortune makes plain enough that he
would be a poor man without her, while whoever rejects a person of good
birth on account of his poverty amply declares that he would be even poorer
than that person if he did not have riches. For if the sufficiency of a sensible
mind[10] and virtuous behavior were superior qualities for those people, as they
should be, they would be obliged, and, what is more, concerned, to accord
them a higher and supreme honor wherever they should meet with them, and
to revere them yet more strongly if they came with inferior rank, not being
able to honor them elsewhere without honoring themselves, nor to disdain
them without disdaining themselves also.

But let us redirect this discourse toward its termination in this Apology
and pursue our objective. At least I have this advantage—that those who
banished me from their good graces when they perceived my misfortune,
whether by withdrawing or by stirring up trouble for me, praised me end-
lessly and greatly while I was able to conceal it; and for a long time they
sought me out and gave me recognition, my house having always been, during that time, heavily frequented and myself freely accessible to all. They are,
moreover, so many—men and women, most of whom are obliged to my
good offices—that, even if they wished to, they could not maintain their last
judgment of me, on the basis of which they reproached or abandoned me,
against their first with the support of the pitiful excuse that they were deceived in my acquaintance. "He that hath a mind to depart from a friend
seeketh occasions: he shall ever be subject to reproach."[11] So says the Sage,
detesting those sorts of moral bankrupts and their pretexts. Let us allow love,

10. The French ("une teste bien faite") is a reminiscence of Montaigne, *Essais*, 1.26.150A.

11. Proverbs 18:1: "Occasiones quaerit, qui recedere vult ab amico: omni tempore erit exprob-
abilis" (word order slightly altered). The Authorized version, "Through desire a man, having
separated himself, seeketh and intermeddleth with all wisdom," does not clearly render the sense
that Gournay conveys by way of the Vulgate verse, which specifies that someone who wishes to
withdraw from a friend seeks occasions to do so. The Sage mentioned in the next sentence is, of
course, Solomon, supposed author of the Proverbs.

at least as usage prescribes, to enjoy its privilege of taking for its device: "As much elsewhere." But in these relations of understanding and fellowship, bound by practical matters, obligation, virtue, or conversations, the only excuse that the deserter can come up with is that foolishness led him hither, and that foolishness and cowardice together draw him away again.

What will they say, after all? I hear him and her—few in number, really—deigning to seek to excuse their retreat, so as to pass themselves off as persons of stability and integrity. For the others take pride in these barbs, and their like, so that they may be hailed in society for their shrewdness. Truly, one must be an honorable man or woman to a high degree to believe that duty or good faith might impose on us an obligation toward the unfortunate. That sort of person, who makes up three-quarters of humankind, or at least of the French of today, would hold duty and good faith in derision, where ingratitude and perfidy cannot be chastised. For the ingrate and deceiver is always a good fellow with his own kind, as long as he whom he injures by these two vices can do no worse than broadcast his complaints to the wind for his revenge (if revenge he desires), so that the rule and essence of their duty consist merely in dodging the blows. Let us continue.

The foolish and the reckless, who from lack of instruction or consideration mistake one thing for another in observing their neighbors, as well as those so feeble-brained that they are not ashamed to be blinded by hatred, so that they spew their spite indiscriminately—they can say anything. But no man or woman of sound judgment and demeanor among my acquaintance could allege, even if they wished me ill, that I am false at heart or capricious in my good feelings or lukewarm in discharging my obligations or unduly secretive or importunate or rash either in manners or company, or less than honorable in my associations (if innocence counts for anything), or, moreover, aggressive. Neither can I be portrayed as disorderly, disputatious, or quarrelsome, as opposed to sensitive, firm, and earnest—qualities which, just as they would amount to thorns, or produce them, in a soul unilluminated by Reason, become seedbeds and nurturers of many laudable effects and necessary to society in those souls enlightened by that torch. I have applied so much effort and zeal, and so many years, to making myself one of that number that henceforth I dare say that I am one without blushing, "Trusting in my morality, not out of arrogance,"[12] just as

---

12. "Fiducia morum, non arrogantia." As noted by Dezon-Jones in her edition of the *Apology* (in *Fragments*, 151 n. 7), the source is the opening of Tacitus, *The Life of Julius Agricola*, where the author declares that, in past times, "plerique suam ipsi vitam narrare fiduciam potius morum quam adrogantiam arbitrati sunt" [many men even counted it not presumption, but self-respect, to narrate their own lives] (in *Agricola, Germania, Dialogus*, 26–27 [1.3]). Rutilius and Scaurus are given as examples in the next phrase—cf. below, 143 and n. 58.

I place myself in the ranks of the supporters of virtue by the same consideration in other places in this treatise—all of this, however, out of mere necessity
of defense, although the Roman poet gives bolder advice: "Accept the proud
honor won by thy merits."[13] And I bring into my conversation that sociable and
mellow humor that I have just described because I know how, not only to refrain scrupulously from offending, but, further, to suffer in patience, to be offended up to a certain point, excusing or disdaining the common stupidity and
the particular. What is more, I know how to guard myself, at all costs, against
rhetorical excesses and misunderstandings that hatch disputes and divi-
sions more often than just causes do. Finally, my demeanor is such that benign
affability does not in the least detract from vigor, nor vigor from benign
affability—a demeanor truly complete with regard to others, the whole without disproportion or incongruity: and to top it all, a very good friend. These
truths cannot be contradicted by man or woman who has cultivated my acquaintance, unless they wish to do themselves more harm than me, so often
have they been proclaimed by their own mouths. And so many other times
these same false friends, men and women, have said expressly, before their
withdrawal, that no one could ever be on bad terms with me unless it was his
fault.

Now, if such truths applied in the past, all the more reason that they
should do so at present, when those persons have vanished, or are vanishing,
from me. For people who live according to pure inclination are ordinarily less
estimable as they age; the contrary is the case with those who live by reason,
because the driving forces of mere inclination, which are physical, deterio-
rate with age, as those of reason improve with it. And I aspire to be among
the adherents of the latter group, if that has not already been said. In conscience, the only reproach that they can impute to me, these male and female
friends, is that the care that I took to retain them, by innumerable praiseworthy efforts, when I sensed the intent of that group, made them act more
quickly. For in this matter, more than in any other, whoever makes himself a
sheep is eaten by the wolf, such persons never dreaming that they have anything to lose in you, if they imagine that you may have something to lose in
them. I declare, moreover, that they measure their interest and advantage in
losing you according to the very interest and care that you bring to retaining
them. Fair-weather friends and well-wishers respect nothing less in their

---

13. Horace, *Odes* (in *Odes and Epodes*, trans. and ed. C. E. Bennett, rev. ed., Loeb Classical Library
[Cambridge, Mass., and London, 1927]), 3.30.14–15: "sume superbiam / quaesitam meritis."
This is part of Horace's conclusion to the *Odes*, in which he anticipates his immortal fame, al-
though these lines are technically addressed to the Muse Melpomene.

friend than the duty that binds them to him, whether it derives from merit or obligation. And their method of operation can be described thus: to grant friendship for a bowl of soup, and consequently, for another bowl of soup, to grant pardon for a cudgeling, if it is useful to them to endure it without murmuring from him who gives it. For a fair-weather friend is nothing but a hired flatterer, who wishes to be the slave, not the companion, of his friend. One of the principal differences between the wise man and the fool, says Seneca, is that riches are prisoners in the wise man's house, queens and mistresses in that of the fool.[14]

But how many arch-fools, then, are these friends, whom we see governed by the riches of neighbors? No one of sound judgment condemns beneficial friendships, provided that honorable ones are found nearby, and that what one does in the first kind out of necessity, one does in the second out of duty and honor. But these vile mercenaries, these charmers, who do nothing except out of mere thirst and regard for profit—do not they show that, like some women, they would rather put up with an insult or a tweak of the nose, as often happens in the households of the powerful, than with a lack of income? Or do they give any just return of gratitude to those who grow fat off their duties or services? (For by such an attitude they would acknowledge that they are not the object of the benefits received but merely the bait, the distributor having directed them only at himself.) And what also galls me to the core is that most of those who cut the learned to pieces in our time, especially if they frequent the court, so highly respect, above others, not only those who can do something or other for their fortunes, but also the providers of good dinners. Let others be, if they wish, the minions of the inner sanctum of the Muses; these gentlemen, more refined, wish to be their minions of the table—if table minions they require. For they have learned letters, not as an ornament and a means of regulating their lives (hence you see their morals and their judgment wandering elsewhere), but as a lucrative profession, and as something not to value but rather, indeed, to possess, because they have not been able to change the natures they were born with, which fashioned them at no higher rate than that of a mercenary and servile artistry.

Would you like to have the proof of their emptiness and of the false luster of that learning with which a shameless boastfulness, so common among them, abuses the credulity of courts so as to break in and pilfer reputation and royal acts of generosity? Shut them up in a room without books with a specific task involving a serious composition or merely an exact version of some

14. Adapted from Seneca, "On the Happy Life," *Moral Essays* 7.26.1.

page from Tacitus or another thorny author: then our learned men are at a total loss.[15] Or, without going so far, observe how their works far exceed their conversation, and you will suddenly recognize that they owe such writings to filching and that the latter do not flow naturally from them—indeed, that the fabricators have not even contributed enough prudence or skill to clothe themselves properly or elegantly in what they have stripped from others. Finally, look at the gaffes in those writings, the base conceptions and rubbish here and there, patched up with irrelevancies; consider the faulty and unhappy judgments mingled with the good ones, the hobbling sequences and transitions, the illogicalities and clashing relationships: this shows plainly that, in the places where things go smoothly, those things are not the author's. With regard to conversation, anyone is capable of pulling a good book—even a mediocre one—out of his brain; what matters is that his own conversation should be nothing but intellect and life. They offend the Muses more than do the purely ignorant, since they deal with them only to dishonor them. But this is all said by the way.

We read that when Friendship, once upon a time, went walking through the world in order to render it happy on all sides beneath the propitious and sweet shelter of her wings, Flattery took her place at the table of Jupiter and, by a feigned resemblance, caused her portion of nectar and ambrosia to be distributed there. Friendship complaining of this theft, the gods ordained that, to remove any uncertainty about recognizing her, they would give her Adversity for a companion, whom the other could not endure. Thus I do not at all repent having made the efforts that I described earlier to retain some of the band of well-wishers, whom I did not deem to be persons of true virtue, since their default in this matter showed the contrary, but nevertheless considered to be on the right path for attaining to the ranks of the virtuous, so that it was a shame they were not yet further advanced—and a shame, too, that what intelligence they possessed, which was not slight, was employed rather to conceal than to heal the diseased state of their morality and sense of responsibility. They may believe what they like, but in truth those who possess the intellect to know without acting accordingly do not possess that for which knowledge and intellect are made, and it must be supposed that they were capable of achieving human perfection, if they had been able to recognize what it consisted in.

I will say, further, that no one is truly endowed with virtue, at least with its principal parts—faith, candor, uprightness—who does not cherish them most strongly and lastingly in his friend, in his neighbor, and in a stranger, because the first quality of such virtues is to make its possessor desire that

15. Gournay had taken same tack as early as the 1595 *Preface* (33–35).

they should reign in the world and there set up and maintain their throne as far as is in his power. Hence, whoever practices virtue without loving it in others exercises it solely out of ambition—that is, does not exercise it at all. And Jesus Christ also teaches us that those who do the will of God, His Father, are his mother and brethren.[16] Prefer persons of that stamp—prefer, I say, the virtuous and their affection, active and passive, above all things. Behold my vengeance—that these deserters have to remember that when I made an effort to stop them, I showed that I saw more clearly regarding their deserts than they did with respect to mine.

And let them, moreover, be so assured of my commitment and my sincerity as to believe for a certainty that I would not thus have failed them in a similar situation. (I include, in all this complaining, the two sexes under the title of one when I name one only, if I have not already made myself sufficiently understood on this point.) Chelonis, wife and daughter of kings of Sparta, once she saw that her husband Cleombrotus had gained the upper hand over Leonidas, her father, in a civil war, attached herself to the one defeated; then, when fortune had relieved him, the tide of circumstance having changed, the wind that impelled them filled better than ever the sails of the conjugal affection of that magnanimous Princess, so that she flew back to her husband.

Good fortune asks for faith, adversity requires it.

Flaminius, too, pursued those who he felt had need of him, distancing himself from others.[17] Also, during the great plague of Athens, it was, for the most part, only honorable men who died, because these regarded nothing more than the shame of abandoning their friends in affliction. In truth, no one is immune to making these retreats when events impoverish a friend, or render him less useful, except by an exertion of heroic virtue. And certainly, besides the fact that it would be cruelty if I were forbidden to relieve my heart by deploring those losses, which I have so little deserved, and which I sought to avoid, as I have said, with such obliging and praiseworthy offices—setting aside for relation in a moment how the diminution of esteem and the bad treatment that follow such retreats have increased my ill fortune and with-

16. Matthew 12:50; Mark 3:34–35; Luke 8:21.

17. The instances of Chelonis and of Flaminius (i.e., Caius Flaminius Nepos, the populist Roman leader who was consul in 223 B.C.E., tribune in 232 B.C.E.) are clearly borrowed from the same passage in Montaigne, *Essais*, 3.13.1100B, who likewise uses them to illustrate his own disposition. The classical sources are *Plutarch's Lives*—respectively, those of Agis and Cleomene (17–18.2), and of Flaminius (1.2). The interpolated quotation, "Poscunt fidem secunda, et adversa exigunt," is taken (with minor variation) from Seneca, *Agamemnon* 934.

drawn the remedies for it—I must complain about those moral bankrupts and counterfeiters of benevolence (let us call them so), even if only because of the obligation that binds me to praise, on the contrary, the openness and religion of your own benevolence, and of that of those few allies, men and women, whom you still have in matters regarding me.

Adversity is good for something, according to an ancient saying: the discovery that others made of my reverses of fortune led me to discover the naked visage of the human race, veiled for those who are in prosperity—so veiled, I say, by the concern and necessity of adversity to disguise that visage from those fortunate ones, so that they remain all their lives the actors of adversity's perpetual farce, in which it makes them play a blind man's part; they are worthy of being hissed doubly because their blindness prevents them from suspecting that they have been playing that role all along. Prudence, seconded by long experience, leads its disciple to acknowledge the pressure put on good-hearted persons and friends as being very clearly present among mankind; but to perceive to what degree it is so—no one has ever arrived at that without ill fortune. For it is the privilege only of him from whom one hopes for nothing, and toward whom one dares anything—like the victim of fortune—to discern in full light what men are, since their hearts never appear in their true colors toward those who elicit hope or fear from them. Innumerable persons are too much concerned, and too much exert themselves, to blind a man of good fortune with regard to their actions and their behavior, for him to hope ever to see clearly into the secret makeup of human beings; but no one bothers to blind a wretch to such matters.

> He who knows how to dress a lavish feast,
> Counsel a poor man, and get him released
> From a great lawsuit that makes his life hell—
> That splendor is followed by a miracle,
> When his mastership's prerogatives extend
> To discerning the true from the false friend.[18]

Or, to express it better, the fortunate man is cognizant of only a quarter of the perfidy, and of the malignant and frivolous mentality and will of the world, on account of the pains they take to control themselves, so as to

---

18. Qui scait donner un plantureux souper,
    Pleiger le pauvre, & le developer
    D'un grand procez qui tourmente sa vie ;
    Ceste splendeur d'un miracle est suivie,
    Lors qu'a son maistrie il peut estre permis,
    De discerner les vrays des faux Amys.

obscure his sight; the unfortunate man perceives and feels it in its entirety, especially amid the enormous laxness of our age, in which someone who cannot revenge injuries has deserved them all, indeed wrongly complains of them, because the common people deem that all resentment, however just it may be, is a vice in him, inasmuch as that sort of person does not believe that generosity is a virtue to which the weak have a right to dare to aspire. For every time he takes offense, these frivolous and crude minds—but always of low quality, who, neither in that quarter nor elsewhere, ever knew how to distinguish the boundaries of much and little, or the true feelings of honor of those who are said to have hair-trigger tempers, or how to consider to what degree the combination of circumstances in such onslaughts can also increase the weight of the offense and justify the bitterness of resentment—these minds say, when the weak person complains, that he takes offense for nothing, and what a pity it is for him to waste his bile, which catches fire so easily. Above all, they attack more readily the moral ardor to which the tutor of all pure and noble actions—that noble glory which the inferior man never recognized in his master—renders the indignity more palpable, seeking there a greater triumph and one more capable of giving a pleasant purge to those to whom they betake themselves afterward to stage their performances, because these persons' tables and favor are milk-cows for them.

In sum, then, to get back to my point, if my ruin, in order to open my eyes, had not again and again raised the mask covering the face of that animal named the human race—myself being a person of better than average social graces, good-natured to the point of foolishness, and of a most obliging temperament—I would have played for all of my life, amid them in the public farce, that role of the blind one out in front of the others. Can I pass on to the next section without going back a step to that discourse regarding the profound and complete abyss of ignominy, offenses, and tyranny, into which the unfortunate man hurled his host? And without remembering the keen shot of a judge who, when he was notified that a wretched old man, whom he was condemning to pay the peasants' tax, was a gentleman, responded, as his only reason, "I am well aware of that, but he is poor"?

It seems possible that these verses are loosely based on Juvenal, *Satire* 1.127–46 (in *Juvenal and Perseus*, trans. and ed. G. G. Ramsay, rev. ed., Loeb Classical Library [London and Cambridge, Mass., 1940]), which has some of the same elements (though differently applied)—legal complications, poor clients at the rich man's table, and the rich man finally mocked (in death) by his erstwhile friends: "nova nec tristis per cunctas fabula cenas: / ducitur iratis pladendum funus amicis" [the new and merry tale runs the round of every dinner-table, and the corpse is carried forth to burial amid the cheers of enraged friends] (145–46). Gournay borrows more directly from the *Satires* below—see 125, 132, and nn. 24 and 33.

The Spaniard who wrote *The Rogue; Or, Guzman de Alfarache*,[19] from whom I believe I recently collected this account, was an author of notable accomplishment, infinitely erudite and having a perfect knowledge of the course and intrigues of human life, and so clear-sighted on the point we are dealing with that he seems to discuss it from experience; he was also a sufficiently honest man to have voluntarily put himself to the test of poverty and what goes with it. Here, then, is the picture he paints of the subject in question in its current version. The poor virtuous man is a coin that is not legal tender, the scum of the town, the refuse of the marketplace, and the beast of burden of the powerful. He eats last, worst, and at greatest cost; his teston is not worth six sous,[20] his pronouncements are ravings, his poise is a caricature, his opinions are folly, his property belongs to everybody, he is insulted by many and loathed by all. If he finds himself in conversation, he is not listened to; if people meet him, they fly from him; if he gives advice, it is ridiculed; if he performs miracles, he is a sorcerer; if he lives honestly, he is a hypocrite. His venial sin is a blasphemy; his mere thought is punished as a crime; he is accorded no rights, and all he can do is to appeal to the next life for the wrong that he receives in this one. All the world persecutes him, finally, and no one grants him a benefit; his necessity finds no person to succor him; he has no one to console his suffering or to accompany his solitude. None relieves him, and all harm him; nobody gives to him, and everybody takes from him; he owes no debt to any, and each makes him his tributary. Feeble as he is, they sell him the hours on the clock; they make him buy the light of midday; and in the same way that a piece of meat, spoiled and tossed into the street, is eaten by dogs, likewise the wise pauper is devoured by fools. This is how the author of *Guzman* speaks of the subject, adding with only too much certainty in another place that the torrent of fashion is so greatly, and to the extent of very hearth and home, in flood against the victim of misfortune that, as good valets elsewhere serve wicked rich masters, good poor masters in their own homes serve wicked valets. And that author writes further in another place that no such miracle ever occurs as the vile and servile spirits of flatterers and corrupt worldlings meeting with a rich fool or a poor sage. This fine book by a Spaniard, almost wholly composed of proverbs, serves as a lesson in the

19. That is, Mateo Aleman (1547–ca. 1614). The work is a picaresque romance; we translate Gournay's *Le Gueux* (The tramp) as "the rogue," in accordance with the English version produced in 1622.

20. It may be relevant that the silver teston had been much devalued during the inflationary period of the civil wars. On the currency and the economy, esp. during the years of extreme difficulty for Gournay's family, see J. H. M. Salmon, *Society in Crisis: France in the Sixteenth Century* (London, 1975), 37–47, 226–27.

special wisdom that nation has shown in enriching its language with that in-structive ornament.

All things considered, isn't the condition of lovers of learning, if they are not of the Church or of the law, a particular target of cacklers in our cli-mate? There is nothing as foolish or ridiculous for them, after poverty, as being clear-sighted and learned; how much more so to be a clear-sighted and learned woman, or simply, like me, to have desired to make oneself so? Among our vulgar class, they fantastically prank up the image of an edu-cated woman—that is, they make of her a stew of extravagancies and chimeras, and they say in general, without bothering with exceptions and distinctions, that such women are shaped on this mold. Whatever may present itself beyond this stereotype to disprove her conformity to it, those vulgar people in no way understand her, and she is no longer seen except in the light of wrongful presumptions and as the image of such a scarecrow. It is marvelous, the fine things that they have her saying and doing while she is asleep, and all the saints of the Legend[21] never performed as many un-heard-of miracles as that poor creature, a true martyr in the mouths of mad-men—I mean, unless she is fortunate enough to be stronger than her wit-nesses. Truly, since they cut out of whole cloth, yapping just for the sake of yapping, they have reason to find full measure in their subject. Thus did the brigand Damastes in Plutarch stretch out his prisoners with exquisite tor-tures if he found them too short for his bed frame; if he found them too long, he cut off their feet.[22]

Now then, having many times heard from these disdainers of the sex, es-pecially if they are nurtured at court, the refrain that learned women are scat-terbrained, I have buried my slight knowledge in obscurity, at little cost, with the intention of seeing whether I might gain with them, if nothing more, the reputation of having good sense, although to speak truly, my letters notwith-standing, the popular breath treated my name well enough, by and large, be-fore the discovery of my misfortune. The story is an old one. Just so, during the decline of the empire, did poverty tarnish a reputation; thus the empire was overthrown by love and estimation of riches. So say, with perfect accu-racy, the greatest of its men: "Financial ruin brought down in its train both rank and reputation."[23] The touchstone of human morality and merit came

21. The reference is undoubtedly to the *Legenda Aurea* (*Golden Legend*). See *Promenade*, n. 52.

22. Damastes, more commonly known as Procrustes—hence, the expression, "Procrustean bed." See *Plutarch's Lives*, Theseus, 11.

23. "Eversio rei familiaris dignitatem ac famam praeceps debat" (Tacitus, *Annals* 6.17)—part of a description of a liquidity crisis in the Roman economy.

from the purse at that time neither more nor less than in our own; these verses make the point:

> If you ask by what precious claim to fame
> A citizen earns a glorious name,
> The question comes down to these points of substance:
> Does the household teem in matters of finance?
> Over grounds and rich dwellings does he hold sway?
> At his heels does there trip a train of valets?
> And does his tasty table offer treasure
> To delight the company at their leisure?
> As for his morals—a pointless concern:
> At the end of the line they take their turn.[24]

In any case, despite the oblivion into which I let my base-metal learning sink, these gentlemen, the pretty boys of the court and their imitators, cannot spare me, unless I resolve to imitate their ways of speaking and acting—a thing totally beyond my capacity (I say this seriously), however much I

24. Si l'on s'enquiert par quels dons precieux,
Un Citoyen rend son nom glorieux,
Sur ces beux poincts la question se fonde:
Si la maison de finances abonde?
S'il est puissant de terre & de palais?
S'il est suivy d'un grand train de valets?
Ou quelque aprest pour resjouir la bande,
D'un long repas sert sa table friande?
Quant à ses moeurs, ce soin importe peu:
Au dernier rang ils seront mis en jeu.

Compare Juvenal, *Satire*, trans. and ed. Ramsay, 3.137–44:

da testem Romae tam sanctum quam fuit hospes
numinis Idaei, procedat vel Numa vel qui
servavit trepidam flagranti ex aede Minervam:
protinus ad censum, de moribus ultima fiet
quaestio. "quot pascit servos? quot possidet agri
jugera? quam multa magnaque paropside cenat?"
quantum quisque sua nummorum servat in arca,
tantum habet et fidei. . . .

[At Rome you may produce a witness as unimpeachable as the host of the Idaean Goddess—Numa himself might present himself, or he who rescued the trembling Minerva from the blazing shrine—the first question asked will be as to his wealth, the last about his character: "How many slaves does he keep?" "How many acres does he own?" "How big and how many are his dessert dishes?" A man's word is believed in exact proportion to the amount of cash that he keeps in his strongbox.]

This leads to a vivid evocation of the indignities of poverty that closely matches Gournay's perspective.

might stretch my mind and spirit to that end. I do not know if this refined troop would imitate mine any better, if they were to make an effort in the other direction, not disdaining to relax their spirits and minds in order to undertake it. O how little account I would make of the miserable scraps that are my Latin, which they rip to pieces in this way, if I did not believe that I knew more French than those who divert themselves by messing with those writings! And I dare to confess it here, although it seems to me that neither they nor their partisans will deign to hear me. It is said that women sew buttons on their clothes but never button their lips.[25] The rule is askew in my case, however, since I scarcely know how to sew and have only a middling fondness for chatting: that is why I find three words of juiceless blather occasionally pardonable in passing.

Now as for letters and learning, whether in men or women, I have not undertaken to busy myself with making an Apology here to establish their value or standing. But for heaven's sake, why won't they let me profit from the passport of ignorance? For it is a fact that either I know nothing, as much on account of a faulty memory as otherwise,[26] or what I do know is so little identified, recognized, and practiced as being learning in our time that every day my ignorance serves as an object of ridicule for the high-spirited among the learned, as my knowledge does for the others. Why would they not laugh, such people, if they come across a woman pretending to learning without formal schooling, because she instructed herself in Latin by rote, aided by setting the translations side by side with the originals, and who therefore would not dare to speak that language for fear of making a false step—a learned woman who cannot unequivocally guarantee the meter of a Latin verse; a learned woman without Greek, without Hebrew, without aptitude for providing scholarly commentary on authors, without manuscripts, without Logic, without Physics or Metaphysics, Mathematics or the rest? Let us add, without old medals in a cabinet, since possessing them is regularly set up as one of the chief accomplishments in our age. So why will the babbling of the world not permit me to rest, without opposing me, in the seat of the learned or of the ignorant, of human beings or of beasts? And this, moreover, when I am someone to whom in all these fields, if I were questioned, there

25. This is as close as we can get to conveying the play on words in the French: "On dit que les femmes n'ont jamais le filet, que pour recoudre leur linge"—literally, "It is said that women never have the little thread except for sewing their linen." *Avoir le filet* ("to have the little thread") means to be "tongue-tied"—the physical condition from which the figurative expression derives.

26. Gournay had accused herself of having a feeble (*tendre*) memory as early as the 1595 *Preface*, 36–37. On this point, as on so many others, she had no difficulty in remembering Montaigne— see *Essais*, 1.9.34A and B.

would duly come, like violins at a wedding, the amusing defeat that Aristippus met with in only one, Logic: "Why would I untie that difficulty if it baffles me when it is tied up?"[27]

To that general condemnation of intellectual women, a particular point is added in my case—that is, my practice of alchemy, which they deem absolute folly in itself. Truly, whether that science is indeed folly, as they say, I do not know. But well I know this—that certain more or less modern emperors, and our more illustrious kings of recent times, have become involved with it, as have also some of the most proficient and most highly distinguished persons in France. I know, further, that it is folly to assert definitively that alchemy is so, since the furthest depth of its secrets and functions is unknown to us, and since it is no small rashness to pronounce on occult subjects, negatively or affirmatively, or to prohibit the practice of them, if that practice lends itself to an exquisite consideration of nature, as does the practice of this one, which is therefore worthy of a curious mind, even if it has no utility but that alone.

I say that it must be tolerated on these two conditions, however, and not otherwise—that the practitioner guard against heavy expenses, so as not to risk things present and assured for those future and uncertain, and then that he banish far off those stupid hopes of the millions and millions that are falsely claimed to be promised in the books of that art, which present the promise only allegorically in these terms, its true fruit being, in all probability, moderate, if it is real. For if the Philosopher's Stone, with these infinite capacities, had ever existed, it would have so inundated the universe with gold and silver that they would no longer be in vogue; yet one cannot plausibly suppose that it exists, if it never has: that is why anyone who believes that its largesse is limitless denies it. It is necessary, moreover, that the practitioner keep from assuring himself of his success, as opposed to simply hoping for it, and that he refrain, in addition, from studying anywhere else but in books. For it is infallible that people never offer to teach it outside of books unless they do not know it.

In this branch of knowledge, as in that of the Muses, vulgar report does me wrong enough in roasting me at the common fire, for as I find myself to

---

27. Compare Diogenes Laertius on Aristippus: "Some one brought him a knotty problem with the request that he would untie the knot. 'Why, you simpleton,' said he, 'do you want it untied, seeing that it causes trouble enough as it is?'" (*Lives of Eminent Philosophers*, trans. and ed. R. D. Hicks, 2 vols. [London and Cambridge, Mass., 1925], 1:199 [2.70]). As Beaulieu and Fournier point out (in *Les Advis; Ou, Les Presens de la Demoiselle de Gournay 1641*, general eds. Jean-Philippe Beaulieu and Hannah Fournier, 3 vols. [Amsterdam and Atlanta, 1997–]), Montaigne also cites this reply (*Essais*, 1.26.171C). On Aristippus, see above, *Equality*, n. 16.

be, if I haven't made it plain enough, beneath the erudite currently in fashion, I consider that I am above run-of-the-mill alchemists: first, in that I do not practice except with the provisos I have just prescribed, which being in place, I maintain that rejecting or disdaining the art is more foolish than practicing it; second, because I am so devoid of the secret information, procedures, and mysteries regarding its vulgar form that it may be said that here I am a step beyond those who have never heard of alchemy, whether of the common sort or of the occult, which is my own. The reason is that, if they do not do it, they do not undo it, while I myself do not do it, yet I undo it, inasmuch as I condemn and oppose it in opinion and action. So let those who meddle with such trickery not be surprised, if occasionally they accost me, to see that I am ignorant of the more vulgar terms and more trivial experiments. But be that as it may, nevertheless—and without regard for those stipulations that I observe—they wrap me up, as I have been saying, in the universal reproaches that dog alchemy in the streets.

Regrettably, the poor state of my fortune, which became apparent only since I have been practicing that odious art, has lent color to these reproaches, at least by way of the expense that they associate with it and that, because of the coincidence in timing, they deemed to be equal in my case to that which devours other alchemists, the talk of the world taking it for the cause of my evil, to which it was nothing but a simple accessory. Now I am such a partisan of Truth that I cannot deny her even where she harms me when I am obliged to speak, the proof being these confessions—proof that I could suppress, in part, or disguise. And someone has lived fifty years with me who has never seen me lie, except to avoid or allay a quarrel with my friends.[28] The first year, then, that I worked on that art cost me, I admit, a not inconsiderable sum (although not greatly excessive), which, of course, came from the productions of my wits and my labors, not from my inheritance. And that excess came about as much because that particular year was naturally more expensive than the others as because I was not then more profoundly acquainted with the means of pursuing that work, hence was compelled to spend while feeling my way. And seven subsequent years, or a little more, during which I undertook diverse operations, have each cost me a hundred or a hundred and twenty ecus.[29] Since that period, two ecus ordinarily, and at unusual times a third as well, do me for a year in this respect, since I have found the means of sparing the extra, with the help of a fire that

28. Gournay refers to her maid, Nicole Jamyn, with whom she had a close relationship—see Ilsley, *A Daughter of the Renaissance*, 123–24.
29. The gold coin known as the *écu au soleil* was the official monetary standard.

is lent me free of charge by the courtesy of the master of the glassworks—a fire, I declare, that was formally the source of my heaviest charge. I have a hundred witnesses that my expenses have by no means gone beyond that, and a hundred others can testify that, to compensate for those of the first and second stages, I cut back on all other spending, customary and, as it were, natural for women of my condition in maintaining themselves, so that I might say that alchemy has not been costing me anything at all, since I have been taking back in those savings what I have been laying out.

Some laugh at my long patience in that work—wrongly, in truth, since one waits an entire year for an ear of grain (a thing, however, as soft and flexible as the materials handled in such an art are resistant and rough). Besides which, even if I did not hope for any success in the work, as I cannot do from now on after such a long time spent without profit, I would not leave off laboring, so that I may see, through the stages of a noble decoction, what the substance will become that I hold over the fire. Isn't that curiosity natural and healthy?[30] And here to conclude the story of my management of resources, I confess, on the other hand, that my generosity, too confident in others, has cost me five hundred ecus, and the vanity of youth five hundred more, although it nevertheless always contained itself, as you know, Monsieur, within the bounds of my condition, which I have acknowledged to be decidedly of a middling sort.

I say this, because I know that there are certain characters—of whom it is no marvel if their words are the scourges of disgrace and ruin, considering the complete picture of their lives—who have fabricated funny stories to make me ridiculous, rather than pitiful, in my misfortunes, by the accusation of vain ostentation; and others have made up similar tales, in order to avoid pardoning me for the fact that they had injured me or paid me with ingratitude. Some have published the claim that I had a page, others rich furniture, others that I kept a lavish table; others have endowed me with two ladies' maids—all equally and publicly false. Except that I once had in my employ a girl of that sort (together with my regular one, of whom I had need), because she played the lute and I wished to learn from her to play certain airs. Besides this, her harmonies were necessary to me at one period to help me charm a certain burdensome sadness, and, having kept her for only eight months, I sent her back to her mother. So if, on occasions since then, more than one girl has been seen with me, that has in truth been just for a brief time, without wages and out of a sense of obligation or pure pity, and it is not

---

30. At this point in the text there is a note by the author: "I have finally thrown it over and abandoned it, however, since the first impression of this book."

reasonable to turn this against me as a reproach of my vanity. I have sometimes had two lackeys, and I acknowledge that that was one too many, but I
have also admitted that youthful vanity cost me something, and I can say
again, truthfully, that, since I had much business to manage, the two were
sufficiently employed.

As for the rest, do they call it keeping a lavish table sometimes to enter-
tain one or two familiar friends—rarely and in moderate style? To which I
will add that not only my personal expenses, as I have represented, but also
my lodgings, my food, and my furniture have always been characterized by
austere frugality, apart from the five hundred ecus that I confess to having too
liberally employed, on the whole, on various occasions: I have always had
just one woolen bed, no matter what the season, scant wall hangings, and the
rest accordingly. Calumny compels me, for the sake of trying to repress it, to
recount this heap of trivialities. With regard to the carriage that I have kept,
that convention originated with women of my station—I simply observed it;
indeed, it is wholly necessary on account of the length and dirtiness of the
Paris streets, especially if such women have on their hands, like me, the day-
to-day business of a paternal succession. Then, the general and tyrannical example of the age renders so great the shame of lacking a carriage that those
women who wish to live with a certain decorum in society are not allowed to
consider whether it costs too much or not. Certain ladies (beautiful in their
youth), in order to curry favor with great persons, have been busying themselves with, among other things, spinning tales about my supposed luxury
where it very much mattered to me—ladies who have never waited for necessity equal to mine in order to seek someone to bankroll luxury for themselves, and who do not stick at accepting from men the means, shamefully solicited, that I have sometimes refused at the hands of women, when they were
becomingly offered, so that they might more becomingly be reserved for
their own need. (Ten thousand people in Guyenne could tell you so.) Forgive
my impatience. Slander does not merely scratch someone it accuses of serious mismanagement of a household: it cuts that person deeply, since good
domestic management is such an easy matter, and means are so necessary,
that anybody who is not willing and able to preserve them, if they can be pre-
served, is unable to do anything and may count himself wholly devoid of prudence—that is, unworthy of the title of a human being.

But the malice of those who accuse me of ruining my finances or of other
kinds of extravagance, as they see fit, further entails taking away my livelihood
and also afflicts with the same stroke those to whom my disposition, which is
not without compassion, would have been able to do good, if fortune had done
good to me. For I have no hope of succor in my necessity except from Kings,

and I am almost entirely losing it, as these chatterers negate any esteem, deserved or not, in which I am held by honorable people, who would have brought me to the favorable notice of Their Majesties. Without this damaging result, a bit of willpower might perhaps restrain me, at least out of contempt, from wasting my time in answering such gossip, since no one has ever been able to escape vulgar prattling who raises himself above the crowd—nor even now, in these decadent times, anyone who, like me, is desirous of raising himself. For in the end, to live with a more far-reaching reputation than one's neighbor means nothing more than pleasing more fools and fewer wise men than he does, unless some external and fortuitous accident has rendered the common people more happy than they are prudent in distributing such esteem. I repeat that, without those consequences of the prattling, which can extend to delivering a ruinous blow, one would perhaps be less concerned about the average person's spitting on one's name, as opposed to one's dress,[31] although my fragile temper balks at being patient with that kind of thing: I have already admitted to this sufficiently at the beginning of this Apology.

Now, after all, I console myself with the fact that most of those who chatter at my expense hold me to be untouchable and proud enough that they are persuaded I would rather submit to their babble than to their examples, whether in words or deeds. I confess, moreover, that I must have more patience than another woman with these verbal escapades—I, who see the origin of the venom they strike me with, and who might even squelch some of them, if I resolved to, at the cost of the damage I would suppose myself to be doing if I modeled myself wholly according to the desires of those people for the sake of checking their drivel—even if any person afflicted by ill fortune could succeed in pleasing them entirely. I say model or fashion myself wholly, for in truth, as is well known, I have somewhat bent in their direction out of practical considerations born of the tyranny of my affairs, and as far as the duty and decency of a person who professes my principles could excuse. Hear what Ronsard has to say:

> Those who have only the body are born for such occupations,
> Those who have only the mind do not willingly perform them.[32]

Finally, all soundness and strength of character are repudiated in our age, and are so in women to an outrageous degree (if they are not dreaded because

31. Gournay had used this image as early as the 1595 *Preface* (69).

32. "Ceux qui n'ont que le corps sont nez pour tels mestiers: / Ceux qui n'ont que l'esprit ne les font volontiers." As Beaulieu and Fournier point out (in Gournay's *Les Advis*), the quotation comes from Ronsard, "À luy-mesme," in *Le Bocage Royal*, in *Oeuvres Complètes*, 2:15–20, lines 197–98.

of the influence of their lineage and living relatives, or of their wealth), inasmuch as the general model of their sex, to which one seeks to make them conform, is found to be, on account of poor intellectual nourishment, a certain degree lower than that of the masculine, which is already extremely low, especially in a court assembly, taken as a whole. Since it falls out that I have the misfortune of being the butt of blather, if not for having achieved that strong and sound condition, at least for aspiring to raise myself to it, what should I do if that wind did not blow from a certain sort of mouth, equally incapable of blaming the bad and of praising the good—

In pardoning the raven, one censures the dove[33]—

and if a certain other sort did not praise me more than I desire (provided that knowledge of my existence carries so far)? I could assign to the latter ranks many of the most distinguished persons of all kinds, even of the court, if I did not fear that this account would be taken as evidence of vanity. At any rate, since the occasion suits me, I will name at least the first in that place to open his mouth in my favor, whether to honor me with his praises or to advance me in the assistance and protection of the King: that is the generous prince to whose glory, natural and inherent as it is, the exalted name of Clèves and of Mantua could add nothing, nor even the throne of that Duchy, so important in Italy, with which he is connected.[34]

If I have any value, the ill will that those jesters display toward me turns directly to their shame, because the best touchstone of the true or false gold of a soul is the application that it can make of praises and reproaches according to merits and demerits, as well as the choice of friends and enemies. How distressed is the evil man by the presence and society of the good one, and the good by that of the evil?

It is lawful for no pure man to cross the accursed threshold.[35]

---

33. "Pardonnant au corbeau la colombe on censure." As Dezon-Jones points out in her edition of the *Apology* (in *Fragments*, 165 n. 15), this derives from Juvenal, *Satire*, trans. and ed. Ramsay, 2.63: "dat veniam corvis, vexat censura columbas" [Our censor absolves the raven and passes judgment on the pigeon!]. The context is significant: a woman is responding to a sneering condemnation of her sex with an indignant attack on male immorality and hypocrisy. The contrast between the contemptible raven and the admirable dove was often attached in Christian tradition to the contrast between the two birds released by Noah to search for land (Gen. 8:6–11).

34. According to Beaulieu and Fournier (in Gournay's *Les Advis*), the reference is to Charles I, who also became Duke of Casal in 1630. Gournay adds this note: "I wrote this some years before his Highness of Mantua moved to Italy."

35. "Nulli fas casto sceleratum insistere limen" (*Aeneid* 6.563) The Sibyl is addressing Aeneas during their journey through the underworld, as they pass by the gate of Tartarus.

Ask Diogenes how important it is for him to choose or refuse individuals and companionship, when he prefers playing with hazelnuts with the children at the gate of the city to governing the state with persons not his true equals.[36] And, by this line of reasoning, let a man show us whom he pleases or displeases and we can show him who he is. This is the case with Homer, who, to discredit Thersites in a few words, limited himself to writing these verses (as translated by Amyot in Plutarch):

> Achilles hated him strongly,
> Ulysses, too, wished him deadly evil.[37]

It must, said a Saint of the primitive Church, be some great good that strongly displeases Nero.[38] And the Philosopher, in my opinion, placed a most worthy inscription on the altar beneath the statue that he dedicated to his divine preceptor: "Aristotle vows this altar to Plato, a man whom impure souls cannot praise without offense."[39]

As in the temple of Pallas Athena there were mysteries for the general populace and others reserved for those professing the religion, so certainly there are persons to be praised and cherished by truly enlightened souls, others for the vulgar. Phocion got what he deserved, when, delivering a speech

36. The reference would be to Diogenes of Sinope, the Cynic philosopher (ca. 400–325 B.C.E.), whose life is recounted by Diogenes Laertius, 6.20–81. The same point is made by many stories attached to his name, but the detail of the hazelnuts may be Gournay's invention—or simply, as Arnould has privately suggested (letter to Hillman, 16 December 1999), her error, for Montaigne (*Essais*, 3.13.1110B) praises Socrates for not disdaining, despite his greatness, to play at hazelnuts with the children. The preceding sentence (1110C) details that philosopher's heroic endurance, at the end, of "la calomnie, la tyrannie, la prison, les fers et le venin" [calumny, tyranny, prison, irons, and poison].

37. "De Pelien le hayssoit bien fort, / Ulysse aussi luy vouloit mal de mort"; the original is *Iliad* 2.220, where Achilles is actually called by his own name rather than by the patronymic "Peleion," and, naturally, the Greek form Odysseus appears for Ulysses. The text of Plutarch in question is "How the Young Man Should Study Poetry," in *Plutarch's Moralia* 30A. The translations of Plutarch by Jacques Amyot (1513–93) had enormous influence within France and beyond. (For example, Thomas North translated Plutarch's *Lives* into English [1579] from Amyot's French.)

38. Tertullian, *Apologeticus* 5.3 (Arnould, letter to Hillman, 16 December 1999). According to Tacitus, the persecutions of Nero were so extreme, and so clearly aimed at creating a scapegoat for the great fire of Rome, that, despite the general loathing of the Christians for their supposed "vices," "there arose a sentiment of pity, due to the impression that they were being sacrificed not for the welfare of the state but to the ferocity of a single man" (*Annals*, trans. and ed. John Jackson, vols. 2–4 of *Tacitus in Five Volumes*, 3:283 and 285 [44]).

39. Arnould has pointed out (letter to Hillman, 16 December 1999) the origin of this story in Aristotelian fragments—see *Fragmenta Aristotelis*, ed. Émile Heitz, in *Aristotelis Opera Omnia* (Paris, 1869), 5:334–35. Gournay's immediate source remains uncertain. Contrary to what might have been expected, the element does not appear either in Diogenes Laertius's life of Aristotle or in his account of Plato's epitaphs (Plato, 3.43–45).

in public, he was vexed by a certain shame at seeing himself, for once in his life, stroked by the adulterous and incestuous praises of the common people (let us adopt these epithets of praise for our language, if we may), and asked his friends who were present if he had inadvertently done or said anything at all out of place.[40] Thus Saint Jerome says to Paulinus that those are most pleasing to the world who are displeasing to Jesus Christ.[41] Now because I have composed a treatise precisely on the antipathy and incompatibility of the opinions, actions, and behavior of low and high minds, I will not speak more of this here.[42]

To finish my digression—which is to the point, however—those who are proud in a small-minded way (clever as they are) conceal at all costs what a hardship it is for them to be cut off from babbling, when this occurs, although everyone sees and knows it. They would deem themselves more degraded and ridiculous by the admission that they would commit that offense than by the offense itself. They do not, in their hearts, believe that anything has value except according to the esteem of the crowd, which they see above them or as their equal, and which therefore carries great weight with them: miserable slaves or, to put it better, the creatures of fools, who wish to be only what such people make them, as it seems to them, by their praises—not daring to evaluate, nor daring to hope that they are worth anything except according to the evaluations they receive from those mouths. The greatly proud, to which number I come close to belonging, who suppose that they have value in their own right, and who see, moreover, the crowd as beneath them, disdain to conceal that eventuality if it occurs to them; for such minds have their greatness apart, like their wisdom. And a tiny quantity of thin efforts to display intellectual sophistication—in a word, all vulgar affectations, stilted facial expressions, and jargon—these prove repulsive to a firm soul and a lofty judgment, when it encounters them.

Truly, petty souls cannot abandon an ounce of their advantages, whether they are imaginary or substantial, without remaining poor; great ones have so many true and real ones, belonging to both present and future, that they can give up something from one and the other without fearing that the loss at all diminishes their worth. My opinion, finally, is that no one believes himself to be an honorable man if he does not seem one, or believes he is one only because he seems one. Horace boasts of nothing so readily as of his base lineage,[43]

40. Gournay cites the same episode in the *Promenade*—see above, 55 and n. 44.

41. See Jerome, letter 53 (to Paulinus, Bishop of Nola), in *Letters*, 4, 5, and 7.

42. Gournay refers to her essay, "Antipathie des ames basses et hautes," originally published in the first collection of her work, *L'Ombre de la Damoiselle de Gournay* (1926).

43. A recurrent point in *Satire* 1.6—see esp. 6, 45–46, and 71.

and I will not further allege (because I cite him in another place), that Greek philosopher who gloried and delighted in telling all comers that he was the son of a slave and a whore.[44] Zeno, too, foremost of the Stoics, having received a slap and a blow of the fist, instead of concealing the bruise, stuck a note on his forehead: "Nicodemus did it."[45] Moreover, Socrates recounts nothing more richly or light-heartedly than the current opinion that he knew how to do nothing but babble, measure the air, and count the stars.[46] In this regard I cannot forget that, in our time, a distinguished Latin poet and old man openly declared that the sole affliction he had was to be beaten by his young wife, and some other personage of the greatest merit did not at all spare, among more than three of his familiar friends, to confess a secret love of his, and that he did not feel his courage sufficient to engage in a duel, although he wore a sword. He admitted these things out of foolishness, it will be said. Ah, truly, if I know anything about it, he was a gracious and judicious fool! The stains that originate or occur, not through the fault of their owner, but through Fortune, through Nature, or through others, should cause blushes only in those who do not have their own virtues with which to cover them, if they should cause blushes in anyone.

I will say, then, leaving this interlude to take up the thread of my defense again, that my ill fortune does not stem from alchemy or from any other excess of mine, and I can prove this by the authoritative testimony of many, oral and written, besides the fact that I am highly scrupulous about never lying and that I consider liars to be as poorly wise as they are impure. And certainly if I wished, for a need, to mask some truth in the hope of concealing a deception, it could not be in the things written about here, above or below, for they are all such that they could not be managed or take place without others present, and such that at least a hundred persons who have served in or frequented my house could refute me if I sought to alter the story in such particulars—without considering that I would have to agree that my proof would melt, especially regarding the things I will come to, if I did not support it by authentic documents, which I offer to show freely.

---

44. Seemingly a reminiscence of Diogenes Laertius's account of Bion the Borysthenite (ca. 325–255 B.C.E.): "Who his parents were, and what his circumstances before he took to philosophy, he himself told Antigonus in plain terms . . . 'my father was a freedman, who wiped his nose on his sleeve. . . . My mother was such as a man like my father would marry, from a brothel. Afterward my father, who had cheated the revenue in some way, was sold with all his family'" (trans. and ed. Hicks, 1:423–25 [Bion, 4.46–47]).

45. "Nicodemus faciebat." This closely resembles an anecdote recounted by Diogenes Laertius, 6.33, but with reference to a gang of nameless young men and the philosopher Diogenes.

46. Compare Plato, *Apology* 2.18B, 3.19C.

The Second Part of the Apology

My father left our household debt free, but my mother, having borrowed much money during the great wars of the League[47] and the minority of all her children—as much to build (an occupation that she was fond of) as to support an elder brother whom we had in Italy, and later in the royal armies—believed, with apparent reason, that, once peace was made, she would be satisfied by means of the amount that had been retained, on account of the king or the evils of the time, from the arrears of various revenues owing to her on the general receipts, the salt, and the clergy, with which she would acquit herself. Dying as she did in the midst of that war, in the year 1591, when peace arrived, it was necessary to pay the liabilities, while those assets were lost for eight whole years. Now, all the substance of us junior siblings—one son, one daughter, and myself sharing it after the elder son was thoroughly provided for, some time before us and separately—rested on those revenues; or further, to put it better, what we had—consisting of two houses in this city of Paris and some furniture—was so far consumed in paying those debts of my mother that only this asset was left to us: a sum that, according to the distribution, amounted to 2,400 and odd pounds of income per annum for each of us. Another of our sisters, the eldest among the younger siblings, instead of participating in the distribution, renounced her inheritance and became a creditor with respect to the dowry contracted by my mother for her marriage with Lord Bourray, our neighbor from Étampes. And the fact that this dowry totaled only eight thousand ecus, of which just a thousand had been advanced at the time of the contract, provides, given our sister's renunciation, another strong proof of our poverty and of the injustice of the reproach leveled against me of causing great loss. For it may be judged whether a daughter would do such harm to the standing of the paternal household as to renounce her inheritance, if she did not believe she would gain thereby, as she did by almost half.

In any case, once that acquittance and discharge relating to the marriage were satisfied by us three sharers in the heritage, together with the other debts, not only did those two houses of our patrimony disappear, as has been stated, but it further cost each of us a hundred ecus of income, with the result

47. The Holy League (*Sainte Ligue*) was the alliance of militant Roman Catholics, under the leadership of the House of Guise and the sponsorship of Spain, that struggled first against Henri III, whom they perceived as too indulgent toward the Protestant minority, then, after that king's assassination in 1589, against his Protestant successor, Henri of Navarre. The latter prevailed militarily, in general, but it was his conversion to Catholicism in 1593 that thoroughly sapped the strength of the League.

that there remained no more than about 2,100 pounds of income apiece. From the remaining revenues must further be deducted the giving up of two or three years of future arrears, which it was necessary to sell at a loss and under legal compulsion, in order to effect the discharge of all the mortgages involved. Indeed, it was necessary to sell mine for even further into the future, because I was in a weaker position than my two coheirs, that younger brother and sister, having lived from my own purse and without drawing on any other money for more than four or five years of that war, since the death of my mother, while they lived in an honorable fashion from the purses of others. And most of the time they lived in this way by my mediation and my credit, as I will now make manifest, inasmuch as I took a maternal care of their youth from the moment when we lost our mother.

Four or five years are long and weigh heavily on the purse for people of poor fortune who borrow in order to live, especially in time of war, for they cannot borrow except on exceedingly unfavorable terms, since the repayment is doubtful. And the Spanish proverb is to the point, which says that to such persons one sells the sun in August. Those four years of saving are another one of the principal causes why the finances of those two cosharers with me in the heritage remained in a somewhat better state than mine, albeit not abundant, besides the marriage of one of them, that young sister, with Lord De la Salle at Cambrai, which in no way sustained her fortune because it came about on those terms. Cambrai was the refuge where I brought them both immediately, when it pleased God to call her who had brought us into the world, and the courtesy of Monsieur the late Maréchal of Balagny took in my brother, as that of Madame la Maréchale, Renée d'Amboise, welcomed my sister, in their court in that unfamiliar city, full of nobility and brilliance, apart from the fact that the great tally of pages he had—my brother being of an age to take livery—and the goodly number of girls she had would have allowed them in good conscience to refuse me.[48] And not only did she take in my sister, but I owe this confession to the tomb of such a generous lady—that she also offered me the same favor, citing as a reason that a person like me did not deserve to be allowed, by those of her rank, to feel the hardships of that miserable destiny. I declined with thanks, fearing to abuse

---

48. Gournay's glowing impression of the court of Cambrai makes for an intriguing contrast with the historical sequel. In fact, Balagny and his wife so exploited and brutalized the population that, when the town was attacked by the Spanish in 1595, there were uprisings in sympathy with the invaders. Balagny was finally forced to withdraw ignominiously, while his wife killed herself. See Léo Mouton, *Bussy d'Amboise et Madame de Montsoreau: D'après des documents inédits* (Paris, 1912), 328–30. Versions of the governor and his wife figure (in a quite different context) in George Chapman's play (ca. 1610), *The Revenge of Bussy d'Ambois.*

her courtesy; but in truth the offer was noble and praiseworthy in many ways. For apart from the fact that that lady was the more deserving for favoring the Muses and intellects because her own was wholly devoid of learning and solely illuminated by the pure splendor of nature (although she was beautiful and vivacious), she could have the more easily dispensed with putting such a value on mine that she would deign to nurture it, because it still remained wholly raw on account of my youth. In addition, she could not have hoped to discharge herself easily of my sister, nor of myself, by the reestablishment of our means, wretched France finding itself at that time so sorely and horribly bruised and confused—the inevitable result of such powerful, irresistible, and venomous forces—that one was led to expect a final ruin, rather than a restoration, of the state.

O how behavior has changed in a short time! And how far are the princes, the great men, and the great ladies of today in France from offering their houses in consideration of intellect and merit! (I always allow for some exceptions, although they are extremely rare.) Perhaps it is that their wisdom is so high above the human variety that they see the latter as having nothing to do with them and that consequently, having no need of human beings as counselors in the conduct of life, or to confide in, or for the pleasures of conversation, they do not choose to seek them out except as valets, and for the qualities of valets. But let us say in passing that whoever wants nothing to do with men except as valets—no wonder if he is rarely capable even of that (namely, choosing a good valet). I rest my case on particular instances, which ordinarily cost the choosers dearly. I am seen so rarely at their gates, moreover, that one may easily believe that I say all of this without any personal stake.

Let me get back to our unfortunate affairs. I will add that the great lawsuit that we had in the Parlement against the heirs of the late Lord Le Châteaupoissy, who sought to rid themselves of one of the two houses we inherited, which they had bought from us, offered ample testimony of our debts to anyone who had not known of them otherwise. Those debts and losses were added to in my case by a bad bargain that I made with my coheirs with respect to their portion of the former arrears of the previously mentioned revenues to increase the sum of mine (I mean the arrears from those eight years of war), for I hoped in vain to profit, as my only resource, from a certain scheme for reimbursement that was proposed to me. But because this story would be too long here, I defer it to whoever would like to hear it from my mouth. Now, if my spending lasted longer than could have been sustained by the miserable remainder of funds that remained to me after all this discharging of debts, charges, and losses, the cause of this was the succor of a good friend, who took pleasure in my making an honorable appearance. Certain loans also supported me and came to my aid, of which I have since paid, thank God, the better part and without borrowing anything new for a long time.

In this, twelve hundred ecus or thereabouts, from the sale of the fourth part of an inheritance of that young brother, Lord Neufvy, assisted me, although in a pitiful way, since the cause was a dear loss in his person. The eldest died without children, but he carried the rest of his funds, which were small after the payment of his debts, on a second voyage to Italy and to Palestine; I mean his personal debts, for we other junior siblings were charged with the common ones. Those distributions among ourselves, the younger ones, the payments of our mother's debts, and the renunciation of her inheritance by our sister, the first married, were effected and may be seen in the registers of the notary La Morlière of about the year 1596, fairly soon after my return from the voyage to Guyenne, where the wife and the daughter of my second father[49] invited me after his death, in order that we might try to console ourselves together, by our company and our discourse, and take possession of the portion that he had mutually given to us—to them in me, and to me in them. They and I lost him in the sixtieth year of his age, three years after our first interview. It seems that Fortune is jealous of the continuance of possessions of such high price.

Anyone who visited me at that time might doubt that my affairs had been as bad as I represent them here, for up to that time I gave indications of being more satisfied with them. The truth is that I lived in hope of obtaining satisfaction from my portion of those eight years of estate revenues in arrears of which I have spoken, which were due to us as inheritors, and also of others of the same kind, which I had purchased from the allotment of my co-heirs; I have described how these arrears, which, however, were lost, comprised my sole resource. Besides which, I further hoped that the sister whose marriage my mother had arranged, providing a dowry of eight thousand ecus, as I have said, would continue as an inheritor, and not a creditor, such as she proved to be when the division mentioned above occurred. Gross calumny—is anything more needed to vindicate myself and confound you? You have the nerve to put it about that I have eaten up fifty thousand ecus, when my sister, born of my own father and mother, by public declaration much preferred eight thousand of the amount to my allotted portion! (I make no mention in any of this of another excellent and virtuous sister, a religious at Chanteloup, since her condition prevented her from taking part.)

49. That is, of course, Montaigne.

What will the chatterers of our time not say concerning such accounts and calculations, indeed of the whole scope, preceding and to come, of this document, so far from social conventions? Patience: every wise person will approve of my frankness, will pity the necessity that has led me to publish this discourse, and will pardon me for seeking to unburden my heart by means of simple truth regarding matters in which so many others would unburden and ease their own by means of artifice and vanity. The effort that the child of Croesus made, in spite of Nature, when he cried out at his father's danger, although he was a natural mute[50]—I do the same, in spite of the modesty I possess from birth and by education, constrained to do by the necessity which accepts no law but itself. Or, like that ancient king who, seeing himself reduced to extremity in his final stronghold, sacrificed his own son in a burnt offering to appease heaven and pierce his enemy's heart with pity,[51] I here sacrifice that virtue, my dear daughter, compelled by a just desire to abate the depraved gossip that does all it can to rob me of one of the sweetest consolations of persons of honor, which consists in the approbation and favor of the wise.

But I would never have dared to expose such declarations and accounts in public, if gossip had not treated me so badly regarding the entire subject of this treatise that I realized I could lose nothing further with the gossipers by doing so. The fact remains that anyone who would wish to subject honorable people to every vulgar convention and formality would resemble those who, to render a king thoroughly accomplished, would wish him to know how to make his own shoes. Did Alexander shrink from taking the very royal diadem from his head in order to bind the wound of an injured man?[52] I will cite only this mark of his contempt for forms, out of a thousand on the part of this prince and those of his station, without mentioning people of other ranks or adding to what degree this action is yet richer and more lustrous in another respect. It should be said of stilted manners, of affectation,

---

50. Herodotus (1.85) recounts that, around 565 B.C.E., Croesus, king of Lydia, was on the point of being killed by the invading Persians at the taking of Sardis when one of his sons, who had hitherto been incapable of speech, called to the soldier to stop. The anecdote was current as proof of the insuperable force of nature–witness its citation by Jean de Rosières, *De la Maladie et mort de monseigneur et tres-illustre Prince Charles Cardinal de Lorraine* (Pont-à-Mousson, 1608), with the comment, "la nature rompit les obstacles, et le fit parler" [nature broke the obstacles and made him speak] (sig. A7r).

51. Reference not traced.

52. Here as elsewhere Gournay may be extrapolating in imagery from a general notion. We have found no reference containing this detail, although Valerius Maximus has a story of Alexander, in a winter encampment, descending from his throne near the fire and with his own hands putting in his place a soldier paralyzed with cold (5.11, Ext. 1).

and of social formalities what one Greek said of the laws—that they are like spiders' webs, which are capable of enmeshing the little flies, whereas a large one pierces and rends them.[53] The only difference lies in this—that the least wise among those of powerful means break the laws, while the wisest among the powerless and the powerful alike dismiss and strongly reject such affectations and formalities, insofar as they may without extraordinary harm. And if the sage Dandamis was unwilling to pardon even Socrates for having to such a degree subjected himself to the laws of his country,[54] how would he have pardoned him for subjecting himself to the petty fashions, formalities, and far-fetched affectations that it devised, as we do, and in a worse way. Further, I owe this Apology, in its full extent, to you and to my other friends, men and women, as many as I still have, in order to justify the defense that you and they have provided for me, when necessary, against the slanderers, so that the reproach directed at my supporters, as if they favored me at the expense of the truth, may rebound upon the assailants.

Finding, therefore, that, because of that withholding in advance, noted in the section previous to the last, of two or three years of arrears, I was deprived of sustenance, along with my revenues, for as many years, what recourse did I have but to fall back on the basics? Consequently, it was necessary to sell—that is, to put it plainly, to give away for a trifle, as much because those in necessity are tormented tyrannically, by the stringency of their need, into parting with what is theirs on any ruinous condition, as because the price is driven down drastically by the fear of debts when one purchases, without its being legally put up for auction, the inheritance deriving from an indebted household, especially an inheritance precarious in itself, as was the one of ours in question. And to proceed under an order is something never done and entails, what is more, an impossible encumbrance of guarantees to which the possessions may be subject, particularly in our family. When I sold, my good faith was trusted, although fearfully, in view of the times we live in and my necessity; no one has ever had to regret this.

Thus I recognized with certainty that, whatever restraint I might practice, my patrimony would at all events be bound to come to ruin, for the reasons that I recently cited, if I was not willing to live in a very low fashion; and

53. Solon, according to Diogenes Laertius: "He compared laws to spiders' webs, which stand firm when any light and yielding object falls on them, while a larger thing breaks through them and makes off" (trans. and ed. Hicks, 1:59 {1.58}). From this there developed a proverbial association that makes its way into English literature—compare John Webster, *The Duchess of Malfi*, ed. John Russell Brown (London, 1964), 1.1.177–80.

54. As pointed out by Beaulieu and Fournier (in Gournay's *Les Advis*), this detail is adapted from Plutarch's life of Alexander, 65.2.

the resolution to live in such a way is extremely difficult to swallow for persons nurtured on honorable appearances, especially young people, who do not yet know to what degree both the world and its plaudits (which follow such appearances) comprise flimsy mirages. I consequently resolved to try to manage it, if possible, that, while my inheritance would hit rock bottom about a year earlier, given a life of honorable appearances, it would in the process sink less miserably. I admit that I still had a hope of restoring my prosperity. (This kind of prudence amounted to trying to reembark before the tide went out.) I had the idea, therefore, of attracting visitors by a certain expenditure at once honorable and restrained, insofar as one in necessity can be restrained, and by means of such visitation to make myself known to those who are close to Their Majesties, so that they might report to the latter that I worthily deserved sustenance at their hands, whether for my personal qualities or for having been ruined in consequence of their affairs. Never would they have seen me, I dare to confess it, as a suitor in my ill fortune, if I had not believed that I deserved in some way that they should share their good fortune with me, although that ill fortune came from their side (however innocently) by the unhappy circumstance of the war, which caused that withholding of estate revenues.

The wise pardon, in oppression, a favorable word about oneself; indeed, Aristotle says that it is cowardice to rate or pay oneself at less than one is worth. "The straight serves to measure both itself and the deviant."[55] And honest people are judges of themselves and of others. Giving credence to this— or, more properly, to his own magnanimity—one of our dukes has not at all spared since that time, in that poem with which he has gratified the Muses, his own ample and deserved praises, as much under the name of Rosny, as under that of Sully.[56] The Trojan prince, too, held up as an exemplar of prudence— does he hide his own good qualities from us? "I am Aeneas the pious"—and a

---

55. Gournay cites, in Latin, from Aristotle, *On the Soul* (*De Anima*), A.1.411a; this remark, which originally carried no moral implication, was included in the medieval compilation known as *Auctoritates Aristotelis* (6.21). (We owe this observation to Arnould, letter to Hillman, 16 December 1999.)

See also the *Eudemian Ethics*, trans. J. Solomon, in *The Works of Aristotle*, gen. ed. W. D. Ross, 11 vols. (Oxford, 1915), 9:1232b–33a (3.5), where the distinction between honor "given by a crowd of ordinary men" and that accorded "by those worthy of consideration" (1232b) is also highly characteristic of Gournay. This is part, moreover, of a discussion of "magnanimity"—a term that Gournay will be using in the next sentence but one (*magnanimité*), and again below (149) in connection with the contemptible judgment of the "vulgar." Cowardice comes in by way of analogy: "It seems characteristic of the magnanimous man to be disdainful; each virtue makes one disdainful of what is esteemed great contrary to reason (e.g., bravery disdains dangers of this kind)" (1232b). Compare also the approval of self-love in the *Nicomachean Ethics* 1168a–69b (9.8).

56. Maximilien de Béthune (1560–1641), seigneur de Rosny, later duc de Sully, prime minister under Henri IV.

bit later, "my fame rises to the heavens."⁵⁷ Socrates, for his part, had his mouth full of his own praises, and of the highest kind, in the two Apologies, particularly in that of Xenophon, just as Scaurus and Rutilius did not forget their own, without, however, being reproached for boastfulness.⁵⁸ And what does the prophet-king say?—"Lord, remember David, and all his meekness."⁵⁹

My mode of proceeding was acceptable on the grounds of its necessity, since it is true that expenditure is the sole unhappy and foolish means of making oneself frequented, known, and valued in France; and, more precisely, it is so for women, who cannot cause themselves to be observed or recognized by means of their activities. I considered also that such a stratagem is employed by junior siblings capable of something good, and that everyone excuses them for making a splash in their torment—for scattering to the winds, I may say, a patrimonial portion that is too skimpy for them, and in conserving which they could equally not fail to be miserable. This is so that, by making themselves seen and showing to the eyes of the world what stuff they are made of, they may advance in their hopes, if possible, by risking the vicissitudes of fortune or by the grace of princes. From time immemorial, moreover, a swift remedy for misfortune in one's affairs has been recommended by the words of the Tragic Sage: "When in danger, take a risky way out," and, elsewhere, "Peril was never vanquished without more of the same."⁶⁰ But if these risks are less freely accessible to our sex, a certain particular esteem, obtained from all the better-born minds in France, if knowledge of me reached them,

57. "Sum pius Aeneas . . . fama super aethera notus" (*Aeneid* 1.378, 379).

58. In Plato's *Apology*, Socrates actually defends himself twice against the appearance of boasting: 5.20E and 26.37A; in Xenophon's version, he does not pull his punches in this way (*Apology* 14–21). Marcus Aemilius Scaurus and Publius Rutilius Rufus were rivals for the Roman consulship in 115 B.C.E., then legal adversaries when Scaurus prevailed. Their memoirs are not extant, and Gournay culled this reference from Tacitus, *Agricola*, who says that they wrote about themselves "without being disbelieved or provoking a sneer" (trans. and ed. Hutton, rev. Ogilvie, 26–27 [1.3]). Compare above, n. 12.

59. "Memento, Domine, David, et omnis mansuetudinis eius" (Ps. 132:1).

60. The "Tragic Sage" could only be Seneca, and the first quotation, from *Agamemnon* 154, had been previously cited by Montaigne in a context likely to increase the appeal for Gournay:

Celuy à qui la fortune refuse dequoy planter son pied et establir un estre tranquille et reposé, il est pardonnable s'il jette au hazard ce qu'il a, puis qu'ainsi comme ainsi la necessité l'envoye à la queste.

[He whom fortune denies the means of settling down and establishing a quiet and restful way of life may be forgiven for throwing what he has to chance, since at all events necessity drives him forth in pursuit.]

(*Essais*, 2.17.645C)

The second quotation may represent a reworking of Seneca's *Hercules Furens*, 326–28 (Arnould, letter to Hillman, 16 December 1999), but the idea there is inevitable vulnerability to danger,

authorized me, with a special passport, in that determination and that plan to aspire to benefits from Their Royal Majesties.

Now if the esteem of Frenchmen rendered me this homage, whether in person or in writing, that of foreigners did not revoke it. Proof of this will be their abundant books from celebrated pens, which are well enough known, and from diverse regions—Flanders, Holland, and recently also from Italy, by the favor of Signors Cesar Chapeco and Carlo Pinto, who make it known in their works that they will not allow the ancient glory of nobly serving the Muses, which was acquired in their great native country, to become tarnished.[61] I cannot forget also the honorable favors received from several sovereigns of the first rank after kings. Nor must I commit the ingratitude of passing over in silence the honor done me at Brussels, where certain business brought me one day toward the beginning of the seventeenth century: I was astonished to see a troop of persons of quality, men and women, till then unknown to me, come to my inn and take me away by gentle force, conducting me and lodging me with a truly noble courtesy in the virtuous home of Lord President Venetten. No more can I omit the welcome and the refined attentions that I received from one of that company, Lord Provider Roberti, who served the Archdukes with renown—a personage truly full of generosity, of love of the Muses and of Virtue.[62] Besides this, shall I keep silent about the receptions and banquets provided by a great number of persons of rank and belonging to the Council, as unknown to my eyes as the first ones, equally in the same city and in Antwerp, and about the portraits of me kept in both of them? Finally, to wind up this dance, the very many honorable words that the late Most Serene James, King of Great Britain, vouchsafed to speak of me to Monsieur le Maréchal de Laverdin, when he was dispatched to His Majesty, the

---

not overcoming it, and it is tempting instead to suspect Gournay of adapting Seneca's well-known lines about avoiding the consequences of crime through crime—see *Agamemnon* 115, and "On Mercy" (["De Clementia"], in *Moral Essays*), 1.13.2; cf. also *Medea* 55.

61. Giulio Cesare Capaccio (1552–1634): prominent and prolific Italian man of letters, secretary for thirty years to the city of Naples and one of the founders of an academy there. As Mario Schiff first observed (*La fille d'alliance de Montaigne, Marie de Gournay* [1910; reprinted, Geneva, 1978], 125), Capaccio included a notice for Gournay, beginning with Lipsius's praise of her as the contemporary Theano (see above, *Promenade*, n. 48), in his *Illustrium Mulierum, et Illustrium Virorum Elogia* [Praise of famous women and famous men (1608–9)], 210–11, while Carlo Pinto (a more obscure figure) supplied some wholly banal supplementary verses.

62. On Gournay's voyage in 1597 to Brussels and Antwerp, where she was warmly received by various statesman, see Ilsley, *A Daughter of the Renaissance*, 82–84, who speaks of her obtaining "just a taste of the renown she craved" (83). (If she also encountered Lipsius on this occasion, as has been conjectured, it seems strange that the *Apology* fails to mention this.) Remacle Roberti, whose brother Jean was a well-known Jesuit theologian, served the state as minister of military provisions, comptroller, and archducal adviser (Beaulieu and Fournier, in Gournay's *Les Advis*).

very many testimonies that he esteemed me worthy of the most honorable royal favors, the favorable display he made to him in his private room of a certain writing that he said came from my hand, in the presence of persons who speak about it to this day at the Louvre—these seal for me with a golden seal those letters which were capable of authorizing my hope of royal favors and acts of generosity.[63] Or, to put it better, that alone should have procured me esteem and good fortune in France, coming as it did from such a powerful monarch, reigning so well and crowned to the point of arousing envy by the hand of the Muses, and by that of humanity.

For sovereign princes appear to be obliged by their glory to cherish Virtue and all that is presented to them, by competent hands, under her name; yea, their own political interests invite them to introduce it in the general crowd of their subjects by the rewarding of particular ones, and, more, to introduce future virtue in them by recompensing that of the present. It was a more illustrious thing, said that elder son of Victory and Greatness, Caesar, to extend the bounds of the intellects of his country than those of his empire. O how fully, then, does the prince merit a great triumph and a greater empire who knows how to extend the limits of the minds of his state, not in a single outstanding one, on the example of Cicero, whom Caesar was speaking of,[64] but in many by the happy influence of his benefices and by his welcoming of rare spirits? To this our young king, indeed, also brings a laudable and generous disposition, as I will say later at greater length. I flee so strongly all that bears the countenance of ostentation, or seems to do so, that the necessity of my affairs would have solicited me in vain to display the kinds of benefits fate has regaled me with, so as to gain me the approbation that could or should do me good, if I had not been obliged to render these thanks, and the just praises that accompany them, to those who have honored me with their favors.

If such risky undertakings as the one of mine I described—exposing an inheritance that was out of proportion to the condition of its possessor— succeed for those who concoct them, they and Fortune must be praised; if not, their originators do not deserve to be blamed for having had bad luck in a scheme that must be considered good because no better could be devised.

---

63. Jean de Beaumanoir, Marquis de Lavardin (1551–1614), was ambassador to England in 1612 (Beaulieu and Fournier, in Gournay's *Les Advis*). It would be interesting to know the precise bearing of Gournay's assertion on the apparent fraud involving her first autobiography (see above, "Introduction to Marie le Jars de Gournay," 10), but the facts and dates remain problematic—see Ilsley, *A Daughter of the Renaissance*, 126–27 and nn. 15 and 16.

64. The detail is taken from Pliny, *Natural History* 7.30.117. Arnould (letter to Hillman, 16 December 1999) has also aptly compared Cicero, *Brutus* 73.255. The relation between Caesar and Cicero was, in fact, a very stormy one.

Whoever provides against an assured evil by an uncertain one does not lose everything. Moreover, if they are thoroughly honest persons, they can say that they should not be deemed truly poor, in the event that they have undone themselves by such a plan, since, if they are wise, the rich cannot do without their advice, services, examples, productions—let us say even their ability, loyalty, consolation, and conversation. Was it not out of this consideration that the King of Wisdom most aptly termed the mouth, vein of life?[65] And such persons should have less shame for falling into total privation of riches, if they are forced to it, because they are most properly the creditors of those who possess wealth and commodities, by dint of the true mortgage acquired upon these things by the virtues with which those persons are replete, and of which the rich are commonly devoid, and devoid also the run-of-the-mill friends from whom the rich seek those virtues when the need arises.

The virtues of such persons rightly and truly acquire a mortgage upon those rich and their wealth, since such means lack zest, or worse, if they are not seasoned by the society of some friend endowed with those precious qualities. This is true, I stress, when the rich themselves possess them; how much more so if they do not? When a race was proposed to the monarch Alexander, he declined, because his competitors were not kings;[66] when philosophy was proposed, he threw himself into the crowd of philosophers without informing himself about their affiliations: his future character, deportment, and worth, the highest pleasures, indeed the life and breath of such a spirit as his depended on the society of that august band.[67] He who disdained elsewhere to associate with those inferior to kings seems to have been declaring these persons kings by his association. Moreover, they repaid him so well that, though unable to make him king, since he was already that by the gift of his birth, they made him king of kings.[68]

He who chooses his company and his friends by their revenues or escutcheons makes it plain enough that he cannot pay, except by these means, for his share in the association; for without doubt, he who would be more of

---

65. The King of Wisdom: again a reference to Solomon; the passage in question is Prov. 10:11, "Vena vitae os iusti, et os impiorum operit iniquitatem"—literally, "The mouth of a just man is the vein of life, and the mouth of the impious conceals injustice." (The Authorized Version diverges substantially: "The mouth of a righteous man is a well of life: but violence covereth the mouth of the wicked.")

66. *Plutarch's Lives*, Alexander, 4.5.

67. On Alexander's love of philosophy, see *Plutarch's Lives*, Alexander, esp. 8.4 and 65.

68. Compare Plutarch's testimony that Alexander loved his tutor Aristotle, "as he himself used to say, more than he did his father, for that the one had given him life, but the other had taught him a noble life" (*Plutarch's Lives*, 7:242–43 [Alexander, 8.3]).

a human being than a gentleman would seek out a human being, of whatever fortune and rank he might be, before a gentleman or, to use the name in vogue with the common people, those rich and titled Milords. And he, moreover, who looks for friendship on the basis of the number of followers and the luxurious trappings of a friend—does he not declare that the stuff of his own friendship, and of himself, is so base that it might be sufficiently paid or compensated for by a picture made for him to hang on his door, in which this friend would be painted in his magnificence, surrounded with such merchandise, as a reminder that the master of that house was honored with a great acquaintance? Surely, anyone who hoped that his person would be esteemed more highly than his wealth would honor the person more than the wealth in others in order to set a good example to all of how to do the same to him.

But it is the ordinary way of the world, and especially in this age, that the virtuous and wise are always at the homes of the powerful, and not the other way round, inasmuch as the former, and not the latter, have read the clever saying of Aristippus: "Refined souls"—which was the appellation given to the philosophers of his time—"well know the need that they have of the rich and powerful; the rich and powerful are ignorant of the need they have of them."[69] Moreover, the wise establish the true definition of the sovereign good of all things in this point—to be and to act in accordance with Nature; hence, the sovereign good of humankind, the highest and most desirable of all its advantages, consists in the employment of Right Reason, that is, in sufficiency and virtue, since humankind was born to be reasonable.[70] They maintain also that all secondary things are matters of indifference, considering that they may be rendered good or bad according to how the mind of the person knows how to use them. In any case, to set the seal on this discourse, a wretched fortune, lodged with a person of such a kind that he does harm, by his merit, to those who permit it when they can relieve it, must be borne more patiently and more proudly by its host. Why would persons of intellect and merit not have the privilege of imputing shame to those who disdain or neglect them, if they alone hold the just rule by which all things should be

69. See, again, Diogenes Laertius on Aristippus: "When Dionysius inquired what was the reason that philosophers go to rich men's houses, while rich men no longer visit philosophers, his reply was that 'the one know what they need while the other do not'" (trans. and ed. Hicks, 1:199 [2.69]).

70. A highly Aristotelian formulation, in keeping with the interest in "the Philosopher" displayed throughout the *Apology*; cf. esp. Aristotle, *Magna Moralia* 1196b–98b (1.34). See also Stephen A. White, *Sovereign Virtue: Aristotle on the Relation between Happiness and Prosperity* (Stanford, Calif., 1992), esp. 104–6. The term "Right Reason" (Gournay's "la droite Raison") was already well established in the English of the period.

valued, and if all things of worth are truly made for them, in that they cannot be made use of elsewhere except by abuse? Why would they not be recognized for lending luster to poverty, if possessions can grant it to so many fools? Or why would they be obscured for lack of riches—those who would not consent, and should not consent, to change places one for one with the rich, if those rich were not adorned with the same intelligence as they and with the same integrity of life? They are, it must be said, the treasure of the nation and of God himself, since the substance and wishes of that nation, let us say further the delight of God, consist above all in such persons. They can become what the rich are, but the greater number, almost all, of the rich cannot become what they are.

And what if, in the worst case, there is nothing left to them but the fate of Polyxena—to fall honorably, since one must fall, and falling is in the course of human affairs?[71] Yea, surely, if it is true that poverty brings its master to see himself reputed contemptible, it is yet more true that riches do not prevent their possessor from ordinarily being so in fact, "since fortunes in life go astray to inappropriate persons."[72] Lands that bear gold and silver never bear fruit. Or, to put it better, is he not rich in the most appealing way who possesses that which he neither would nor should exchange for any riches, and who would not consent for the gold or jewels of the Indies to commit a wicked act or to cause unjust affliction to anyone—who, finally, can observe in poverty, when doing so is difficult, those same laws and duties as others can scarcely at all observe in a state of plenty, when doing so is easy?

Someone termed contempt for gold the essence of justice, another

---

71. According to post-Homeric accounts of the Trojan war, Polyxena, the daughter of Priam and Hecuba, gained the love of Achilles and, after the fall of Troy, either committed suicide or was sacrificed by Achilles' vengeful son, Neoptolemus or Pyrrhus. Gournay's stoical interpretation most closely accords with that of Seneca in *Troades* (also cited in the *Equality*—see above, 88 and n. 60), esp. 1137–59, where Polyxena's gloriously transfiguring courage, as she faces the stroke of Pyrrhus, enacts a kind of moral revenge on Achilles: "cecidit, ut Achilli gravem / factura terram, prona et irato impetu" [she fell, as if thus to make the earth heavy on Achilles, prone and with an angry thud] (*Tragedies*, trans. and ed. Frank Justus Miller, 2 vols., Loeb Classical Library [London and Cambridge, Mass., 1917], 1:1158–59). Such a perspective notably matches the self-sacrifice of Alinda in the *Promenade*. Compare Boccaccio, *Concerning Famous Women*, 67 (chap. 31); and Flavius Philostratus, *The Life of Apollonius of Tyana*—a work on which Gournay will shortly be drawing (see below, 149, 153, and nn. 74 and 90)—where a contrasting reading in terms of *Liebestod* is attributed to the ghost of Achilles, who maintains that Polyxena "came of her own free will to the sepulcher, and that so high was the value she set on her own passion for him and his for her, that she threw herself upon a drawn sword" (*The Life of Apollonius of Tyana, the Epistles of Apollonius, and the Treatise of Eusebius*, trans. and ed. F. C. Conybeare, 2 vols., Loeb Classical Library [London and New York, 1912], 1:381 [4.16]).

72. "Quia sors deerrat ad parum idoneos": a generalizing adaptation of a comment in Tacitus regarding the awarding of prefectures by lot (*Annals* 13.29).

adding that gold is to man what a touchstone is to gold, because most of what is required of a human being consists in disdaining it.[73] And the famous Apollonius compared the poor possessions allotted to great and worthy masters to a noble and precious image of the gods lodged in an unsuitable temple, then went on to wonder at how much more that was worth than the inverse.[74] Thus said Cato the Elder—that he would much rather debate concerning virtue with the virtuous than concerning riches with the rich.[75] Add to this the opinion of the Stoics: honesty, they say, should be reputed the sole good of a happy life because, if life admits anything else as its good, it opens itself to all the injuries of fate by the danger of loss, while that alone cannot be snatched from it. Moreover, in this way one is in harmony with Providence, which every day gives to honest people what is called evil, and vice-versa. Besides, magnanimity is displayed in disdaining what the vulgar judge to be great. That is what those philosophers say. In conclusion, if the plan for my resources that I mentioned succeeds, so much the better, although it can now succeed only belatedly; if success is denied it, if I have to be poor, I prefer to suffer, having acted prudently to try as best I could to make a means of rising from the little I had, rather than not having done so. And I owe this testimony to the generous bounty and liberality of the King and the Queen, his mother—that

73. These are philosophical commonplaces for which we have not identified definitive sources. The first statement is close to the *chreia* (moral saw or anecdote) attributed to Aristides, said to have defined justice as "Not desiring the possessions of others" (Ronald F. Hock and Edward N. O'Neil, *The Chreia in Ancient Rhetoric*, vol. 1, *The Progymnasmata*, Society of Biblical Literature Texts and Translations, Texts and Translations 27/Graeco-Roman Religion Series 9 [Atlanta, 1986], 308 [no. 8]). The remark about gold as a means of testing the human being is strongly reminiscent of Seneca's *Moral Epistles to Lucilius*. Arnould has particularly drawn attention (letter to Hillman, 16 December 1999) to no. 17, with its emphasis on riches as an obstacle to wisdom—see esp. 17.3; the idea of the moral test is perhaps more prominent in 20.11.

74. As the mention of Thespesion below confirms (153), the reference is pretty clearly to Apollonius of Tyana, a wandering ascetic of the Neopythagorean persuasion who lived in the very early Christian era (he is said to have foretold the imminent assassination of the Emperor Domitian in 96 C.E.) and whose biography is fancifully recounted by Philostratus. We have not found a precise equivalent of Gournay's reference, but cf. the sage's opinion that persons should pray to receive whatever they deserve: "For . . . the holy . . . surely deserve to receive blessings, and the wicked the contrary. Therefore the gods, as they are beneficent, if they find anyone who is healthy and whole and unscarred by vice, will send him away, surely, after crowning him, not with golden crowns, but with all sorts of blessings; but if they find a man branded with sin and utterly corrupt, they will hand him over and leave him to justice, after inflicting their wrath upon him all the more, because he dared to invade their Temples without being pure" (Philostratus, *Life of Apollonius of Tyana*, trans. and ed. Conybeare, 1:26–29 [1.11]).

75. Cato the Elder: Marcus Porcius Cato (234–149 B.C.E.), i.e., Cato Major or Cato the Censor. The remark is translated by Perrin as follows: "I prefer to strive in bravery with the bravest, rather than in wealth with the richest" (*Plutarch's Lives*, 2: 333 [Marcus Cato, 10.4]). Arguably, Gournay's paraphrase is closer to the Greek.

they have lent a certain praiseworthy beginning to that success, in which matter Monsieur le Président Jeannin, Superintendent of Finances, that personage distinguished in councils of state and for his uprightness, did me service with their Majesties by his recommendation and the preface that he honored me by writing.

This Treatise was begun in the youth of King Louis XIII.[76]

The royal father of that good prince, just a month before his death, had commanded me to frequent the court, although I had little inclination to do so. And many of the most honorable persons of this part of the world know with what an eye he looked on me and in what way he checked the excessive license of certain wits whom my Latin and my ill fortune had induced to tell him frivolous tales about me. That gave hope to the clear-sighted that he would have alerted the King his son to honor me with his largesse, if death had not prevented him.

If my substance had been, not even according to my condition, which my second father says is another nature for everyone,[77] but merely approaching it, I would have kept myself from running the risk of hazarding my remainder. But that substance was such (if I have not sufficiently described it) that I could scarcely, in keeping with my birth, as mediocre as that is, take worse lodgings than it provided for me. If it is a pity for any other reason that I have remained in a poor state, it is certainly also so on account of the infinite and painful efforts that I have endured for the sake of avoiding it, and on account of my disposition—active, industrious, provident, of some small understanding in business, and suited to initiating and controlling income and expenditure in their proper time and place. I dare say this to you, Monsieur, who have condescended to observe me. That capacity is not such a glorious thing that I can be accused of crediting myself with it out of vanity; besides which, persons who know how to read Latin have need of such a justification in our society, which believes that those who are good at books

76. Gournay seems to have intended this italicized sentence as an explanatory note.

77. She is speaking of the "style to which she has been accustomed," with "custom" the crucial factor, according to Montaigne:

Appellons encore nature l'usage et condition de chacun de nous. . . . Car jusques là il me semble bien que nous avons quelque excuse. L'accoustumance est une second nature, et non moins puissante. . . . Et aymerois quasi esgalement qu'on m'ostat la vie, que si on me l'essimoit et retranchoit bien loing de l'estat auquel je l'ay vescue si long temps.

[Let us further term nature the practice and condition of each of us. . . . For we have good reason, it seems to me, to extend it so far. Custom is a second nature, and no less compelling. . . . And I would nearly like equally to lose my life as to have much diminished and cut back the situation in which I have lived for such a long time.]

(*Essais*, 3.10.1009–10B)

are good only at that. In truth, I would triumph more in these qualities of domestic economy with an ample and moderate task of administration than with a reduced one, but I would still not fail in the latter case to ensure that the assets would not fail me first.

What, however, are our efforts but a dam of reeds against the rushing torrent of Fortune? It fills up the two pages of life, so said the ancient proverb, and the rich Greek merchant declared of it that he acquired small possessions with great effort, large ones easily, because they cannot come into being except by the bold and surreptitious intervention of fate.[78] "No man gives a reason for his prosperity."[79] Joseph (nurtured, however, under other teachings) maintains that that blind goddess surmounts all human prudence; Sallust subscribes to this; Pliny offers her no other incense but insults; my second father, too, calls good luck and bad the sovereign deities of the world.[80] I still see the memory of a Flemish man of reputation attacked by certain pens for having,

78. As Arnould has pointed out (letter to Hillman, 16 December 1999), this reference to Lampis, which comes from Plutarch's essay, "Whether an Old Man Should Engage in Public Affairs," *Moralia* 787A, was also collected in Lycosthenes, *Theatrum vitae humanae*, "De Divitiis et Opibus" [On riches and wealth]. In Plutarch, the point concerns not fortune but rather the relative ease of preserving great political power and reputation once acquired.

79. "Rationem felicitatis nemo reddit." Dezon-Jones (in her edition of the *Apology* in *Fragments*, 182 n. 32) has identified the source of this statement as Decimus Magnus Ausonius (the poet and teacher of the fourth century C.E.), "The Thanksgiving of Ausonius of Bordeaux, the Vasate, for his Consulship, Addressed to the Emperor Gratian," *Ausonius* 5. In connection with his theme, Ausonius is commenting on the unaccountability of divine (and quasi-divine) blessings; the fact that he was a Christian helps to explain Gournay's subsequent reference to Josephus, who was Jewish.

80. Gournay's words ("mon second Pere appelle aussi l'heur & le mal heur, souveraines Deïtez du Monde") are indeed close to Montaigne's: "L'heur et le mal'heur sont à mon gré deux souveraines puissances" [Happiness and unhappiness are, in my view, two sovereign powers] (*Essais*, 3.8.934B).

Joseph: i.e., Flavius Josephus; Gournay follows Montaigne's account of an occasion when Fortune displayed extraordinary power in saving the life of Josephus "outre toute raison humaine" [beyond all human reason] (2.3.355A); the allusion is clearly to Josephus's *Life* 28–29, where, however, that author actually speaks of putting his trust in God and employing a successful stratagem. Sallust states bluntly (in words cited in Latin by Montaigne, 2.16.621C), "But beyond question Fortune holds sway everywhere. It is she that makes all events famous or obscure according to her caprice rather than in accordance with the truth" (*Sallust*, trans. and ed. J. C. Rolfe, rev. ed., Loeb Classical Library [London and Cambridge, Mass., 1931], 14–15 [The War with Cataline, 7.1]). The Pliny intended is probably the Younger—Caius Plinius Caecilius Secundus (ca. 61–112 C.E.). Arnould has suggested (letter to Hillman, 16 December 1999) that Gournay recalled mainly Pliny's *Letters*, 4.24, where the vicissitudes of fortune are accentuated; she may also have had in mind Pliny's account in 4.11 of an exiled Roman praetor, newly become a teacher of rhetoric, who began his lectures by attacking Fortune with "a sarcasm so full of gall, that I fancy he turned rhetorician on purpose to utter it" (*Letters*, trans. and ed. William Melmoth, rev. ed. by W. M. L. Hutchinson, 2 vols., Loeb Classical Library [London and Cambridge, Mass., 1915], 1:303).

in their opinion, extended the prerogatives of destiny too far;[81] and Theophrastus speaks of it in this fashion: "Fate, not Prudence, guides our lives."[82] Moreover, Plato attributes all things to destiny,[83] a statement I believe the Stoics are not far from endorsing—nor the Epicureans from saying as much, if not of destiny, at least of chance.

And not only is he who deserves and serves felicity not happy, but (a strange matter!) he is not unhappy who seeks out and serves unhappiness: witness some ancient examples and the rich diamond of the Tyrant Polycrates, voluntarily thrown into the sea by its master so that he might find a source of affliction in this, then carried back to him,[84] Fortune thwarting his foolish intention of thereby paying some of the tribute that her vicissitudes and revolutions require of us—in her own fashion, however, not in ours. Shall I forget a marvel of our times—that those two deluded and tragically impaired minds, Poltrot and Clément, could never be found out, although they had revealed their schemes to everyone and those schemes were so momentous and clamorous in themselves?[85] A story drawn from a certain comedy would not be beside the point in this discussion.[86] According to this,

---

81. The reference is clearly to Lipsius. The latter's Neostoicism, as set out in the enormously popular *De Constantia* (On constancy [1584]), assigns a large role to fate, and he was indeed accused of reverting to pagan ideas. Arnould has particularly signaled (letter to Hillman, 16 December 1999) the attack of the Jesuit controversialist François Garasse in the revealingly entitled work (of over a thousand pages in quarto!), *La Doctrine curieuse des beaux esprits de ce temps, ou prétendus tels, contenant plusieurs maximes pernicieuses à la religion, à l'Estat et aux bonnes moeurs, combattue et renversée* . . . [The strange doctrine of the great minds of this age, or those who claim to be such, containing various maxims pernicious to religion, to the state, and to sound morality, combated and overthrown . . .] (Paris, 1623), 343. See also Gerhard Oestreich, *Neostoicism and the Early Modern State*, ed. Brigitta Oestreich and H. G. Koenigsberger, trans. David McLintock (Cambridge, 1982), esp. 23 and 29.

82. Theophrastus (ca. 370–285 B.C.E.) was the disciple and successor of Aristotle. Cicero (*Tusculan Disputations* 5.9.25) defends him for endorsing this statement and is, in turn, followed by Montaigne (*Essais*, 3.9.984C).

83. Gournay appears to have in mind the account of Necessity and of the Fates, her daughters, in *The Republic* 10.616C–10.621A. See also *Laws* 818B–D.

84. As noted by Beaulieu and Fournier (in Gournay's *Les Advis*), the reference is to Polycrates of Samos (sixth century B.C.E.); see Herodotus, 3.41–42, where the jewel, however, is actually an emerald set in gold.

85. The Huguenot gentleman Jean de Poltrot, seigneur de Méré, assassinated François, duke of Guise, leader of the radical Catholic faction, in 1563—an incident "avenged" during the massacre of Saint Bartholomew (1572) by Guise's son and heir, Henri, upon the supposed instigator, Gaspard de Châtillon, Admiral Coligny. In turn, the murder of Henri III in 1589 by the Dominican Friar, Jacques Clément, was largely in retribution for the king's assassination, in the last days of the previous year, of the same Henri, duke of Guise, and his brother, the cardinal of Lorraine. Gournay, then, is carefully straddling the religious and political fence.

86. We have not identified the "comedy."

a great tree planted in the naval of the universe measures the sphere of the earth with the extent of its branches, in which are scattered all sorts of good and evil gifts hanging among the leaves, and Fortune, seated at the top of that tree, incessantly beats the branches with a long rod of gold, whence it happens that as men, by chance, go restlessly to and fro beneath it day and night, sometimes riches tumble upon them, sometimes poverty—here the cap of a counselor, there the robe of a pauper, here a scepter, there a fool's bauble, and so forth, without choice or purpose. Aristotle tops that opinion, maintaining that, to have more fully the honor of great successes, that goddess deliberately extends them to those least able to attribute them to their prudence.[87] And Solomon has always seen, he says in Ecclesiastes, the brave without victory, the wise man without bread.[88] "Somehow or other poverty is sister to good sense"—so said a celebrated Roman courtier.[89] In this regard, we must not forget the opinion of Thespesion, the notable Gymnosophist, who, on the example of Palamedes, Socrates, Aristides, and Phocion, concluded and preached that the gods had ordained that equity can never be happy in this world: "It seemed otherwise to the gods."[90] Likewise Ezekiel intones that God scourges every child he recognizes as his own[91]—"and even the Son of man has found no stone on which to rest his head."[92]

In the end, the prudence of mankind has never been able to square the justice of the decrees of Divine Providence with human fortunes, which are

87. Arnould (letter to Hillman, 16 December 1999) has aptly suggested a reworking of the *Nicomachean Ethics* 1099b (1.9), whose subject includes the role of fortune in producing happiness. Gournay may also have had in mind, again, the *Eudemian Ethics*, where Aristotle takes up fortune and prudence (1246b–48b [7.14]). In both cases, she would be skewing the philosopher's perspective in making it ironic and absolute. White, *Sovereign Virtue*, 119–22, usefully discusses fortune in the Aristotelian context.

88. Compare Eccles. 9:11: "I returned, and saw under the sun, that the race is not to the swift, nor the battle to the strong, neither yet bread to the wise, nor yet riches to men of understanding, nor yet favor to men of skill; but time and chance happeneth to them all."

89. That is, Petronius Arbiter (first century C.E.); the wry comment ("Nescio quo fato bonae mentis soror est paupertas") is found in his *Satyricon* 84.

90. "Diis aliter visum" (*Aeneid* 2.428)—with reference to the fall of the most deserving and fairminded of the Trojans. The distinguished men named all suffered unjustly from betrayal or ingratitude; with the exception of Phocion, all of them are indeed cited by Thespesion, the chief of the so-called naked sages, in conversation with Apollonius in Philostratus, *Life of Apollonius* 6.21. Socrates, moreover, compares himself to Palamedes in the *Apologies* of both Plato (41B) and Xenophon (26). In addition to the life of Phocion, previously cited, Plutarch also wrote that of Aristides.

91. The theme runs throughout Ezekiel. Perhaps the most closely parallel passage is the following: "Behold, all souls are mine; as the soul of the father, so also the soul of the son is mine: the soul that sinneth, it shall die" (18:4).

92. Compare Matt. 8:20, Luke 9:58.

commonly, to our eyes, so inappropriate, in good and in bad, to the objects on which they are conferred. Let us leave off these disagreeable speeches and say, or reiterate, Monsieur, that I have crafted this Apology in writing so that, by means of it, you may deign, and be able more easily, to defend me against the follies of popular gossip, since it places in the hands of your prudence and your affection, already disposed to render me that service, exact knowledge of my actions and my affairs—knowledge, however, largely present in you in outline, thanks to the long acquaintance with you that I have had the honor of enjoying. God bless your person and all your actions, the perfection and crown of which consist only in following their accustomed course.

BIBLIOGRAPHY

PRIMARY WORKS

Agrippa, Henricus Cornelius. *Declamation on the Nobility and Preeminence of the Female Sex.* Translated and edited by Albert Rabil, Jr. The Other Voice in Early Modern Europe. Chicago: University of Chicago Press, 1996.

Alberti, Leon Battista (1404–72). *The Family in Renaissance Florence.* Translated by Renée Neu Watkins. Columbia: University of South Carolina Press, 1969.

Arenal, Electa, and Stacey Schlau, eds. *Untold Sisters: Hispanic Nuns in Their Own Works.* Translated by Amanda Powell. Albuquerque: University of New Mexico Press, 1989.

Ariosto, Ludovico (1474–1533). *Orlando Furioso.* Translated by Barbara Reynolds. 2 vols. New York: Penguin Books, 1975, 1977.

Astell, Mary (1666–1731). *The First English Feminist: Reflections on Marriage and Other Writings.* Edited and with an introduction by Bridget Hill. New York: St. Martin's Press, 1986.

Atherton, Margaret, ed. *Women Philosophers of the Early Modern Period.* Indianapolis: Hackett Publishing, 1994.

Aughterson, Kate, ed. *Renaissance Woman: Constructions of Femininity in England: A Source Book.* London and New York: Routledge, 1995.

Barbaro, Francesco (1390–1454). *On Wifely Duties* (preface and bk. 2). Translated by Benjamin Kohl. In *The Earthly Republic: Italian Humanists on Government and Society,* edited by Benjamin Kohl and R. G. Witt, with Elizabeth B. Welles, 179–228. Philadelphia: University of Pennsylvania Press, 1978.

Behn, Aphra. *The Works of Aphra Behn.* 7 vols. Edited by Janet Todd. Columbus: Ohio State University Press, 1992–96.

Boccaccio, Giovanni (1313–75). *Concerning Famous Women.* Translated and edited by Guido R. Guarino. Rutgers, N.J.: Rutgers University Press, 1963.

———. *Corbaccio; Or, the Labyrinth of Love.* Translated by Anthony K. Cassell. 2d rev. ed. Binghamton, N.Y.: Medieval and Renaissance Texts and Studies, 1993.

Bruni, Leonardo (1370–1444). "On the Study of Literature (1405) to Lady Battista Malatesta of Moltefeltro." In *The Humanism of Leonardo Bruni: Selected Texts.* Translated and with an introduction by Gordon Griffiths, James Hankins, and David Thompson, 240–51. Binghamton, N.Y.: Medieval and Renaissance Studies and Texts, 1987.

Castiglione, Baldassare (1478–1529). *The Book of the Courtier.* Translated by George Bull. New York: Penguin, 1967.

Cerasano, S. P., and Marion Wynne-Davies, eds. *Readings in Renaissance Women's Drama: Criticism, History, and Performance, 1594–1998.* London and New York: Routledge, 1998.

Christine de Pizan (1365–1431). *The Book of the City of Ladies.* Translated by Earl Jeffrey Richards. Foreword Marina Warner. New York: Persea Books, 1982.

————. *The Treasure of the City of Ladies.* Translated by Sarah Lawson. New York: Viking Penguin, 1985.

————. *The Treasure of the City of Ladies.* Translated by and introduction by Charity Cannon Willard. Edited and with an introduction by Madeleine P. Cosman. New York: Persea Books, 1989.

Clement of Alexandria. *The Miscellanies (Stromata), Bks. 2–8.*Vol. 2 of *The Writings of Clement of Alexandria.* Translated by William Wilson. Ante-Nicene Christian Library, vol. 12. Edinburgh: T. & T. Clark, 1869.

Crawford, Patricia, and Laura Gowing, eds. *Women's Worlds in Seventeenth-Century England: A Source Book.* London and New York: Routledge, 2000.

Elizabeth I: Collected Works. Edited by Leah S. Marcus, Janel Mueller, and Mary Beth Rose. Chicago: University of Chicago Press, 2000.

Elyot, Thomas (1490–1546). *Defence of Good Women.* In *The Feminist Controversy of the Renaissance: Facsimile Reproductions.* Edited by Diane Bornstein. Delmar, N.Y.: Scholars' Facsimiles and Reprints, 1980.

Erasmus, Desiderius (1467–1536). *Erasmus on Women.* Edited by Erika Rummel. Toronto: University of Toronto Press, 1996.

Erauso, Catalina De. *Lieutenant Nun: Memoir of a Basque Transvestite in the New World.* Translated by Michele Ttepto and Gabriel Stepto; foreword by Marjorie Garber. Boston: Beacon Press, 1995.

Ferguson, Moira, ed. *First Feminists: British Women Writers, 1578–1799.* Bloomington: Indiana University Press, 1985.

Glückel of Hameln (1646–1724). *The Memoirs of Glückel of Hameln.* Translated by Marvin Lowenthal. New introduction by Robert Rosen. New York: Schocken Books, 1977.

Gournay, Marie le Jars de. *Les Advis; Ou, Les Presens de la Demoiselle de Gournay 1641.* Gen. eds. Jean-Philippe Beaulieu and Hannah Fournier. 3 vols. Amsterdam and Atlanta: Rodopi, 1997–.

————. *Égalité des hommes et des femmes, Grief des dames, Le Proumenoir de Monsieur de Montaigne.* Edited by Constant Venesoen. Textes littéraires français. Geneva: Droz, 1993.

————. *"The Equality of Men and Women and The Ladies' Grievance."* Translated with a biographical introduction by Maja Bijvoet. In *Women Writers of the Seventeenth Century,* edited by Katharina M. Wilson and Frank J. Warnke, 3–29. Athens: University of Georgia Press, 1989.

————. *Fragments d'un discours féminin.* Edited by Élyane Dezon-Jones. Paris: Corti, 1988.

————. *"Imitation of the Life of Damoiselle de Gournay."* Translated by Élyane Dezon-Jones. In *Writings by Pre-Revolutionary French Women: From Marie de France to Élisabeth Vigée–Le Brun,* edited by Anne R. Larsen and Colette H. Winn, 237–41. Women Writers of the World, vol. 2. Garland Reference Library of the Humanities, vol. 2111. New York: Garland, 2000.

———. *Oeuvres complètes.* Edited by J.-C. Arnould, E. Berriot, C. Blum, A.-L. Franchetti, M.-C. Thomine, and V. Worth, under the direction of J.-C. Arnould. Paris: Champion, 2002 (in press).

———. *"Of the Equality of Men and Women* and *The Complaint of the Ladies."* Translated by Eva M. Sartori. *Allegorica* 9 (Winter 1987): 135–63.

———. *L'Ombre de la damoiselle de Gournay.* Paris: Jean Libert, 1626.

———. "Préface de 1599 publiée dans *Le Proumenoir."* Edited by Anna Lia Franchetti. *Montaigne Studies: An Interdisciplinary Forum* 8, nos. 1–2 (1996): 179–92.

———. "Préface to Montaigne's '*Essais*' (1595)." In *La première réception des Essais de Montaigne (1580–1640)*, edited by Olivier Millet, 79–128. Études montaignistes, 24. Paris: Champion, 1995.

———. *Preface to the Essays of Michel de Montaigne by His Adoptive Daughter, Marie le Jars de Gournay.* Translated with supplementary annotation by Richard Hillman and Colette Quesnel from the ed. prepared by François Rigolot. Tempe, Ariz.: Medieval and Renaissance Texts and Studies, 1998.

———. "Preface to the 1617 Edition of the *Essais.*" Edited by Mary McKinley. *Montaigne Studies: An Interdisciplinary Forum* 8, nos. 1–2 (1996): 203–19.

———. *Le Proumenoir de Monsieur de Montaigne (1594) by Marie le Jars de Gournay: A Facsimile Reproduction with an Introduction by Patricia Francis Cholakian.* Delmar, N.Y.: Scholars' Facsimiles and Reprints, 1985.

———. *Le Promenoir de Monsieur de Montaigne: Texte de 1641, avec les variantes des éditions de 1594, 1595, 1598, 1599, 1607, 1623, 1626, 1627, 1634.* Edited by Jean-Claude Arnould. Études montaignistes, 26. Paris: Champion, 1996.

Gregory of Nyssa, Saint. *The Life of St. Macrina.* In *Ascetical Works.* Translated by Virginia Woods Callahan, 163–91. Fathers of the Church, 58. Washington, D.C.: Catholic University of America Press, 1967.

Guillaume de Lorris, and Jean de Meun. *The Romance of the Rose.* Translated by Charles Dahlbert. Princeton, N.J.: Princeton University Press, 1971; reprinted, Hanover, N.H.: University Press of New England, 1983.

Henderson, Katherine Usher, and Barbara F. McManus, eds. *Half Humankind: Contexts and Texts of the Controversy about Women in England, 1540–1640.* Urbana: University of Illinois Press, 1985.

Jerome, Saint. *Against Jovinianus.* In *The Principal Works of St. Jerome.* Translated by W. H. Fremantle, G. Lewis, and W. G. Martley, 346–416. A Select Library of Nicene and Post-Nicene Fathers of the Christian Church, 2d ser., vol. 6. New York: Christian Literature Co., 1893; reprinted in facsimile, Grand Rapids, Mich.: Eerdmans Publishing, 1989.

———. *In Sophoniam Prophetam.* In *Commentarii in Prophetas Minores,* pt. 1.6 of *S. Hieronymi Presbyteri Opera,* edited by M. Adriaen, 655–711. Corpus Christianorum Series Latina, vol. 76A. Turnhout: Brepols, 1970.

———. *Letters.* In *The Principal Works of St. Jerome.* Translated by W. H. Fremantle, G. Lewis, and W. G. Martley, 1–295. A Select Library of Nicene and Post-Nicene Fathers of the Christian Church, 2d ser., vol. 6. New York: Christian Literature Co., 1893; reprinted in facsimile, Grand Rapids, Mich.: Eerdmans Publishing, 1989.

Joscelin, Elizabeth. *The Mothers Legacy to Her Unborn Childe.* Edited by Jean leDrew Metcalfe. Toronto: University of Toronto Press, 2000.

Kaminsky, Amy Katz, ed. *Water Lilies, Flores del agua: An Anthology of Spanish Women Writers from the Fifteenth through the Nineteenth Century.* Minneapolis: University of Minnesota Press, 1996.

Kempe, Margery (1373–1439). *The Book of Margery Kempe.* Translated by Barry Windeatt. New York: Viking Penguin, 1986.

King, Margaret L., and Albert Rabil, Jr., eds. *Her Immaculate Hand: Selected Works by and about the Women Humanists of Quattrocento Italy.* 2d rev. ed. Binghamton, N.Y.: Medieval and Renaissance Texts and Studies, 1991.

Klein, Joan Larsen, ed. *Daughters, Wives, and Widows: Writings by Men about Women and Marriage in England, 1500–1640.* Urbana: University of Illinois Press, 1992.

Knox, John (1505–72). *The Political Writings of John Knox: The First Blast of the Trumpet against the Monstrous Regiment of Women and Other Selected Works.* Edited by Marvin A. Breslow. Washington, D.C.: Folger Shakespeare Library, 1985.

Kors, Alan C., and Edward Peters, eds. *Witchcraft in Europe, 1100–1700: A Documentary History.* Philadelphia: University of Pennsylvania Press, 1972.

Krämer, Heinrich, and Jacob Sprenger. *Malleus Maleficarum (ca. 1487).* Translated by Montague Summers. London: Pushkin Press, 1928; reprinted, New York: Dover, 1971.

Larsen, Anne R., and Colette H. Winn, eds. *Writings by Pre-Revolutionary French Women: From Marie de France to Elizabeth Vigée-Le Brun.* New York and London: Garland Publishing Co., 2000.

Marguerite d'Angoulême, Queen of Navarre (1492–1549). *The Heptameron.* Translated by P. A. Chilton. New York: Viking Penguin, 1984.

Montaigne, Michel de. *The Complete Essays of Montaigne.* Translated by Donald M. Frame. Stanford, Calif.: Stanford University Press, 1958.

———. *Les Essais de Michel de Montaigne.* Edited by Pierre Villey. Reissued under the direction of, and with a preface by, V.-L. Saulnier. Paris: Presses Universitaires de France, 1965.

Plutarch. *Bravery of Women.* In *Plutarch's Moralia.* Translated and edited by Frank Cole Babbitt, 471–581. 14 vols. Loeb Classical Library, vol. 3. London: Heinemann; Cambridge, Mass.: Harvard University Press, 1931.

Russell, Rinaldina, ed. *Sister Maria Celeste's Letters to Her Father, Galileo.* San Jose, Calif., and New York: Writers Club Press, 2000.

Taillemont, Claude de. *Discours des Champs faëz: A l'honneur, et exaltation de l'Amour et des Dames [1553].* Edited by Jean-Claude Arnould. Textes littéraires français. Geneva: Droz, 1991.

Teresa of Avila, Saint (1515–82). *The Life of Saint Teresa of Avila by Herself.* Translated by J. M. Cohen. New York: Viking Penguin, 1957.

Weyer, Johann (1515–88). *Witches, Devils, and Doctors in the Renaissance: Johann Weyer, De praestigiis daemonum.* Edited by George Mora with Benjamin G. Kohl, Erik Midelfort, and Helen Bacon. Translated by John Shea. Binghamton, N.Y.: Medieval and Renaissance Texts and Studies, 1991.

Wilson, Katharina M., ed. *Medieval Women Writers.* Athens: University of Georgia Press, 1984.

———, ed. *Women Writers of the Renaissance and Reformation.* Athens: University of Georgia Press, 1987.

Wilson, Katharina M., and Frank J. Warnke, eds. *Women Writers of the Seventeenth Century.* Athens: University of Georgia Press, 1989.

Wollstonecraft, Mary. *A Vindication of the Rights of Men and a Vindication of the Rights of Women.* Edited by Sylvana Tomaselli. Cambridge: Cambridge University Press, 1995.

———. *The Vindications of the Rights of Men, the Rights of Women.* Edited by D. L. Macdonald and Kathleen Scherf. Peterborough, Ontario: Broadview Press, 1997.

Women Writers in English, 1350–1850. 15 vols. Oxford: Oxford University Press. (Projected 30-vol. series suspended.)

Wroth, Lady Mary. *The Countess of Montgomery's Urania.* 2 pts. Edited by Josephine A. Roberts. Tempe, Ariz.: Medieval and Renaissance Texts and Studies, 1995, 1999.

———. *The Poems of Lady Mary Wroth.* Edited by Josephine A. Roberts. Baton Rouge: Louisiana State University Press, 1983.

Zayas, Maria de. *The Disenchantments of Love.* Translated by H. Patsy Boyer. Albany: State University of New York Press, 1997.

———. *The Enchantments of Love: Amorous and Exemplary Novels.* Translated by H. Patsy Boyer. Berkeley: University of California Press, 1990.

SECONDARY WORKS

Akkerman, Tjitske, and Siep Sturman, eds. *Feminist Thought in European History, 1400–2000.* London and New York: Routledge, 1997.

Albistur, Maïté, and Daniel Armogath. *Histoire du féminisme français du moyen âge à nos jours.* [Paris]: Éditions des Femmes, 1977.

Angenot, Marc. *Les Champions des femmes: Examen du discours sur la supériorité des femmes.* Montreal: Presses de l'Université du Québec, 1977.

Arnould, Jean-Claude, ed. *Marie de Gournay et l'Édition de 1595 des Essais de Montaigne: Actes du Colloque organisé par la Société Internationale des Amis de Montaigne les 9 et 10 juin 1995, en Sorbonne.* Paris: Champion, 1996.

Barash, Carol. *English Women's Poetry, 1649–1714: Politics, Community, and Linguistic Authority.* New York and Oxford: Oxford University Press, 1996.

Battigelli, Anna. *Margaret Cavendish and the Exiles of the Mind.* Lexington: University of Kentucky Press, 1998.

Bauschatz, Cathleen M. "Imitation, Writing, and Self-Study in Marie de Gournay's 1595 'Préface' to Montaigne's Essais." In *Contending Kingdoms: Historical, Psychological, and Feminist Approaches to the Literature of Sixteenth-Century England and France,* edited by Marie-Rose Logan and Peter L. Rudnytsky, 346–64. Detroit: Wayne State University Press, 1991.

———. "'Les Puissances de Vostre Empire': Changing Power Relations in Marie de Gournay's *Le Proumenoir de Monsieur de Montaigne* from 1594 to 1626." In *Renaissance Women Writers: French Texts/American Contexts,* edited by Anne R. Larsen and Colette H. Winn, 189–208. Detroit: Wayne State University Press, 1994.

———. "Marie de Gournay's 'Préface de 1595': A Critical Evaluation." *Bulletin de la Société des Amis de Montaigne* 3–4 (1986): 73–82.

Beilin, Elaine V. *Redeeming Eve: Women Writers of the English Renaissance.* Princeton, N.J.: Princeton University Press, 1987.

Benson, Pamela Joseph. *The Invention of Renaissance Woman: The Challenge of Female Independence in the Literature and Thought of Italy and England.* University Park: Pennsylvania State University Press, 1992.

Blain, Virginia, Isobel Grundy, and Patricia Clements, eds. *The Feminist Companion to Literature in English: Women Writers from the Middle Ages to the Present.* New Haven, Conn.: Yale University Press, 1990.

Bloch, R. Howard. *Medieval Misogyny and the Invention of Western Romantic Love.* Chicago: University of Chicago Press, 1991.

Boase, Alan M. *The Fortunes of Montaigne: A History of the Essais in France, 1580–1669.* 1935; reprinted, New York: Octagon Books, 1970.

Bonnefon, Paul. *Montaigne et ses amis: La Boétie, Charron, Mlle de Gournay.* 2 vols. 1898; reprinted, Geneva: Slatkine, 1969.

———. "Une supercherie de Mlle de Gournay." *Revue d'histoire littéraire de la France* 3 (1896): 71–89.

Bornstein, Daniel, and Roberto Rusconi, eds. *Women and Religion in Medieval and Renaissance Italy.* Translated by Margery J. Schneider. Chicago: University of Chicago Press, 1996.

Brant, Clare, and Diane Purkiss, eds. *Women, Texts and Histories, 1575–1760.* London and New York: Routledge, 1992.

Briggs, Robin. *Witches and Neighbours: The Social and Cultural Context of European Witchcraft.* New York: HarperCollins, 1995; New York: Viking Penguin, 1996.

Brown, Judith C. *Immodest Acts: The Life of a Lesbian Nun in Renaissance Italy.* New York: Oxford University Press, 1986.

Cervigni, Dino S., ed. *Women Mystic Writers.* Volume 13 of *Annali d'Italianistica* (1995).

Cervigni, Dino S., and Rebecca West, eds. *Women's Voices in Italian Literature.* Volume 7 of *Annali d'Italianistica* (1989).

Charlton, Kenneth. *Women, Religion and Education in Early Modern England.* London and New York: Routledge, 1999.

Chojnacka, Monica. *Working Women in Early Modern Venice.* Baltimore: Johns Hopkins University Press, 2001.

Chojnacki, Stanley. *Women and Men in Renaissance Venice: Twelve Essays on Patrician Society.* Baltimore: Johns Hopkins University Press, 2000.

Cholakian, Patricia Francis. "The Identity of the Reader in Marie de Gournay's *Le Proumenoir de Monsieur de Montaigne* (1594)." In *Seeing the Woman in Late Medieval and Renaissance Writings,* edited by Sheila Fisher and Janet E. Hailley, 207–32. Knoxville: University of Tennessee Press, 1989.

———. *Rape and Writing in the "Heptameron" of Marguerite de Navarre.* Carbondale and Edwardsville: Southern Illinois University Press, 1991.

———. *Women and the Politics of Self-Representation in Seventeenth-Century France.* Newark: University of Delaware Press, 2000.

Davis, Natalie Zemon. *Society and Culture in Early Modern France.* Stanford, Calif.: Stanford University Press, 1975. See, esp., chaps. 3 and 5.

———. *Women on the Margins: Three Seventeenth-Century Lives.* Cambridge, Mass.: Harvard University Press, 1995.

Debaisieux, Martine. "Marie de Gournay cont(r)e la tradition: Du *Proumenoir de Monsieur de Montaigne* aux versions de l'Énéide." *Renaissance and Reformation/Renaissance et Réforme,* n.s., 21, no. 2 (1997): 45–58.

DeJean, Joan. *Ancients against Moderns: Culture Wars and the Making of a Fin de Siècle.* Chicago: University of Chicago Press, 1997.

————. *Tender Geographies: Women and the Origins of the Novel in France.* New York: Columbia University Press, 1991.

Desan, Philippe. "The Book, the Friend, the Woman: Montaigne's Circular Exchanges." Translated by Brad Bassler. In *Contending Kingdoms: Historical, Psychological, and Feminist Approaches to the Literature of Sixteenth-Century England and France,* edited by Marie-Rose Logan and Peter L. Rudnytsky, 225–62. Detroit: Wayne State University Press, 1991.

Dezon-Jones, Élyane. "Marie de Gournay: le je/u/ palimpseste." *L'Esprit créateur* 23, no. 2 (1983): 26–36.

————. "Marie le Jars de Gournay (1565-1645)." In *French Women Writers: A Bio-bibliographical Source Book,* edited by Eva M. Sartori and Dorothy Wynne Zimmerman, 198–217. New York: Greenwood, 1991.

Dixon, Laurinda S. *Perilous Chastity: Women and Illness in Pre-Enlightenment Art and Medicine.* Ithaca, N.Y.: Cornell University Press, 1995.

Dolan, Frances, E. *Whores of Babylon: Catholicism, Gender and Seventeenth-Century Print Culture.* Ithaca, N.Y.: Cornell University Press, 1999.

Donovan, Josephine. *Women and the Rise of the Novel, 1405–1726.* New York: St. Martin's Press, 1999.

Duby, George, Michelle Perrot, and Pauline Schmitt Pantel, eds. *A History of Women in the West.* Vol. 1, *From Ancient Goddesses to Christian Saints,* edited by Pauline Schmitt Pantel. Vol. 2, *Silences of the Middle Ages,* edited by Christiane Klapisch-Zuber. Vol. 3, *Renaissance and Enlightenment Paradoxes,* edited by Natalie Zemon Davis and Arlette Farge. Cambridge, Mass.: Harvard University Press, 1992–93.

Erickson, Amy Louise. *Women and Property in Early Modern England.* London and New York: Routledge, 1993.

Ezell, Margaret J. M. *Writing Women's Literary History.* Baltimore: Johns Hopkins University Press, 1993.

Ferguson, Margaret W., Maureen Quilligan, and Nancy J. Vickers, eds. *Rewriting the Renaissance: The Discourses of Sexual Difference in Early Modern Europe.* Chicago: University of Chicago Press, 1987.

Fletcher, Anthony. *Gender, Sex and Subordination in England, 1500–1800.* New Haven, Conn.: Yale University Press, 1995.

Frye, Susan, and Karen Robertson, eds. *Maids and Mistresses, Cousins and Queens: Women's Alliances in Early Modern England.* Oxford: Oxford University Press, 1999.

Gallagher, Catherine. *Nobody's Story: The Vanishing Acts of Women Writers in the Marketplace, 1670–1820.* Berkeley: University of California Press, 1994.

Ganley, Anne Hunter. "The Journal of Marie le Jars de Gournay." Master's thesis. Louisiana State University in Shreveport, 1992.

Gelbart, Nina Rattner. *The King's Midwife: A History and Mystery of Madame du Coudray.* Berkeley: University of California Press, 1998.

Goldberg, Jonathan. *Desiring Women Writing: English Renaissance Examples.* Stanford, Calif.: Stanford University Press, 1997.

Goldsmith, Elizabeth C., ed. *Writing the Female Voice.* Boston: Northeastern University Press, 1989.

Goldsmith, Elizabeth C., and Dena Goodman, eds. *Going Public: Women and Publishing in Early Modern France.* Ithaca, N.Y.: Cornell University Press, 1995.

Greer, Margaret Rich. *Maria de Zayas.* University Park: Pennsylvania State University Press, 2000.

Hall, Kim F. *Things of Darkness: Economies of Race and Gender in Early Modern England.* Ithaca, N.Y.: Cornell University Press, 1995.

Hampton, Timothy. *Literature and the Nation in the Sixteenth Century: Inventing Renaissance France.* Ithaca, N.Y.: Cornell University Press, 2001.

Hardwick, Julie. *The Practice of Patriarchy: Gender and the Politics of Household Authority in Early Modern France.* University Park: Pennsylvania State University Press, 1998.

Haselkorn, Anne M., and Betty Travitsky, eds. *The Renaissance Englishwoman in Print: Counterbalancing the Canon.* Amherst: University of Massachusetts Press, 1990.

Herlihy, David. "Did Women Have a Renaissance? A Reconsideration." *Medievalia et Humanistica,* n.s., 13 (1985): 1–22.

Hill, Bridget. *The Republican Virago: The Life and Times of Catharine Macaulay, Historian.* New York: Oxford University Press, 1992.

Hillman, Richard. "Hamlet et la *Préface* de Marie de Gournay." *Renaissance and Reformation/Renaissance et Réforme,* n.s., 18, no. 3 (1994): 29–42.

———. *Self-Speaking in Medieval and Early Modern English Drama: Subjectivity, Discourse and the Stage.* Basingstoke: Macmillan; New York: St. Martin's, 1997.

Holmes, Peggy P. "Mlle de Gournay's Defence of Baroque Imagery." *French Studies* 8 (1954): 122–31.

Horowitz, Maryanne Cline. "Aristotle and Women." *Journal of the History of Biology* 9 (1976): 183–213.

———. "Marie de Gournay, Editor of the *Essais* of Michel de Montaigne: A Case-Study in Mentor-Protégée Friendship." *Sixteenth Century Journal* 17 (1986): 271–84.

Hufton, Olwen H. *The Prospect before Her: A History of Women in Western Europe.* Vol. 1, *1500–1800.* New York: HarperCollins, 1996.

Hull, Suzanne W. *Chaste, Silent, and Obedient: English Books for Women, 1475–1640.* San Marino, Calif.: Huntington Library, 1982.

Hutner, Heidi, ed. *Rereading Aphra Behn: History, Theory, and Criticism.* Charlottesville: University Press of Virginia, 1993.

Hutson, Lorna, ed. *Feminism and Renaissance Studies.* New York: Oxford University Press, 1999.

Ilsley, Marjorie Henry. *A Daughter of the Renaissance: Marie le Jars de Gournay: Her Life and Works.* The Hague: Mouton, 1963.

James, Susan E. *Kateryn Parr: The Making of a Queen.* Aldershot and Brookfield: Ashgate Publishing, 1999.

Jankowski, Theodora A. *Women in Power in the Early Modern Drama.* Urbana: University of Illinois Press, 1992.

Jed, Stephanie H. *Chaste Thinking: The Rape of Lucretia and the Birth of Humanism.* Bloomington: Indiana University Press, 1989.

Joran, Théodore. *Les Féministes avant le féminisme.* Paris: Savaète, 1910.

Jordan, Constance. *Renaissance Feminism: Literary Texts and Political Models.* Ithaca, N.Y.: Cornell University Press, 1990.

Kelly, Joan. "Did Women Have a Renaissance?" In her *Women, History, and Theory.* Chicago: University of Chicago Press, 1984. Reprinted in *Becoming Visible: Women in European History,* edited by Renate Bridenthal, Claudia Koonz, and Susan M. Stuard. 3d ed. Boston: Houghton Mifflin, 1998.

———. "Early Feminist Theory and the Querelle des Femmes." In her *Women, History, and Theory.* Chicago: University of Chicago Press, 1984.

Kelso, Ruth. *Doctrine for the Lady of the Renaissance.* Foreword by Katharine M. Rogers. 1956; reprinted, Urbana: University of Illinois Press, 1978.

King, Carole. *Renaissance Women Patrons: Wives and Widows in Italy, c. 1300–1550.* New York and Manchester: Manchester University Press, 1998.

King, Margaret L. *Women of the Renaissance.* Foreword by Catharine R. Stimpson. Chicago: University of Chicago Press, 1991.

Krontiris, Tina. *Oppositional Voices: Women as Writers and Translators of Literature in the English Renaissance.* London and New York: Routledge, 1992.

Kuehn, Thomas. *Law, Family, and Women: Toward a Legal Anthropology of Renaissance Italy.* Chicago: University of Chicago Press, 1991.

Kunze, Bonnelyn Young. *Margaret Fell and the Rise of Quakerism.* Stanford, Calif.: Stanford University Press, 1994.

Labalme, Patricia A., ed. *Beyond Their Sex: Learned Women of the European Past.* New York: New York University Press, 1980.

Larsen, Anne R., and Colette H. Winn, eds. *Renaissance Women Writers: French Texts/American Contexts.* Detroit: Wayne State University Press, 1994.

Laqueur, Thomas. *Making Sex: Body and Gender from the Greeks to Freud.* Cambridge, Mass.: Harvard University Press, 1990.

Lerner, Gerda. *The Creation of Patriarchy.* Women and History, vol. 1. New York: Oxford University Press, 1986.

———. *Creation of Feminist Consciousness: From the Middle Ages to Eighteen-Seventy.* Women and History, vol. 2. New York: Oxford University Press, 1994.

Levin, Carole, and Jeanie Watson, eds. *Ambiguous Realities: Women in the Middle Ages and Renaissance.* Detroit: Wayne State University Press, 1987.

Levin, Carole, et al. *Extraordinary Women of the Medieval and Renaissance World: A Biographical Dictionary.* Westport, Conn.: Greenwood Press, 2000.

Lindsey, Karen. *Divorced, Beheaded, Survived: A Feminist Reinterpretation of the Wives of Henry VIII.* Reading, Mass.: Addison-Wesley Publishing, 1995.

Lochrie, Karma. *Margery Kempe and Translations of the Flesh.* Philadelphia: University of Pennsylvania Press, 1992.

MacCarthy, Bridget G. *The Female Pen: Women Writers and Novelists, 1621–1818.* Preface by Janet Todd. Cork: Cork University Press, 1946–47; reprinted, New York: New York University Press, 1994

Maclean, Ian. *The Renaissance Notion of Woman: A Study of the Fortunes of Scholasticism and Medical Science in European Intellectual Life.* Cambridge: Cambridge University Press, 1980.

———. *Woman Triumphant: Feminism in French Literature, 1610–1652.* Oxford: Clarendon Press, 1977.

Matter, E. Ann, and John Coakley, eds. *Creative Women in Medieval and Early Modern Italy.* Philadelphia: University of Pennsylvania Press, 1994. This collection is the sequel to the Monson collection, below.

McKinley, Mary. "An Editorial Revival: Gournay's 1617 Preface to the *Essais.*" *Montaigne Studies: An Interdisciplinary Forum* 8, nos. 1–2 (1996): 193–201.

Ménage, Gilles. *The History of Women Philosophers.* Translated with an introduction by Beatrice H. Zedler. Lanham, Md.: University Press of America, 1984.

Mendelson, Sara, and Patricia Crawford. *Women in Early Modern England, 1550–1720.* Oxford: Clarendon Press, 1998.

Monson, Craig A., ed. *The Crannied Wall: Women, Religion, and the Arts in Early Modern Europe.* Ann Arbor: University of Michigan Press, 1992.

Newman, Karen. *Fashioning Femininity and English Renaissance Drama.* Chicago and London: University of Chicago Press, 1991.

Okin, Susan Moller. *Women in Western Political Thought.* Princeton, N.J.: Princeton University Press, 1979.

Ozment, Steven. *The Bürgermeister's Daughter: Scandal in a Sixteenth-Century German Town.* New York: St. Martin's Press, 1995.

Pacheco, Anita, ed. *Early Women Writers: 1600–1720.* New York and London: Longman, 1998.

Pagels, Elaine. *Adam, Eve, and the Serpent.* New York: HarperCollins, 1988.

Panizza, Letizia, ed. *Women in Italian Renaissance Culture and Society.* Oxford: European Humanities Research Centre, 2000.

Panizza, Letizia, and Sharon Wood, eds. *A History of Women's Writing in Italy.* Cambridge: Cambridge University Press, 2000.

Perry, Ruth. *The Celebrated Mary Astell: An Early English Feminist.* Chicago: University of Chicago Press, 1986.

Raven, James, Helen Small, and Naomi Tadmor, eds. *The Practice and Representation of Reading in England.* Cambridge: Cambridge University Press, 1996.

Regosin, Richard. "Montaigne's Dutiful Daughter." *Montaigne Studies* 3 (1991): 103–27.

Richardson, Lula McDowell. *The Forerunners of Feminism in French Literature of the Renaissance from Christine of Pisa to Marie de Gournay.* Johns Hopkins Studies in Romance Literatures and Languages, 12. Baltimore: Johns Hopkins University Press, 1929; reprinted, New York: Johnson Reprint Corporation, 1973.

Riddle, John M. *Contraception and Abortion from the Ancient World to the Renaissance.* Cambridge, Mass.: Harvard University Press, 1992.

———. *Eve's Herbs: A History of Contraception and Abortion in the West.* Cambridge, Mass.: Harvard University Press, 1997.

Rigolot, François. Introduction to *"Préface à l'édition des* Essais *de Montaigne* (Paris: Abel L'Angelier, 1595)." By Marie de Gournay. Edited by François Rigolot. *Montaigne Studies: An Interdisciplinary Forum* 1 (1989): 8–20.

Rose, Mary Beth, ed. *Women in the Middle Ages and the Renaissance: Literary and Historical Perspectives.* Syracuse, N.Y.: Syracuse University Press, 1986.

Rosenthal, Margaret F. *The Honest Courtesan: Veronica Franco, Citizen and Writer in Sixteenth-Century Venice.* Foreword by Catharine R. Stimpson. Chicago: University of Chicago Press, 1992.

Sankovitch, Tilde A. *French Women Writers and the Book: Myths of Access and Desire.* Syracuse, N.Y.: Syracuse University Press, 1988.

Sartori, Eva M., and Dorothy Wynne Zimmerman, eds. *French Women Writers: A Biobibliographical Source Book.* New York: Greenwood, 1991.

Sayce, Richard A., and David Maskell. *A Descriptive Bibliography of Montaigne's Essais, 1580–1700.* London: Bibliographical Society, in conjunction with the Modern Humanities Research Association, 1983.

Schiebinger, Londa. *The Mind Has No Sex? Women in the Origins of Modern Science.* Cambridge, Mass.: Harvard University Press, 1991.

———. *Nature's Body: Gender in the Making of Modern Science.* Boston: Beacon Press, 1993.

Schiff, Mario. *La fille d'alliance de Montaigne, Marie de Gournay.* 1910; reprinted, Geneva: Slatkine, 1978.

Shemek, Deanna. *Ladies Errant: Wayward Women and Social Order in Early Modern Italy.* Durham, N.C.: Duke University Press, 1998.

Sobel, Dava. *Galileo's Daughter: A Historical Memoir of Science, Faith, and Love.* New York: Penguin Books, 2000.

Sommerville, Margaret R. *Sex and Subjection: Attitudes to Women in Early-Modern Society.* London: Arnold, 1995.

Spencer, Jane. *The Rise of the Woman Novelist: From Aphra Behn to Jane Austen.* Oxford: Basil Blackwell, 1986.

Spender, Dale. *Mothers of the Novel: 100 Good Women Writers before Jane Austen.* London and New York: Routledge, 1986.

Sperling, Jutta Gisela. *Convents and the Body Politic in Late Renaissance Venice.* Foreword by Catharine R. Stimpson. Chicago: University of Chicago Press, 1999.

Stanton, Domna C. "Autogynography: The Case of Marie de Gournay's *Apologie pour celle qui escrit.*" In *Autobiography in French Literature,* 18–31. French Literature Series 12. Columbia: Department of Foreign Languages and Literatures, College of Humanities and Social Sciences, University of South Carolina, 1985.

———. "Woman as Object and Subject of Exchange: Marie de Gournay's *Le Proumenoir* (1594)." *L'Esprit créateur* 23, no. 2 (1983): 9–25.

Steinbrügge, Lieselotte. *The Moral Sex: Woman's Nature in the French Enlightenment.* Translated by Pamela E. Selwyn. New York: Oxford University Press, 1995.

Stuard, Susan M. "The Dominion of Gender: Women's Fortunes in the High Middle Ages." In *Becoming Visible: Women in European History,* edited by Renate Bridenthal, Claudia Koonz, and Susan M. Stuard. 3d ed. Boston: Houghton Mifflin, 1998.

Summit, Jennifer. *Lost Property: The Woman Writer and English Literary History, 1380–1589.* Chicago: University of Chicago Press, 2000.

Teague, Frances. *Bathsua Makin, Woman of Learning.* Lewisburg, Pa.: Bucknell University Press, 1999.

Tetel, Marcel, ed. "Montaigne and Marie de Gournay." Special issue of *Journal of Medieval and Renaissance Studies,* vol. 25 (1995).

———, ed. *Montaigne et Marie de Gournay: Actes du Colloque international de Duke Études Montaignistes,* 30. Paris: Champion, 1997.

Todd, Janet. *The Secret Life of Aphra Behn.* London: Pandora, 2000.

———. *The Sign of Angelica: Women, Writing and Fiction, 1660–1800.* New York: Columbia University Press, 1989.

Venesoen, Constant. *Études sur la littérature féminine au XVIIe siècle: Mademoiselle de Gournay, Mademoiselle de Scudéry, Madame de Villedieu, Madame de Lafayette.* Birmingham, Ala.: Summa, 1990.

Villey, Pierre. *Montaigne devant la postérité.* Paris: Boivin & Cie, 1935.

Waithe, Mary Ellen. "Finding Bits and Pieces of Hypatia." In *Hypatia's Daughters: Fifteen Hundred Years of Women Philosophers,* edited by Linda Lopez McAlister, 4–15. Bloomington: Indiana University Press, 1996.

———, ed. *A History of Women Philosophers.* Vol. 1, *Ancient Women Philosophers, 600 B.C.–A.D. 500.* Vol. 2, *Medieval, Renaissance, and Enlightenment Women Philosophers, 500–1600.* Dordrecht: Kluwer, 1987–89.

Walsh, William T. *St. Teresa of Avila: A Biography.* Rockford, Ill.: TAN Books & Publications, 1987.

Warner, Marina. *Alone of All Her Sex: The Myth and Cult of the Virgin Mary.* New York: Knopf, 1976.

Warnicke, Retha M. *The Marrying of Anne of Cleves: Royal Protocol in Tudor England.* Cambridge: Cambridge University Press, 2000.

Watt, Diane. *Secretaries of God: Women Prophets in Late Medieval and Early Modern England.* Cambridge: D. S. Brewer, 1997.

Welles, Marcia L. *Persephone's Girdle: Narratives of Rape in Seventeenth-Century Spanish Literature.* Nashville: Vanderbilt University Press, 2000.

Whitehead, Barbara J., ed. *Women's Education in Early Modern Europe: A History, 1500–1800.* New York and London: Garland Publishing, 1999.

Wiesner, Merry E. *Women and Gender in Early Modern Europe.* Cambridge: Cambridge University Press, 1993.

Willard, Charity Cannon. *Christine de Pizan: Her Life and Works.* New York: Persea Books, 1984.

Wilson, Katharina, ed. *An Encyclopedia of Continental Women Writers.* 2 vols. New York: Garland, 1991.

Woodbridge, Linda. *Women and the English Renaissance: Literature and the Nature of Womankind.* Urbana: University of Illinois Press, 1984.

Woods, Susanne. *Lanyer: A Renaissance Woman Poet.* New York: Oxford University Press, 1999.

Woods, Susanne, and Margaret P. Hannay, eds. *Teaching Tudor and Stuart Women Writers.* New York: Modern Language Association, 2000.

INDEX

174   *Index*